Other Bible in Dialogue publications

The Gospel of Mark in Dialogue
Ed G. Wallen

Additional titles in preparation

The
Gospel

of

Matthew
in Dialogue

ED G. WALLEN

WESTBOW
PRESS®
A DIVISION OF THOMAS NELSON
& ZONDERVAN

New Revised Standard Version Bible, copyright © 1989, Division of
Christian Education of the National Council of the Churches of Christ in
the United States of America. Used by permission. All rights reserved.

WestBow Press books may be ordered through booksellers or by contacting:

WestBow Press
A Division of Thomas Nelson & Zondervan
1663 Liberty Drive
Bloomington, IN 47403
www.westbowpress.com
1 (866) 928-1240

ISBN: 978-1-5127-2283-3 (sc)
ISBN: 978-1-5127-2284-0 (hc)
ISBN: 978-1-5127-2282-6 (e)

Library of Congress Control Number: 2015920487

Print information available on the last page.

WestBow Press rev. date: 02/01/2016

Contents

Abbreviations and Terms used in the Bible in Dialogue vii

To the Reader ix

Acknowledgments xv

Names and Order of the Books of the Old and New
    Testament with the Apocryphal/Deuterocanonical Books ... xvii

The Cast for Matthew 1

Introduction to the Gospel of Matthew 19

Matthew 23

Sources in Matthew 249

Additional Reading 259

Cast Index 261

Abbreviations and Terms used in the Bible in Dialogue

Apoc	Apocrypha
B in D	Bible in Dialogue
b.	born
BCE	Before the Common Era (= BC)
ca	circa (about)
CE	Common Era (=AD)
CEB	Common English Bible (2011)
cf.	compare with
Ch, chs	Chapter, chapters
CMS	*The Chicago Manual of Style, Fifteenth Edition*
CWMS	*The Christian Writer's Manual of Style*
D	Deuteronomic or Deuteronomistic source (of Torah)
d.	died
E	Elohist or Elohistic source (of Torah)
Ecclus	Ecclesiasticus
e.g.	for example
Esd	Esdras
etc.	and so on
Gk	Septuagint, Greek version of the Old Testament
Heb	Hebrew of the consonantal Masoretic Text of the OT
i.e.	*id est,* that is
J	Jahwist or Yahwist source (of Torah)
Josephus	Flavius Josephus (Jewish historian about 37 to 95 CE)
KJV	King James Version of the Bible (1611)

LXX	Septuagint, the oldest translation of the OT into Greek
M	One hundred and fifty verses on the sayings of Jesus only found in Matthew and not available in Mark and Luke
Macc	The book(s) of the Maccabees
Ms(s)	Manuscript(s)
MT	The Hebrew of the pointed Masoretic Text of the OT
NIV	New International Version (1973)
NRSV	New Revised Standard Version of the Bible (1989)
NT	New Testament
OT	Old Testament, Hebrew Bible
P	Priestly source (of Torah)
Q	Q_1 the earliest writings about Jesus of Nazareth compiled about the mid 50's CE. Q_2 compiled in the late 60 or early 70s. Q_3 The smallest collection of the Gospel of Q compiled about 80 CE
Q Ms(s)	Manuscript(s) found at Qumran by the Dead Sea.
RSV	Revised Standard Version of the Bible (1946-52, 1971)
Sam	Samaritan Hebrew text of the OT
Syr	Syriac Version of the OT
Syr H	Syriac Version of Origen's Hexapla
Tg	Targum, Aramaic translation of Hebrew Bible
NJPS	New Jewish Publication Society, the Tanakh (1999)
TNIV	Today's New International Version (2002, 2004)
Vg	Vulgate, Latin Version of the OT
Webster's	*Merriam-Webster's Collegiate Dictionary, Eleventh Edition*
Wisd of Sol	Wisdom of Solomon

To the Reader

Conversing with God through study, prayer and worship has been a regular part of my faith journey. However, imagine my surprise when I heard the words one night, "Write my Word in dialogue." My immediate reaction was, "You have to be kidding." In the morning, I shared what happened with my wife and a few others who know I am not prone to hearing voices. Their response was both positive and enjoyable. The following night the same voice was heard, "Write my Word in dialogue."

So, what version should be used? Today, the reader can choose between many excellent versions of the Bible. Whenever I look at my copy of the King James Version (1611), a smile crosses my face because duct-tape holds it together. When I was in Seminary, this copy of the KJV was replaced with a Revised Standard Version (1952) because of its closeness to the Hebrew and Greek languages. When it became necessary to replace this Bible, because of use, the only RSV available was the Catholic edition. The New Revised Standard Version (1989) was selected, complete with the Apocrypha. Since the NRSV continues to be my version of choice, it was selected for the Bible in Dialogue. Placing the NRSV in a dialogue format does not change the text; it provides the reader the opportunity to experience God's Word, much as you would enjoy a dramatic production.

The traditional chapter and verse division found in the printed Bible provides an indispensable system of references, even if they do not always follow the original divisions within the text. The divisions into chapters resulted from medieval Christian scholarship, and it did not always join or separate the paragraphs, sentences and even parts of sentences in the correct manner. The reader has only to compare Genesis (Gen 7.24-8.1) in the NJPS and the NRSV to recognize the issue. "And when the waters had swelled on the earth one hundred and fifty days, God remembered Noah and all the beasts and all the cattle that were with him in the ark, and God caused a wind to blow across the earth and the waters subsided" (NJPS). "And the waters swelled on the earth for one hundred fifty days. However, God remembered Noah and all the wild animals and all the domestic animals that were with him in the ark. And God made a wind blow over the earth, and the water subsided; (the sentence continues through verse two ending following the first half of verse three in NRSV)." Readers have long understood that in the Jewish Bible the first verse of many Psalms included the subscription of the Psalm or a part, making it difficult to reference the same verse in both biblical versions. The Bible in Dialogue does not eliminate the divisions between chapters and verses; it emphasizes the stories and the voices within them.

The practice of using a period between chapter and verse (1.1) instead of a colon (1:1) is followed in the NRSV, Mt 4.4 is Matthew, chapter 4, verse 4. Over seventy individuals or groups participate in the gospel of Matthew in dialogue. When it applies, the meaning of a name is in square brackets with some information and scriptural references. A cast index is at the back of the B in D material to provide a page reference. The page reference for primary cast members, such as God and Jesus, is for the first time it appears in a chapter.

Italicized type in the notes indicates a quotation or word from the New Revised Standard Version (NRSV) of the passage under discussion. In addition, in scripture references to a letter (a, b, etc.) appended to a verse number indicates a clause within the verse; an additional Greek letter indicates a subdivision within the clause. When no book is named, the book under discussion is understood. When another verse is quoted, it will be shown within quotes.

Old Testament quotes or paraphrases cited in NT books will be placed in round brackets with a footnote on the location. The original cast member in the OT quote will be in the NT, with attention given to the identification of the editor when available. In Mt 5.43b, **Moses.**

x

(P) "You shall love your neighbor and hate your enemy." In Leviticus (Lev 19.18) Moses is the speaker, according to the (P) Priestly editor.

Where do we capitalize or use the lowercase form? In the OT terms such as "Temple" (Temple at Jerusalem) and "Synagogue" are capitalized, but not in the NT. The word "gospel" will not be capitalized unless it is part of the actual title, per the *CWMS*.

The careful reader will notice in the OT the word LORD printed in small capital letters. The name "LORD" was used in the OT instead of Yahweh in most Jewish and English versions, to follow the common Jewish practice of substituting the Hebrew word "Adonai" translated as "LORD" instead of saying the name of YHWH (with no vowels). In the NT, where the LORD speaks in an OT quote, the LORD remains even if the text uses Lord.

Many biblical books resulted from a redaction process, meaning later individual writers or groups used one or more local or area traditions and edited them in developing a particular book or books of the Bible. In the Book of Genesis, at least seven editors used varied terms and traditions to identify God. Why was it important for the writers to maintain those traditions? What contribution do the individual traditions make to the total picture of the faith community? What issues moved later editors to unite the differing faith traditions? Scholars accept that many OT books, including the Psalter are a collection of many writers. However, the NT is not held to the same criteria.

Before canonization, the NT endured its share of reworking by later writers or editors to address current issues or expand upon previous statements. Matthew used a variety of materials, including the OT to proclaim Jesus as the Messiah, the new Moses. Matthew's gospel contains most of the narrative of Mark, the collection of the sayings of Jesus, known today as Q, and material identified as "M." Burton, Ernest DeWitt and Goodspeed, Edgar Johnson, *A Harmony of the Synoptic Gospels,* Charles Scribner's Sons, New York, 1917, makes it possible to identify one hundred and fifty verses found only in Matthew. These designated passages are in round brackets. Even if the reader does not agree that (M) is a separate document, to read the gospel of Matthew giving attention to the marked passages reveals some of the writer's personality.

In 1838, a German scholar, Christian Hermann Weisse, expressed what he believed to be the teachings of Jesus under the surface of the gospels of Matthew and Luke. These teachings or sayings are called *Quelle,* German for "the source," and are commonly known as Q. Some scholars believe the gospel of Q represents at least three collections of the sayings or teachings of Jesus and have identified them as Q_1, Q_2, and Q_3.

Q_1 was a collection of the early sayings of Jesus, compiled about the mid 50's CE. In this collection, there was no attempt to identify Jesus as the Son of God, because Jesus had something else in mind. Here, Jesus was a great teacher, who taught what the people needed to understand.

Q_2, compiled in the late 60s or early 70s, made up more than half of the gospel of Q. Q_2 presented Jesus as a teacher of great wisdom, making it easier to observe the evolution of beliefs in contrast to those of the Pharisees. This collection provides insights into the interactions between the followers of Jesus and those of John the Baptist. The Dead Sea Scrolls illuminated this issue for the reader. In addition, in Q_2 there is the introduction of an apocalyptic vision not evident in Q_1

The smallest collection of the gospel of Q was Q_3, compiled about 80 CE, after the fall of Jerusalem and close to the appearance of the gospels of Matthew and Luke. In this collection, a tone of reproach was evident for those refusing to listen and Jesus was more a Son of God than he was a wise teacher. In the B in D, the three collections of Q will be contained in brackets.

Some believe Moses or a few authors wrote the Torah in a single setting. Others believe the Bible reflected the history of God's people covering many centuries. The B in D approaches the biblical material from the position that several writers collected and interpreted both oral and written texts in light of current circumstances. While everyone may not agree on the identification of the editors or the different sources, to examine the material in this manner opens possibilities for some creative reflection upon the Word of God. Scholars mostly agree that each author or editor had a reason for what they presented. What is that reason? What is it that made their world different from ours? History, secular or religious, was written in response to an event that had altered the status quo. America is different since 9/11, and so were the biblical people after the destruction of the temple and Jerusalem in 70 CE. How did the ministries of Jesus and Paul change the Jewish and Greek communities? How did these major events and others affect the writings of the NT and the early Christian church?

Ed G. Wallen

Acknowledgments

Thanks to those at the Salem United Methodist Church, Wapakoneta, Ohio, who have used the B in D material over the past several years. Thanks to the Seek and Serve Sunday school class, the Alpha Group, the Brats in the Belfrey, the Monday Bible Study Group, the Wednesday Evening Study Group, and an Internet group called Education without Walls (Ew/oW). They each read parts of the material and enriched it with their questions and comments. Thanks to Reverends Gregory Roberts, Shawn Morris, and John Foster for giving faithful support, and for using this material in different settings. Special thanks to Darlene and Wayne Arnold, Bev Foster, Don and Marj Kachelries, Sarah Klaus, Kathy Latimer, Amy Miller, Stephanie Mosler and Wes McPheron for their faithfulness during this project. Thanks to Stephanie Mosler and Marguerite Wallen, for their questions, insights, and editorial skills, they are appreciated beyond words. My deepest gratitude is to my wife, Marguerite, whose love becomes more evident by her silence, when she does not agree with me, and yet she continues to encourage me. My prayer is that God will continue to bless each in this group, because they provide me with a loving climate that continues to encourage my efforts. Believe me, it makes a difference.

Names and Order of the Books of the Old and New Testament with the Apocryphal/Deuterocanonical Books

Abbreviations for the books of the Bible
Old Testament

Gen	Genesis	2 Chr	2 Chronicles	Dan	Daniel
Ex	Exodus	Ezra	Ezra	Hos	Hoses
Lev	Leviticus	Neh	Nehemiah	Joel	Joel
Num	Numbers	Esth	Esther	Am	Amos
Deut	Deuteronomy	Job	Job	Ob	Obadiah
Josh	Joshua	Ps	Psalms	Jon	Jonah
Judg	Judges	Prov	Proverbs	Mic	Micah
Ruth	Ruth	Eccl	Ecclesiastes	Nah	Nahum
1 Sam	1 Samuel	Song	Songs of Songs	Hab	Habakkuk
2 Sam	2 Samuel	Isa	Isaiah	Zeph	Zephaniah
1 Kings	1 Kings	Jer	Jeremiah	Hag	Haggai
2 Kings	2 Kings	Lam	Lamentations	Zech	Zechariah
1 Chr	1 Chronicles	Ezek	Ezekiel	Mal	Malachi

Apocryphal/Deuterocanonical Books

Tobit	Tobit	Sus	Susanna
Jdt	Judith	Bel	Bell and the Dragon
Add Esth	Addition to Esther (Gk)	1 Macc	1 Maccabees
Wis	Wisdom	2 Macc	2 Maccabees
Sir	Sirach (Ecclesiasticus)	1 Esd	1 Esdras
Bar	Baruch	Pr Man	Prayer of Manasseh
Let Jer	Letter of Jeremiah	Ps 151	Psalm 151
Song of Thr	Prayer of Azariah and The Song of the Three Jews	3 Macc	3 Maccabees
		2 Esd	2 Esdras
		4 Macc	4 Maccabees

New Testament

Mt	Matthew	Eph	Ephesians	Heb	Hebrews
Mk	Mark	Phil	Philippians	Jas	James
Lk	Luke	Col	Colossians	1 Pet	1 Peter
Jn	John	1 Thess	1 Thessalonians	2 Pet	2 Peter
Acts	Acts	2 Thess	2 Thessalonians	1 Jn	1 John
Rom	Romans	1 Tim	1 Timothy	2 Jn	2 John
1 Cor	1 Corinthians	2 Tim	2 Timothy	3 Jn	3 John
2 Cor	2 Corinthians	Titus	Titus	Jude	Jude
Gal	Galatians	Philem	Philemon	Rev	Revelation

The Cast for Matthew

Aaronic priesthood. The Aaronic priesthood traced its origin through Eleazar, son of Aaron (Num 20.23-28; 25.7-13; 33.37-39; 1 Chr 6.1-15; 24.4). Jesus in his lament over Jerusalem used a quote from Psalms attributed to the Aaronic priesthood (Ps 118.26; Mt 23.39).

Angels. Belief in angels became widespread after the exile. These winged creatures, with supernatural powers, surrounded the LORD (1 Kings 22.19; Isa ch 6), ready to serve as his messengers (Gen 28.12; 32.1-2; Mt 1.20; 2.13, 20; Lk 2.8-20; 22.43; Acts 10.1-18; Gal 4.14; Rev 18.4-8). John observed three angels flying in midheaven with an eternal gospel for those living on earth (Rev 14.4-13). However, for Joshua (Josh 5.14) and Matthew (Mt 26.52), angels were part of the LORD's army. John recorded Michael and his angels defeating the ancient serpent and his angels (Rev 12.7-9). Some believed angels were God's Senate, and he did nothing without consulting them. "Let us make humankind in our image, according to our likeness" (Gen 1.26). Angels did not always agree with God, and they objected to the creation of human life.

There were angels over the water (Rev 16.1), fire (Rev 14.18), hail, thunder, and the lightning. Recording angels wrote down every spoken word. There were destroying angels and angels of punishment. There was Satan, the prosecuting angel, which on every day, except on the Day of Atonement, brought charges against men and women before God. The angel of death went out to do God's bidding and impartially delivered his summons to both good and evil people.

Every individual, even children, and nations had a guardian angel (Mt 18.10). There were two angels at the Jesus' empty tomb with a message for Mary Magdalene (Jn 20.13). Apollos wanted to prove that Jesus was not an angel, but he was superior to angels (Heb 1.1-4).

Asaph singer. [He that gathered or removed reproach] Asaph was believed to be the father or ancestor of Joah, Hezekiah's recorder (2 Kings 18.18, 37; Isa 36.3, 22). Asaph was the founder of one of the three chief families or guilds of Levite temple musicians, the "sons of Asaph" (1 Chr 6.39). In the Chronicler's history of Judah, the sons of Asaph participate as singers in every major temple celebration, both before and after the exile (1 Chr 9.15; Ezra 2.41; Neh 7.44; 11.17, 22; 1 Esd 5.27, 59, Mt 13.35). Psalms 50; 73-83 were all ascribed to Asaph.

Blind. Jesus healed several individuals of their blindness, but Bartimaeus was the only one identified by name (Mt 9.27-36; 20.29-34; Lk 18.35-43). John recorded that Jesus healed a blind individual on the sabbath (Jn 9.1-41) and the Pharisees questioned the blind person with his parents (*see* Parents).

Bridegroom. In the parable of the wise and foolish bridesmaids, the bridegroom rejected those not prepared (Mt 25.1-12).

Bridesmaids. In the parable of the wise and the foolish bridesmaids, the foolish bridesmaids did not prepare for the bridegroom's lengthy delay and experienced a shortage in oil for their lamps. The wise bridesmaids were prepared by taking flasks that contained extra oil (Mt 25.1-13).

Bystanders. Bystanders were individuals who observed what took place, but limited their involvement (Mt 26.73; 27.40, 49; Mk 11.5).

Caiaphas. [A searcher] Joseph Caiaphas, a Sadducee, the son-in-law of Annas, was high priest of the Judeans for eighteen years (Mt 26.3, 57). At the trial of Jesus, Caiaphas presided over a meeting of some chief priests, scribes and elders to decide Jesus' fate. Determined to find Jesus guilty, he displayed a disregard for the traditional and accepted forms of Jewish law (Mt 26.57-58, 62-66; Jn 11.49, 53; 18.24; Acts 4.5).

Centurion. The title centurion identified a non-Jewish military officer in command of fifty to one hundred soldiers (Mt 8.6, 8).

Chief priests. The chief priests, an exclusive group of two hundred highborn Judeans, supervised the temple priests, the temple services, the temple treasury, and maintained the sacred vessels. They reported directly to the high priest and challenged anyone they perceived to be a danger to the temple system. They seldom acted alone, except to determine the fate of Lazarus (Jn 11.10), to strike a deal with Judas (Mt 26.14; Mk 14.10-11), to interact with Pilate (Jn 18.36; 19.15, 21) or to grant authority to Paul to persecute Christians (Acts 9.14, 21).

Children. The importance of children in the Bible was evident by the number of times they appeared. Jesus used the children in the marketplace to compare with the present generation. One group played the "wedding" game of rejoicing, while the other group played the "funeral" game of mourning (Mt 11.17). Later children outside the temple were overheard singing praises to Jesus as the Son of God by the chief priests and scribes (Mt 21.15).

Christ. Christ was a title applied to the coming king expected by the Judeans, the Messiah, the Anointed One. In the NT, Christ was commonly connected with Jesus (*see* Jesus).

Citizens. These individuals were usually residents of a location, like Jerusalem (Mt 21.11). However, citizens in the parable of the ten pounds were those who rejected the nobleman's rule (Lk 19.14).

Congregation. This term described an assembly of believers or faithful. It usually appeared in the Psalter, where the congregation played a minor role in worship. At certain points, they would shout "amen," or hallelujah," or "forever and ever." They were also described as the, "quiet in the land" (Ps 35.10), "assembly of the faithful" (Ps 149.1), "assembly of the peoples" (Ps 5.7), or "assembly of the holy ones" (Ps 79.5). In the NT, the term usually appeared when it was part of a quote from a Psalm (Acts 2.28; 4.25; Rom 4.7).

Crowd. The crowd represented a group or groups of Jewish people who reacted both positively and negatively to the ministry of Jesus. Outside the feeding of the four (Mt 15.32-39; Mk 8.1-10) and five thousand (Mt 14.13-21; Mk 6.30-44; Lk 9.10-17; Jn 6.1-15), it was not known how many people made up a crowd. Christians usually presented the crowds embracing the teachings of Jesus while the Jewish religious leaders perceived them to be indifferent and even hostile to Jesus' ministry.

Daniel. [God is my judge] During the exile, Daniel was taken to Babylon and trained with others to serve the king (Ezek 14.14, 20; 28.3; Dan 1.6, 21). Instead, he became a model of Jewish faithfulness to God. The first part of the book of Daniel, written in 164 BCE was in Aramaic (A) and the rest was in Hebrew (H). Matthew used Daniel to support the belief that Jesus was the Son of Man (Mt 24.30; 26.64).

David. [Beloved] David, the youngest of Jesse's eight sons, was the second and greatest king of Israel. Trained to tend sheep, yet, the LORD raised David from a low estate and placed him on the throne. David's psalms were mostly contained in book 1 of the Psalter (Pss 1-41) and quoted in the NT (Mt 22.41-46; Mk 12.36; Lk 20.42; Acts 2.34; Rom 3.4; 15.9; Heb 7.21).

Demoniac. (Gerasene) The Gerasene or Gadarene demoniac was a mentally disturbed inhabitant of the city or the surrounding district of Gadara, the capital of Perea. Matthew had Jesus curing two demoniacs (Mt 8.28-30) while Mark and Luke only mentioned one demoniac (Mk 5.1-20; Lk 8.26-39).

Disciples. (John the Baptist's) Followers of John the Baptist were disciples of John, some continued even after his death. The only one identified by name was Andrew (Jn 1.40).

Disciples. A disciple was a learner or pupil who accepted and followed a doctrine or teacher. As with Jesus, a teacher invited a disciple to become a student. The term referred to the Twelve Jesus selected to follow him. However, a majority of the times it referred to more than the Twelve (Mt 8.2; Mk 3.7; Lk 6.13; 10.1-16; 19.3 7; 6.66-67). John the Baptist had several disciples, including Andrew (Jn 1.40). The Pharisees had disciples, often identified as lawyers or scribes, whose primary responsibilities were to study the Scriptures (Mt 22.16-21).

Editor. Many editors wrote or compiled the OT material. The differing editors responsible for material quoted in the NT are noted in the cast.

Elders. The Elders of Israel were individuals with status or personality within the community. They conducted their business at the gates of the community (Gen 23.12; 50.7; Ex 3.15; Mt 21.23, 31, 41; 26.5; 27.4-7, 42-43).

Father. The father was the head of the family and expected honor and obedience. In the Bible, the word "father" was frequently used to describe the nature of God (Prov 3.11-12, 34; Mt 21.28; 25.8-11; Mk 9.14-29; Lk 5.11-32; 9.34-42; Heb 12.5; James 4.6; 1 Pet 5.5).

God. In the Bible, it was inappropriate to ask the question, "Did God exist?" rather the question should be, "Who was your God?" The name given to the Divine in the OT revealed the nature of the Divine and the relationship between the Divine and the people. In the account of the burning bush, Moses hesitated to accept a task from the God of the Ancestors, the God of Abraham, the God of Isaac, and the God of Jacob (Ex 3.6). A later editor (LJE) then identified God as LORD or "ha-Shem" (Ex 3.7), but the issue remained. If Moses went back to the people in Egypt and said, "The God of your ancestors has sent me," they would ask, "What was his name?" He would have to identify God as, "I AM WHO I AM" (Ex 3.14), meaning, "I cause to be what comes into existence" and "I will be with you." The LORD sent Moses back to Egypt to assure the Israelites he could deliver what he proclaimed. He then humiliated the most powerful ruler of that time and called upon the forces of nature to fulfill his will, the deliverance of the Israelites. The LORD said to the Israelites, at the consecration of the tent of meeting and the altar, "I will meet with the Israelites there, and it shall be sanctified by my glory; I will consecrate the tent of meeting and the altar; Aaron also and his sons I will consecrate, to serve me as priests. I will dwell among the Israelites, and I will be their God. And they shall know that I am the LORD their God, who brought them out of the land of Egypt that I might dwell among them; I am the LORD their God" (Ex 29.43-46).

Herod. [Son of the hero] Herod the Great (73-4 BCE) was appointed governor of Syria with the promise of a later appointment as king of Judea. The Judeans, who allied with him, received high honors, and his opposition, including members of the Sanhedrin, received bitter vengeance. He had ten wives and fifteen children, of which ten were sons, setting up an inevitable domestic struggle for the throne (Mt 2.8). His son, Herod Antipas by a Samaritan wife named Maithace, governed as Prince of Galilee and Perea (Transjordan) until his death in 39 CE (Mt 14.2; Lk 9.9).

Herodians. Individuals who regarded the Herodian dynasty as the best solution to the Judean problem were Herodians. These Herodian sympathizers united forces with the Pharisees in opposing Jesus (Mt 33.15-22; Mk 3.6; 12.13-17; Lk 20.20-26).

Homeowner. Homeowner was a term used to identify someone who owned a house or home and wanted to protect it against evil doers (Mt 13.28-30; Mk 4.26-29; Lk 11.7; 13.25-27).

Isaiah. [The LORD is Helper] The book of Isaiah contained at least three distinct sections, from three periods, and was written by at least three authors, and maybe reworked by many later editors. Isaiah (I) chapters 1-39 were mostly the work of the prophet Isaiah, who lived in Jerusalem during the eighth century BCE. Chapters 24-27 were identified as the Isaiah Apocalypse, because of its themes concerning the end of the age. Chapters 36-39 was an appendix, taken from the book of Kings, sometime around the last half of the fourth century and the early part of the second century BCE.

Many Jewish and Christian scholars agree that chapters 40–55 of Isaiah, known as Deutero-Isaiah or Second Isaiah (D-I), reflected another historical setting, the Babylonian exile of the sixth century. The author of Deutero-Isaiah was in the Babylonian exile writing to his fellow Judeans. Some believe Deutero-Isaiah may have been one of the later editors to change chapters 1-39.

Chapters 56–66, known as Trito-Isaiah (T-I), are thought to have been written by disciples of Deutero-Isaiah. This editor made sure the master's writings were brought to Judah from Babylon. Since Trito-Isaiah quoted or pointed to Deutero-Isaiah, this indicated he wrote after the exile. Later editors may have added or inserted additional material even as late as the first half of the second century BCE. There are almost a hundred quotes in the NT from the book of Isaiah.

Jairus. [He will enlighten] Jairus was the leader of a synagogue whose daughter Jesus raised from the dead (Mk 5.22; Lk 8.41).

James and John. James and his younger brother, John, sons of Zebedee, a Galilean fisherman, were disciples of Jesus. Tradition holds that their mother Salome was the sister of Mary, the mother of Jesus. James was killed by Herod Agrippa with a sword (Mt. 4.21; 10.2; 17.1; 20.22; Mk 1.19, 29; 3.17; 5.37; 9.2; 10.35, 41; 13.3; 14.33; Lk 5.10; 6.14; 8.51; 9.28, 54; Acts 1.13; 12.2).

James. (Brother of Jesus) Those who believed Mary remained a virgin suggested that James was a child of Joseph by a former marriage, or the word "brother" was loosely used and may be "cousin". He was not considered a believer during Jesus' lifetime (Mt 13-57; Lk 7.20-21; Jn 2.12; 7.3, 10). After Jesus' death, James became the leader of the Jewish Christian church at Jerusalem (Acts 12.17; 15.4-34; 21.18, 19; Gal 2.1-10). He was called James the Just because of his piety and honesty. He was beheaded in 60 CE.

Jesus. [Jehovah is Salvation] Joseph was told that Mary, his wife, was to have a son, and he should name him Jesus (Mt 1.21). During his teaching and healing ministry in Palestine, Jesus received other names including: Advocate (Jn 14.15-16), Prophet (Jn 1.21; 614; 7.40), Messiah (Jn 1.41; 4.25), Christ (Mt 16.16), Anointed One, Judge (Jn 12.47-49), Rabbi (Jn 1.38, 49; 6.25; 9.2), Galilean (Mk 1.9, 14; 4.15), Master, Teacher (Mt 5.21-22), Son of Man (Mk 2.10; Jn 5.27), John the Baptist, Elijah, Jeremiah, Mediator, King of Israel (Mk 11.9-10; Lk 19 38; Jn 1.49; 12.13) High Priest (Heb 10.21-25), Servant of God (Jn 1.49), Lamb of God (Jn 1.29, 36, 41), Light of the World (Jn 6.16-21; 8.12), Son of David, Judge, Holy One of God, Lord (Mt 28.20), Savior (Jn 4.42), King, Word (Logos) (Jn 1.1-3; Heb 1.1-2), Son of God (Mk 14.61-64; Jn 5.18; 10.33), and the Good Shepherd (Mk 14.7; Jn 10.15-18; 13.37-38; 15.13). These names all described his unique relationship with God and raised the messianic expectations of the people. The NT contained the story of Jesus' life, death, and resurrection, as he became the founder of the Christian faith.

John the Baptist. The Synoptic Gospels considered John the Baptist to be the forerunner of the Messiah. (Lk 1.16, 76). Jesus identified John the Baptist as Elijah (Mt 17. 10-11). When asked by the priests and Levites from Jerusalem, if he was the prophet, John responded, "No" (Jn 1.21). Early Christians regarded John the Baptist to be the prophet who was the forerunner of the Messiah. However, the Baptist's disciples considered him the final prophet who prepared the way for God himself (Lk 1.15), expressing the belief that the Messiah was the same as the "eschatological prophet."

Judas Iscariot. [Praise of the LORD] Judas, son of Simon, was not only one of the Twelve, but he was the treasurer of the group (Jn 6.71; 12.6; 13.26, 29). The word "Iscariot" may mean "man from Kerioth", a town in southern Judea, making Judas the only Judean among the Twelve. His name was always listed, "the one who betrayed Jesus." According to Matthew, after the betrayal of Jesus, Judas threw the money down in the temple and then hung himself (Mk 27.3-10). However, Luke in Acts recorded a different account (Acts 1.18-19) where Judas bought a field with the betrayal money; and falling headlong, he burst open in the middle, and all his bowels gushed out.

King. A king was the ruler of an area or country. In the Royal Psalms (Pss 2; 18; 20; 21; 45; 72; 89; 101; 110; 132; 144) the kings were not identified by name. In several parables, Jesus used the term king to identify the ruler. However, in the interpretation, the king referred to God (Mt 18.37; 22.8-13; 25.34-45; Acts 4.11).

Lawyer. Matthew (Mt 22.34-40) and Luke (Lk 10.25-37) used the term lawyer in place of Mark's "scribe" to identify someone educated in the religious law.

Leper. A leper was expected to separate himself and to cry "Unclean, unclean" as a warning to others of his condition (Deut 13.45-46). It would have been unlawful for a leper to approach anyone (Mt 8.1-4). In Luke's gospel, Jesus healed ten lepers, and only one returned to thank him (Lk 17.10-19).

LORD. The name "LORD" was used in the OT instead of Yahweh in most Jewish and English versions, to follow the common Jewish practice of substituting the Hebrew word "Adonai" translated as "LORD" instead of saying the name of YHWH (with no vowels).

LORD God. The designation "LORD God" or "ha-Shem" was a translation of "Yahweh" and "Elohim" indicating a unity between the Yahwist (J) and Elohist (E) traditions. Its designation was in the story of the Paradise and the fall (Gen 2-3). A variation of the two traditions was the Lord, my God.

Lord GOD. (*see* Lord God)

Magi. The wise men may have been a Median tribe of priests. An embassy of Parthian magi paid homage to Nero at Naples in 66 CE and returned by another route. "Magi" denoted astrologers and magicians regarded in the NT and Rabbinical writings as evil (magicians), but Matthew thought of them as part of a learned class of Babylonian astrologers. While the number of wise men was not stated, the number of gifts presented to Jesus suggested the number to be three.

Mary Magdalene. Mary was one of the most prominent Galilean women to follow Jesus. Luke introduced her as "Mary called Magdalene, from whom seven demons had come out" (Lk 8.2). Her devotion to Jesus and his ministry was evident, as she provided for Jesus and his disciples out of her resources (Mk 15.40-41; Lk 8.3). She accompanied Jesus and his followers to Jerusalem for his final appeal to the nation (Mk 15.40; Jn 19.25), was present at the cross, came to the tomb to anoint the body (Mk 16.1; Lk 23.55-24.1), reported the empty tomb and the angel's message to the disciples (Lk 24.1-11), and met Jesus after the resurrection (Jn 20.11-18).

Mary. (the mother of Jesus) It becomes difficult to describe Mary as an historical person. Tradition holds her "as the servant of the Lord" (Lk 1.38), who became the instrument for God to visit humanity in a child born of a virgin, that he may redeem them from sin and death and lead them into his blessed kingdom. She was a devout Jewess, who lived in Nazareth. She may have been of Levite descent because of her relationship with Elizabeth. A second century writing (*Protoevangelium of James*) identified her parents as Joachim and Anna. She was engaged to Joseph, from the house of David, when she conceived. This was a shock to Joseph, but his fears were put to rest by the assurances of an angel (Mk 1.20-21).

It is not clear how early the doctrine of the virgin birth became a part of the early church, because it did not appear in the NT except in Matthew (Mt 1.23) and Luke (Lk 1.34-35), but this does not deny the possibility that Jesus was virgin born, making him unique at birth. Mary's offering at the end of her period of uncleanness of "a pair of turtledoves or two young pigeons" indicated the humble lifestyle of this new family (Lev 12.6-8). There remains little information about the childhood of Jesus and his relationship with his parents, except for their annual visit to Jerusalem during the festival of the Passover, but it was different when Jesus was twelve years of age (Lk 2.41-52).

John had Mary appearing at the beginning of Jesus' ministry at the wedding at Cana (Jn 2. 1-11). Mark had Mary and Jesus' brothers seek Jesus in order to have him return home with them. Instead of welcoming them, he told his hearers that his real relatives were those who joined him in obedience to the will of God (Mk 3.31-35). Mary appeared at the foot of the cross with the beloved disciple (Jn 19.25-27), when Jesus gave them to each other, and he took her into his home.

Mary appeared again in Acts (Acts 1.14) where she participated in a prayer meeting, following Jesus' resurrection and ascension, with the apostles and the brothers of Jesus. Legend holds that Mary died in Jerusalem (other legends that she died in Ephesus) attended by the apostles. Legend also had it that a Jewish priest, during the funeral, laid his hands on the bier to overturn it, only to discover that he could not free his hands until he had confessed faith in Mary's divine Son. After the body of Mary was placed in a new sepulcher, Jesus appeared with a band of angels, and at his command, the angels carried her into paradise.

Mary. (The sister of Martha) Mary was the sister of Martha and Lazarus of Bethany (Jn 11.1-12.2). At the death of her brother, Lazarus, she received a message from Martha of Jesus' presence and admonished Jesus for not being there (Jn 11.32). After the resurrection of Lazarus, Mary anointed the feet of Jesus while Martha served at a dinner for Jesus (Jn 12.1-8). Mark (Mk 14.3-9) had this meal in the house of Simon, the leper and that an unnamed woman anointed Jesus.

Matthew. [Gift of the Lord] **(Mt)** Matthew may have written his gospel of Jesus Christ in Hebrew or Aramaic, about 85 CE in or about Antioch. However, only early copies were available in Greek. Matthew regarded Mark's gospel as incomplete, as he rearranged it and added material from the Jewish Scriptures, the OT, to present Jesus as the Messiah and to legitimize the Christian movement. Matthew presented Jesus as the new Moses and the early church as the people of the Lord. Jesus and his disciples gave the gospel to the Jewish people, but since they refused it, Jesus' last command to his followers was to offer it to all humanity (Mt 28.19).

Meander. A friend, an associate and perhaps a pupil of Theophrastus, Meander was on intimate terms with the Athenian dictator Demetrius of Phalerum. Meander authored more than a hundred comedies and became one of the favorite writers of antiquity. According to a note in the *Ibis of Ovid,* he drowned while bathing and his countrymen honored him with a tomb on the road leading to Athens. Numerous supposed busts of him survive, including a well-known statue in the Vatican, formerly thought to represent Gaius Marius. Paul quoted Meander to warn the Corinthians about their morals (1 Cor 15.33).

Messenger. An individual, who carried a message from its sender to the intended reader, with no other identification was the messenger (Mt 12.47; 25.6).

Messiah. (false) There were several individuals during the period before and after Jesus, who falsely claimed to be the messiah. Theudas appeared in 45 CE during the reign of Cuspius Fadus (Acts 5.36) and misled four hundred men. Later Judas the Galilean convinced people to follow him, but he was killed (Acts 5.37). In 54 CE, a Jewish Egyptian was put to death by Felix (Acts 21.38), after persuading thirty thousand people to follow him to the Mount of Olives promising that upon his command the walls of Jerusalem would fall. Then there was Simon bar Kochba whose revolt was smashed in 135 CE (Mt 24.24; Mk 13.22; Lk 21.28).

Moses. [Taken out of the water] Moses was the youngest son of Amran and Jochebed, his wife, of the tribe of Levi, the third son of Jacob. Moses was among the greatest Hebrew leaders and legislators for the Israelite people.

Nobleman. Jesus in the parable of the ten pounds (Lk 19.11-27; talents, Mt 25.14-20) used the nobleman as someone who equiped his slaves with adequate resources, and expected them to continue the business during his absence.

People. In the biblical text, there were several gatherings of people with or without additional information. Sometimes a location provided additional information, such as, people from the home of Simon the leper (Mk 14.3-9) or the home of Jairus (Mk 5.35). In other NT places, they might be identified as "crowd" (*see* Crowd) or just "people" (Mt 11.18-19; Mk 2.18; 3.21; 7.37; 14.4; Lk 7.33-34; 20.16; Jn 6.14; 7.25-42).

Peter. [A rock] Peter, also known as Simon Peter, began as a fisherman and became a "rock." Jona or Jonah was his father and Andrew was his brother. The brothers were fishermen on the Lake of Galilee and may have been in partnership with Zebedee and his two sons, James and John. Peter's brother Andrew introduced him to Jesus, and he was to become his friend, disciple, and apostle. Peter was impulsive (Mt 14.28; 17.4), tenderhearted, and affectionate (Mt 26.75; Jn 13.9; 21.15-17). He possessed spiritual insight (Jn 6.68), and yet found it difficult to understand (Mt 15.15-16), courageous and yet he denied Jesus (Mt 16.16; Jn 6.69; Mk 14.67-71), self-sacrificing and at other times self-seeking (Mt 19.27). He became the leader of the early apostles and became a miracle worker. He carried the gospel message to the Gentiles and in 61 CE traveled to Rome before Paul's release from prison. A few years later, Peter suffered martyrdom by crucifixion but pleaded to be crucified upside down.

Pharisees. The leading Jewish party or sect was the Pharisees, a group of middle class, substantial citizens, mostly devout and intelligent laity. The Pharisees' origin came be traced to when the Jewish people returned from exile. They could not follow the exclusive path of the religious leaders, and so they separated themselves. Over the centuries, they became exclusive and separated themselves from the unclean to observe the ritual purity of the Law. They believed the Law was perfect and permanent, and the purpose of life was absolute obedience. Among the Pharisees, there were elders, people older in age, scribes, who studied and interpreted the Law, and Zealots, who were ready to lay down their lives in the struggle for freedom. Some of Jesus' harshest words were directed against the hypocrisy of the Pharisees, who were his chief enemies.

Pilate. [One armed with a dart] After being tried before the Sanhedrin, Jesus was presented to Pontius Pilate, the Roman procurator of Judea (26-36 CE), to be tried and crucified (Mt 27.1-26; Mk 15.1-15; Lk 23; Jn 18.28-19.16).

Pilate's wife. While unnamed in the NT (Mt 27.19), the extra canonical material, identified her as Procula or Procla. The Coptic church honors Pilate and Procla on June 25, making them both saints and martyrs.

Rich young ruler. The title, rich young ruler, resulted from combined information from the Synoptics. Mark called him a "rich man" (Mk 10.17-31), and Matthew called him a "young man" (Mt 19.16-30). Luke identified him as a "ruler," a member of the governing body of a synagogue (Lk18.18-30)

Righteous followers. This term identified the loyal followers of the king in Jesus parable on the Great Judgment (Mt 25.31-46).

Sadducees. The Sadducees were the biblical fundamentalists of ancient Palestine. They were a group of conservative, aristocratic, landowning, and priestly families whose lives centered on the Jerusalem temple. They insisted that a faithful believer needed to understand the Torah. They rejected what they believed to be the modern traditions of the scribes and the doctrine of the resurrection. Their fellow Judeans hated these Sadducees, because of their collaboration with Rome, their zeal for the Law, and their unwillingness to address the concerns of the people. The Sadducees disappeared from Jewish history following the destruction of Jerusalem and the temple in 70 CE.

Salome. There were two women with the name Salome. The first was a Galilean follower of Jesus, probably the wife of Zebedee and the mother of James and John (cf. Mt 20.20-24; Mk 10.35-41). The second was the daughter of Herodias, who danced for Herod Antipas and his guests and requested the head of John the Baptist for payment. (Mt 14.6; Mk 6.22).

Scoffers. Scoffers responded with words of contempt or insincerity (Mt 7.21; 24.23-26; Lk 14.30; see Rom, Cor and 2 Pet).

Scribes. The Pharisees were the only group to have scribes, and they were experts in the religious law. It was also a term that gave way to the title "rabbi."

Servant girl. This individual may have been one of the slaves or servants of Caiaphas who inquired if Peter was a follower of Jesus (Mt 26.71; Mk 14.67; Lk 22.56).

Slave. An individual or individuals under the complete control of others are slaves. The high priest (Jn 18.10, 26) and officials had slaves (Jn 4.43-54). Jesus used the term, slaves, to teach a parable on forgiveness (Mt 25.14-30; Lk 19.12-27). Paul healed a slave girl with a spirit of divination, and it angered her owners (Acts 16.16-21).

Soldiers. It remains unclear if the text referred to the Roman military (Mt 8.8; 27.27-29; Lk 7.8; Acts 12.4; 21.32), or if they were temple guards under the direction of the chief priest (*see* temple police). Whenever the Roman governor traveled from Caesarea to Jerusalem, it was with a cohort of soldiers (five thousand) to keep order during one of the Feasts.

Son. This was a term used to describe a male descendant. It usually needed additional information to describe the person, such as the first son, meaning the oldest in the family (Mt 21.29). The elder son represented the older son in Jesus' parable of the lost son (Lk 15.11-32), who remained at home and faithfully carried out his duties. However, he became jealous of the younger son, who received forgiveness and a party upon returning home after wasting his share of the inheritance. Then there was the parable of the two sons and the vineyard (Mt 22.28-32).

Synagogue members. A Jewish synagogue was comprised of at least ten Jewish adults.

Temple singer. In late Jewish times, during the daily offering two priests with silver horns would stand behind the singing choir and at every section of the psalm there would be a pause, the priests would blow on their horns and the congregation would fall down in worship. A presenter, temple singer, or priest usually began the hymns followed by a response from the temple choir. Or, the hymn might be sung by two temple choirs, as evident in Psalm 136. This practice would be more like the responsive readings conducted in most churches today.

Temple tax collectors. Individuals who collected a half-shekel tax from every Jewish male, over the age of twenty, in March of each year, for the upkeep of the temple were called temple tax collectors (Ex 30.14-15; Mt 17.24).

Tempter/Devil. In the OT, the tempter or devil played only a minor role. Even in the late book of Job, he was only one of the angels whose duty it was to call God's attention to the shortcomings of God's people. However, in the intertestamental literature, under the influence of Persian dualism (Ahriman against Ormazd), the tempter took on the character of an evil deity opposed to God and was accepted by the early church. For Paul, he was "the god of this world" who had "blinded the minds of the unbelievers" (2 Cor 4.4). Jesus thought of the devil and "his kingdom" (11.8), as did his Jewish contemporaries and later Christians, as the great obstacles preventing the rule of God.

Tenants. In Jesus' parable of the vineyard, the landowner planted a vineyard, put a fence around it, dug a winepress in it and built a watchtower. Then he leased it to tenants while he went to another country. At harvest time, he sent his slaves to the tenants to collect his produce, but they beat one, killed another, and stoned another. They also killed the landowner's son. (Mt 21.33-46).

Those at the left hand. In Jesus' parable of the great judgment, this was the location of some people at the left hand of God (Mt 25.44).

Unemployed. In the parable of the laborers in the vineyard, these individuals remained unemployed by five o'clock in the afternoon with no reason given (Mt 20.1-16).

Vineyard owner. In the parable of the vineyard, God was the owner of the vineyard, and the vineyard represented Israel. The tenants were the leaders of Judaism, and the slaves were the OT prophets. Jesus was the beloved son murdered by crucifixion. The destruction of the wicked was the destruction of the temple, and the new tenants were the apostles and the early church (Mt 21.33-36).

Witnesses. (two false) Since Jewish law required that two witnesses give testimony before putting anyone to death (Num 35.30; Deut

19-15), two false witnesses provided this testimony against Jesus (Mt 26.61).

Woman. The function and status of women in the Bible, as wives and mothers, were strongly influenced by the patriarchal form of family life. Here, a woman was not identified by name, but by region, Canaanite (Mt 15.22-27; 27.54), Samaritan (Jn 4.1-42), at the gate of the high priest (Jn 18.17), or by an illness (Mt 9.21-22).

Zechariah. [Jehovah is renowned] There were several individuals in the Bible bearing the name of Zechariah. The most familiar one was Zachariah, the prophet in Judah who wrote the eleventh book among the Minor Prophets, quoted in Matthew (Mt 21.5) and John (Jn 12.15). Another well-known Zachariah was the father of John the Baptist (Lk 1.57-80).

Introduction to the Gospel of Matthew

The Jewish Christian movement failed to have fellow Jews embrace the gospel message of Jesus as the Messiah. For the most part, the nation that gave birth to its founder and its early followers disowned him. The early followers of Jesus must have identified with Moses when the Israelites rejected him. However, the rejection of Jesus was more frustrating, because they believed Jesus to be the crown and completion of Judaism. Jesus, as the Jewish Messiah, would usher in the nation's high hopes of spiritual triumph. On the other hand, the Jewish establishment refused to recognize Jesus as the long-expected deliverer and naturally rejected his gospel. Who was right? The prophets had anticipated a redeemed and glorified nation, but the nation had refused to be redeemed and glorified by such a Messiah. It seemed the Lord's divine program had broken down and was destined for failure.

However, the gospel was being received among the Greeks of the Roman Empire in increasing numbers. Gentiles were taking places the Jewish prophets predicted would be occupied by their countrymen. The church was rapidly becoming a Roman affair. Many Gentiles and Romans were ready to accept the Messiah (Christ) and make him their own. To a Christian, with Jewish training, this only magnified the problem. How could the messiahship of Jesus be harmonized with the nation's rejection of him? The prophets associated the messianic deliverer with the redeemed nation, but the events of history were not being fulfilled as predicted and expected. What did all this mean? Were the prophets wrong, or was Jesus a false Messiah? In addition, if Jesus was a false Messiah, why did the

Gentiles and Romans embrace him as the Messiah? Paul recognized the problem and in his writings to the Romans proposed a solution. Paul felt the Jewish people would ultimately turn to the Gospel, and all Israel would be saved. However, after Paul wrote his letter to the Romans relations between the Jewish people and Christians did not improve, in fact, the separation grew greater, and Paul's solution seemed more improbable than ever.

When the Romans destroyed Jerusalem and the temple in 70 CE, the entire world for both Jews and Christians changed. Matthew, a Jewish Christian, believed Jesus was the Messiah of the prophets. Jesus presented himself as the Messiah before the assembly in Jerusalem, at its great annual Feast and offered the kingdom of heaven to the Jewish people. However, the nation misled by its religious leaders rejected him and drove him to his death. Matthew looked upon the fall of Jerusalem and the temple as God's punishment of the Jewish nation for their rejection of the Messiah, and by this rejection, it proved the gospel was intended for all nations. Clearly, Matthew was not a Judaizer, someone who believed to be a Christian you must first become a Jew. Nor did he belong to any exclusive Jewish Christian sect evidenced by his radical break from the position of the scribes and Pharisees.

Matthew made extensive use of the OT, especially the prophecies, and some thirteen times he stated, "All this took place to fulfill what had been spoken by the LORD through the prophet" (1.22). Matthew considered this fulfillment theme necessary for his readers as he laid out his gospel into five great discourses: "The Sermon on the Mount" (5.1-7.27), "Commissioning and instruction of the Twelve" (10.1-11.1), "Teaching in parables" (13.1-52), "Sayings on humility and forgiveness" (18.1-35), and "On the end of the age" (24.1-26.2).

With great skill, Matthew worked his material, from Q (oral teachings) and other sources, into an account of the life and teachings of Jesus, and what might be called the first historical defense for universal Christianity. It was a biography of Jesus, who descended from Abraham through the royal line of David, who was born into a unique relationship with God. This unequaled relationship affirmed at his baptism took form during the temptation conflicts. Jesus presented the message of God's kingdom or the rule of God by using a series of great sermons and miracles. In one of his sermons, known as "the Sermon on the Mount," Jesus called his disciples to a higher standard of righteousness than required by the Jewish law (teaching). He followed these bold demands with a series of prophetic and messianic acts that revealed his right to make such demands. The Jewish leaders were not convinced and quickly became hostile toward Jesus, as they believed Jesus to be a false Messiah, even if his closest disciples recognized him as the Messiah. Soon afterward, his disciples in the transfiguration experience received a new image of the spiritual and prophetic nature of the Messiah, where they saw him associated with Moses and Elijah, the great prophetic molders of the Jewish religion.

Aware that his time on earth was limited, Jesus continued to preach and turned toward Jerusalem where he would put the nation in a position to either accept or refuse his message. When they refused, he predicted the nation's doom as a result. The kingdom of God would be taken away from them and given to a nation that would produce the fruits of the kingdom. Jesus, in some final discourses, denounced the wickedness and hypocrisy of the nation's religious leaders and pronounced the destruction of the temple and the city of Jerusalem, followed shortly by the triumphant return of the Messiah in judgment. The Jewish leaders were offended by his claims of authority, and in response, had him arrested and executed. However, after three days he reappeared to some women of the disciples' company, and afterward to the disciples, with the charge for them to carry his gospel about the kingdom of God to all the nations.

For Matthew during Jesus' earthly ministry, his message was confined to his disciples and the Jews. However, since they refused the gospel, his last command to his followers was to offer it to all humanity. Therefore, the curtain fell on the Gospel of Matthew leaving Jesus as an abiding presence with his disciples.

The Jewish war of 66-70 CE reminded Jesus' followers of his predictions and teachings. Jesus did not come to destroy Law (teaching) or prophets; his work and its fortunes stood in close relationship with them. For Matthew, the solution to the problem was a simple and complete one, so much so that few people today stop to think about the possibility of a triumphal Messiah apart from a triumphal nation. As a result, the Gospel according to Matthew was a success for the early believers and even for our present generation.

We should not dismiss lightly the tradition of the authorship of the book by the apostle Matthew around 85 CE. If Matthew regarded Mark's earlier gospel as inadequate in his dealing with Jesus' teaching, yet he included almost everything in Mark's account, but freely rearranged the events, as though he somehow knew best. Certainly, this was not the first time that a good book had become the basis for a better one. Nor was it anything against Matthew's authorship that he made use of a document or two used again by Luke.

The reader might assume when Matthew, living in Antioch, received Mark's book about Jesus, from his perspective, there was apparent weakness, and he used it as the foundation of his account. Forty years after Matthew's book was written it was quoted by those at Antioch as "The Gospel," and probably was the first book to bear that title. Some twenty years later, when the Christian leaders, for some reason, collected the Gospels of Matthew, Mark, Luke and John, first place was given to Matthew, and the name "Gospel" was extended to all of them. As a result, a new designation was made that would distinguish between them, so it became "The Gospel according to Matthew."

Matthew

Chapter 1
Jesus' royal descent, 1.1-17
(Lk 3.23-38)

Matthew. (M)(An account of the genealogy[a] of Jesus the Messiah,[b]the son of David, the son of Abraham.

[2]Abraham was the father of Isaac, and Isaac the father of Jacob, and Jacob the father of Judah and his brothers, [3]and Judah the father of Perez and Zerah by Tamar, and Perez the father of Hezron, and Hezron the father of Aram, [4]and Aram the father of Aminadab, and Aminadab the father of Nahshon, and Nahshon the father of Salmon, [5]and Salmon the father of Boaz by Rahab, and Boaz the father of Obed by Ruth, and Obed the father of Jesse, [6]and Jesse the father of King David.

And David was the father of Solomon by the wife of Uriah, [7]and Solomon the father of Rehoboam, and Rehoboam the father of Abijah, and Abijah the father of Asaph,[c] [8]and Asaph[d] the father of Jehoshaphat, and Jehoshaphat the father of Joram, and Joram the father of Uzziah, [9]and Uzziah the father of Jotham, and Jotham the father of Ahaz, and Ahaz the father of Hezekiah, [10]and Hezekiah the father of Manasseh, and Manasseh the father of Amos,[e] and Amos[f]

---

[a] Or *birth*
[b] Or *Jesus Christ*
[c] Other ancient authorities read *Asa*
[e] Other ancient authorities read *Amon*
[f] Other ancient authorities read *Amon*

the father of Josiah, ^{11} and Josiah the father of Jechoniah and his brothers, at the time of the deportation to Babylon.

^{12}And after the deportation to Babylon: Jechoniah was the father of Salathiel, and Salathiel the father of Zerubbabel, ^{13}and Zerubbabel the father of Abiud, and Abiud the father of Eliakim, and Eliakim the father of Azor, ^{14}and Azor the father of Zadok, and Zadok the father of Achim, and Achim the father of Eliud, ^{15}and Eliud the father of Eleazar, and Eleazar the father of Matthan, and Matthan the father of Jacob, ^{16}and Jacob the father of Joseph the husband of Mary, of whom Jesus was born, who is called the Messiah.^{g}

^{17}So all the generations from Abraham to David are fourteen generations; and from David to the deportation to Babylon, fourteen generations; and from the deportation to Babylon to the Messiah,^{h} fourteen generations.)

Jesus' birth and infancy, 1.18-2.25
(Lk 1.26-2.40)

Matthew. (M)(^{18}Now the birth of Jesus the Messiah^i took place in this way. When his mother Mary had been engaged to Joseph, but before they lived together, she was found to be with child from the Holy Spirit.^{19}Her husband Joseph, being a righteous man and unwilling to expose her to public disgrace, planned to dismiss her quietly. ^{20}But just when he had resolved to do this, an angel of the Lord appeared to him in a dream and said,

Angel. "Joseph, son of David, do not be afraid to take Mary as your wife, for the child conceived in her is from the Holy Spirit. ^{21} She will bear a son, and you are to name him Jesus, for he will save his people from their sins."

Matthew. ^{22}All this took place to fulfill what had been spoken by the Lord through the prophet:

g Or *the Christ*
h Or *the Christ*
i Or *Jesus Christ*

Isaiah. (I)([23]"Look, the virgin shall conceive and bear a son, and they shall name him Emmanuel,"

Matthew. which means,

Isaiah. "God is with us" [j])

Matthew. [24]When Joseph awoke from sleep, he did as the angel of the Lord commanded him; he took her as his wife, [25]but had no marital relations with her until she had borne a son;[k] and he named him Jesus.)

Chapter 1 Notes
Jesus' royal descent, 1.1-17

Matthew began his gospel with a genealogy to prove that Jesus was the rightful Messiah according to Jewish law by linking him to Abraham through David. Luke in contrast connected Jesus' line with Adam, the first man (Lk 3.23-38). The original list may have been compiled by a Jewish Christian, who believed that Jesus was the son of David through Joseph and who regarded James, the Lord's brother, and others of Jesus' family leaders of the church after the resurrection. Genealogies were important for several reasons, including the establishment of priestly descent. Matthew's list contained errors that could be easily corrected by the Bible, so he probably obtained it from a source rather than compiling it himself. Matthew ended his gospel with a world outlook and mission (Mt 28.19), but he began it recognizing Israel's national heritage and hope for a Messiah, who for Matthew was Jesus Christ.

1: *Messiah,* the Hebrew word meaning "anointed one," or "restorer" was translated into Greek as "Christos" or Christ. The Jewish people did not universally believe that the Messiah was the son of David, but after 63 BCE, it became the popular opinion. The

[j] Isa 7.14
[k] Other ancient authorities read *her firstborn son*

accepted doctrine included "the promise made to Abraham and his seed" (Gen 22.18). **3-6:** Women were not usually included in Jewish genealogies, yet Rahab, Ruth, and Bath-sheba are included here, along with Tamar. Ruth was a foreigner, and scandals were attached to the other names. However, the God of Israel, in his infinite power and love, could make great kings out of the descendants of even these women (Ruth 4.18-22; 1 Chr 2.1-15). **8:** For the sake of the pattern (v 17), the names of Ahaziah, Joash, and Amaziah (1 Chr 3.11-12) have been omitted; such omission followed the Jewish practice of forming genealogies. **11:** *The deportation* was a reference to the exile into Babylon as it marked a new relationship between God and Israel (2 Kings 8-16; Jer 27.20). **12:** *Jechoniah* may also be translated as Jehoiachin (2 Kings 24.6; 1 Chr 3.16). *Salathiel* apparently transmitted the line of legal descent from *Jechoniah* to *Zerubbabel* (Ezra 3.2; Hag 2.2; Lk 3.27), although the Chronicler traced it through Pedaiah (1 Chr 3.16-19). **13-16:** The persons from *Abiud* to *Jacob* are otherwise unknown.

16: Some ancient authorities read, "Jacob the father of Joseph, to whom the virgin Mary having been betrothed bore Jesus called Christ." Other ancient authorities read, "Jacob the father of Joseph. Joseph, to who was betrothed the virgin Mary who bore Jesus the Christ." In addition, other ancient authorities read, "Jacob, the father of Joseph the husband of Mary who bore Jesus who is called Christ." **17:** The practice of making three groups of names is an aid to memory. *Fourteen* is the numerical value of the three letters in the name David in Hebrew (DWD).

Jesus' birth and infancy, 1.18-2.23

18: *Jesus the Messiah,* or Jesus or Christ; Jesus. A Jewish engagement (betrothal) could only be dissolved by the man giving the woman a writ of divorce, and a betrothed virgin would be a widow if her fiancé died. **19:** *A righteous* man observed the Jewish law. Joseph had two options: he could expose Mary by bringing her before the court and *expose her to public disgrace,* or he could *dismiss her quietly,* by giving her a writ in the presence of two witnesses. **20:** *Angel of the Lord* probably should read "Angel of the LORD" (*see* Angels). In the OT, the word Lord was used two ways (*see* LORD). **21:** The name Jesus was the Greek form of the Hebrew name Joshua that means, "Yahweh is salvation" or "Yahweh saves." Matthew understood this when *the angel of the Lord* said, *"and you are to name him Jesus, for he will save his people from their sins."* In Jewish thought, *from their sins,* was not an essential part of the Messiah's role, but it was believed that in the days of the Messiah that sin would disappear. The Messiah would judge and destroy sinners and demons, and then pour out his Spirit, which would cause holiness (*Testament of Judah*, 24). **22-23:** Matthew to explain the importance of Jesus' birth as a sign from the LORD reached back to Isaiah (Isa 7.10-16). The LORD urged Ahaz to request a sign, a sign that was "as deep as Sheol or high as heaven," that what he had been told was the truth. Ahaz refused the offer and defended his decision, claiming he did not want to test the LORD, while in reality he was relying on the intervention of the Assyrian king (2 Kings 16.7-9). Ahaz's response was understood to be one of profound unbelief (2 Kings 16.1-4). The term "sign" had great importance within the Scriptures, because a particular event, be it normal or miraculous, confirms the prophetic word, be it positive or negative. The rainbow was God's promise to never again destroy the world by water (Gen 9.12-15). Samuel promised that Saul would rule over Israel (1 Sam 10.1). The prediction was that the entire house of Eli would be destroyed (1 Sam 2.34). These are only a few examples that lead the people to expect a sign from God before some pending divine action. "Therefore the Lord himself will give you a sign. Look, the young woman is with child and shall bear a son, and shall name him Immanuel. He shall eat curds and honey by the time he knows how to refuse the evil and choose the good...the land will be deserted" (Isa 7.14-15). Scholars differ on whether the sign was the woman's pregnancy, the child's birth, his name, his diet, or when this would happen. The *Septuagint* (LXX) translated "young woman" as *"virgin"* leading Christians to connect these verses with Mary and the birth of Jesus. In Luke, the angel of the LORD tells the shepherds, "This will be a sign for you: you will find a child wrapped in bands of cloth and lying in a manger" (Lk 2.12). Jewish scholars agree the sign refers to a young woman of marriageable age, whether married or not, will bear a son, and his name will be Immanuel (God is with us). The message of the sign was two-fold; God is with us, to both protect (Isa 7.16) and to punish (Isa 7.17). **25:** *Bore a son* in other ancient authorities reads "her firstborn son," or "she bore him a son."

Chapter 1 Study Guide

1. State the purpose for Matthew's gospel.
2. Why does Matthew's list of ancestors differ from that of Luke (Lk 3.23-34)?
3. Why do you think the list of Jesus' ancestors is through Joseph rather than Mary?
4. Why did Joseph plan to dismiss Mary quietly before the birth of Jesus?
5. What does the virgin birth mean to you?

Chapter 2
The wise men (Magi), 2.1-12

Matthew. (M)(In the time of King Herod, after Jesus was born in Bethlehem of Judea, wise men[a] from the East came to Jerusalem, [2]asking,

Magi. "Where is the child who has been born king of the Jews? For we observed his star at its rising,[b] and have come to pay him homage."

Matthew. [3]When King Herod heard this, he was frightened, and all Jerusalem with him; [4]and calling together all the chief priests and

---

[a] Or *astrologers*; Gk *magi*
[b] Or *in the East*

scribes of the people, he inquired of them where the Messiah^c was to be born. ⁵They told him,

Chief priests and Scribes. "In Bethlehem of Judea; for so it has been written by the prophet:

Lord. ⁶'And you, Bethlehem, in the land of Judah, are by no means least among the rulers of Judah; for from you shall come a ruler who is to shepherd^d my people Israel.'"^e

Matthew. ⁷Then Herod secretly called for the wise men^f and learned from them the exact time when the star had appeared. ⁸Then he sent them to Bethlehem, saying,

Herod. "Go and search diligently for the child; and when you have found him, bring me word so that I may also go and pay him homage."

Matthew. ⁹When they had heard the king, they set out; and there, ahead of them, went the star that they had seen at its rising,^g until it stopped over the place where the child was. ¹⁰When they saw that the star had stopped,^h they were overwhelmed with joy. ¹¹On entering the house, they saw the child with Mary his mother; and they knelt down and paid him homage. Then, opening their treasure chests, they offered him gifts of gold, frankincense, and myrrh. ¹²And having been warned in a dream not to return to Herod, they left for their own country by another road.)

Escape to Egypt and return, 2.13-23

Matthew. (M)([13]Now after they had left, an angel of the Lord appeared to Joseph in a dream and said,

Angel. "Get up, take the child and his mother, and flee to Egypt, and remain there until I tell you; for Herod is about to search for the child, to destroy him."

Matthew. [14]Then Joseph[i] got up, took the child and his mother by night, and went to Egypt, [15]and remained there until the death of Herod. This was to fulfill what had been spoken by the Lord through the prophet,

Lord. (Je)("Out of Egypt I have called my son."[j]**)**

Matthew. [16]When Herod saw that he had been tricked by the wise men,[k] he was infuriated, and he sent and killed all the children in and around Bethlehem who were two years old or under, according to the time that he had learned from the wise men.[l] [17]Then was fulfilled what had been spoken through the prophet Jeremiah:

Lord. (B)([18]"A voice was heard in Ramah, wailing and loud lamentation, Rachel weeping for her children; she refused to be consoled, because they are no more."[m]**)**

Matthew. [19]When Herod died, an angel of the Lord suddenly appeared in a dream to Joseph in Egypt and said,

Angel. [20]"Get up, take the child and his mother, and go to the land of Israel, for those who were seeking the child's life are dead."

---

[i] Gk *he*
[j] Hos 11.1
[k] Or *astrologers*; Gk *magi*
[l] Or *astrologers*; Gk *magi*
[m] Jer 31.15

Matthew. [21]Then Joseph[n] got up, took the child and his mother, and went to the land of Israel. [22]But when he heard that Archelaus was ruling over Judea in place of his father Herod, he was afraid to go there. After being warned in a dream, he went away to the district of Galilee. [23]There he made his home in a town called Nazareth, so that what had been spoken through the prophets might be fulfilled.)

Isaiah. (I)("He will be called a Nazorean." [o])

Chapter 2 Notes
The wise men (Magi), 2.1-12

The account of the wise men (Magi), like other narratives in this chapter, can not be found in any other first-century Christian writing. Therefore, its validity cannot be established, but its value does not depend on its accuracy, the story is a work of art. When heard during the Christmas or Epiphany season, Christians recognize its value. Jesus was born among the Jewish people and men came from great distances and by many means to worship Christ. Matthew felt that nothing, not even nature remained unmoved by this stupendous event and he has Jesus controlling what happened from his cradle, before he says or does anything. The absence of any activity by the Jewish leaders concerning the birth of Jesus was noted in this chapter. They knew where the King of the Jews was to be born and yet they made no inquiry of the Magi.

1-2: *Herod* the Great was appointed King of the Jews by the Roman Senate in 40 BCE and gained control of his realm a few years later. He died in the spring of 4 BCE (*see* Herod). *Bethlehem of Judea,* the birthplace of David, was five miles south of Jerusalem and a church there marks the traditional site of Jesus' birth. *Wise men* may have been a Median tribe of priests (*see* Magi). An embassy of Parthian magi paid homage to Nero at Naples in 66 CE and returned

---

[n] Gk *he*
[o] Isa 11.1

by another route. *We observed his star at its rising* reflected the ancient belief that a star appeared at the birth of a great person or a great event, and they had *come to pay him homage.* **3-4:** It was understandable that Herod felt threatened, but it was not clear why *all Jerusalem* was frightened. Unless they were in fear of what Herod might do, or maybe they feared the report of the chief priests and scribes. *Chief priests* were probably members of the high priests' families (*see* Chief priests). *Scribes of the people* were probably the scribes of the Pharisees (*see* Scribes). **5-6:** *They* (Chief priests and scribes) *told* Herod *it had been written by the prophet* Micah (Mic 5.2-4) that the Messiah, the shepherd king, would not be born in Jerusalem, but like David, in Bethlehem, among the insignificant clan of Judah (Gen 35.19; Ruth 4.11; 1 Sam 7.12). They probably related to Herod the hardship that Israel must endure before the Messiah would come. The NJPS comment on Micah (Mic 5.2-4) may provide a reason for the people's fear. "Rab said: 'The son of David will not come until the [Roman] power enfolds Israel for nine months, as it is written, Therefore will he give them up, until the time that she which travaileth hath brought forth: then the remnant of his brethren shall return unto the children of Israel.' Ulla said: 'Let him [The Messiah] come, but let me not see him.' Rabbah said likewise: 'Let him come, but let me not see him.' Abaye enquired of Rabbah: 'What is your reason [for not wishing to see him]? Shall we say, because of the birth pains [preceding the advent] of the Messiah?' But it has been taught, R. Eleazar's disciples: 'What must a man do to be spared the pangs of the Messiah?' [He answered,] 'Let him engage in study and benevolence; and your Master do both.'" (b. *Samh.* 986b [Soricino ET]). The Messiah would usher in a time of security and stability for Israel and because of his unlimited power would not be challenged by other nations. It would be a time when Israel would be rescued by the LORD and transformed into a strong nation that would live unthreatened and invulnerable in the midst of the nations. It shall be a blessing upon those who receive them and a curse upon those who reject them (Gen 12.2-3; Gal 3.8).

7: Such news would have caused Herod some concern and *the exact time when the star had appeared* would enable him to determine the age of the child. **11:** *Frankincense* was a fragrance from white gum resin imported to Palestine from Arabia, that was ground into a powder, and when burned would give off a balsam like odor. According to Levitical regulations, frankincense was one of the major ingredients of the incense for the LORD. Using this incense for purposes other than those specified in the priestly rituals was forbidden. Frankincense was set before the holy of holies with the Bread of the Presence (Lev 24.7). *Myrrh* was the fragrant resin found mostly in S. Arabia. It was an important ingredient of the sacred anointing oil (Ex 30.23) and in perfumes used for beauty treatments (Esther 2.12; Song of Sol 5.5) and for scenting clothes. **12:** *Warned* in the Greek can be translated "instructed by an oracle."

Escape to Egypt and return, 2.13-23

13-14: Matthew identified the opposition to Jesus starting with his birth, and continuing until his death. For additional information on *the angel of the LORD, (see* Angels). *Egypt* at its nearest point was not far from Bethlehem. It is not clear how long they stayed in Egypt only *until the death of Herod* in the spring of 4 BCE. At the beginning of the second century CE, a Jewish story emerged that Jesus learned magic while he was in Egypt. **15:** Again, Matthew used the OT to support his claim concerning Jesus as the Messiah. As the quote from Hosea, *"Out of Egypt I have called my son"* (Ex 4.22; Hos 11.1) where the LORD concerning Israel was not merely events that might have happened, but fulfilling the LORD's purpose, delayed but never replaced.

16: Herod, when he realized he was tricked by the wise men, became *infuriated, and he sent and killed all the children in and around Bethlehem who were two years old or under.* Because no record of this massacre exists in any other historical source, some believe it was a legend. On the other hand, Herod was ruthless and reacted violently to any threat to his throne, and there were similar stories of infants being killed because of prophecy. Others used this as reference to Pharaoh's hostility to Moses and the children of Israel (Ex 1.16). **18:** This verse is from Jeremiah (Jer 31.15), *Rachel,* wife of Jacob, died in childbirth and according to Genesis (Gen 35.16-20) was buried near Bethlehem. *Ramah,* an Ephraimite town, eight miles north of Jerusalem was the scene of national grief (Jer 40.1) inflicted by an enemy.

20: *Those who were seeking the child's life* referred to Herod and maybe those who had been commanded to kill the newborn king of the Jews. **22:** *Archelaus,* who was almost as cruel as his father Herod, reigned from 4 BCE to 6 CE, and because of his brutality was replaced by a Roman procurator until Palestine was ruled by King Herod Agrippa I (41-44 CE). **23:** There was a similarity in sound and possibly, in meaning between the Aramaic word for Nazareth and the Hebrew word translated branch (Isa 11.1). Nazareth was in a secluded valley in lower Galilee, a little north of the Esdraelon plain. There was no mention of Nazareth in the OT or to any prophecy concerning any residency there. Matthew apparently uses *"Nazareth"* as a play on words for the Greek title *"a Nazorean"* (19.19; Acts 24.5) that came from the Hebrew "nasar" that means "to guard" or "to observe" and should be compared with the name "nasorayya" that was given to the Mandaean sect, known to be followers of John the Baptist. Josephus recorded John the Baptist was arrested because he raised the messianic expectations in the people. John, the Evangelist (Jn 18.7), expressed that it was difficult within Jesus' lifetime to separate the movement of John the Baptist from that of Jesus. There are those who hold that the Mandaean sect resisted pressures from the Christian church for centuries and may have even been an influence in the origin of the Islamic religion.

Chapter 2 Study Guide

1. What is the purpose of the visit of the wise men from the East?
2. Why was Herod and all Jerusalem frightened at the wise men's inquiry, "Where is the child who has been born king of the Jews?"

3. How do you explain that Luke reports that Jesus was born in a manger (Lk 2.7, 1 3) while Matthew has the wise men visiting in a house?

4. Why kill all of the children in and around Bethlehem two years old and under?

5. Explain the term "Nazorean."

Chapter 3
Activity of John the Baptist, 3.1-12
(Mk 1.1-8; Lk 3.1-18; Jn 1.6-8, 19-28)

Matthew. (M)(In those days) **[Q₂]**[John the Baptist appeared in the wilderness of Judea,] proclaiming,

John the Baptist. (M)(²"Repent, for the kingdom of heaven has come near."ª)

Matthew. ³This is the one of whom the prophet Isaiah spoke when he said,

Isaiah. (D-I)("The voice of one crying out in the wilderness:

Messenger. 'Prepare the way of the Lord, make his paths straight.' "ᵇ)

Matthew. (M)(⁴Now John wore clothing of camel's hair with a leather belt around his waist, and his food was locusts and wild honey.) ⁵Then the people of Jerusalem and all Judea were going out to him, and all the region along the Jordan, ⁶and they were baptized by him in the river Jordan, confessing their sins. **[Q₂]**[⁷But when he saw many Pharisees and Sadducees coming for baptism, he said to them,

---

ª   Or *is at hand*
ᵇ   Isa 40.3

John the Baptist. "You brood of vipers! Who warned you to flee from the wrath to come? [8]Bear fruit worthy of repentance. [9]Do not presume to say to yourselves,

Pharisees and Sadducees. 'We have Abraham as our ancestor';

John the Baptist. for I tell you, God is able from these stones to raise up children to Abraham. [10]Even now the ax is lying at the root of the trees; every tree therefore that does not bear good fruit is cut down and thrown into the fire.]

[Q_2][[11] "I baptize you with[c] water for repentance, but one who is more powerful than I is coming after me; I am not worthy to carry his sandals. He will baptize you with[c] the Holy Spirit and fire. [12]His winnowing fork is in his hand, and he will clear his threshing floor and will gather his wheat into the granary; but the chaff he will burn with unquenchable fire."]

Jesus' baptism, 3.13-17
(Mk 1.9-11; Lk 3.21-22; Jn 1.31-34)

Matthew. [13]Then Jesus came from Galilee to John at the Jordan, to be baptized by him. (**M**)([14]John would have prevented him, saying,

John the Baptist. "I need to be baptized by you, and do you come to me?"

Matthew. But Jesus answered him,

Jesus. [15]"Let it be so now; for it is proper for us in this way to fulfill all righteousness."

Matthew. Then he consented.) [Q_1][[16]And when Jesus had been baptized, just as he came up from the water, suddenly the heavens

---

[c] Or *in*

were opened **(M)**(to him) and he saw the Spirit of God descending like a dove and alighting on him. [17]And a voice from heaven said,

God. "This is my Son, the Beloved,[d] with whom I am well pleased."]

Chapter 3 Notes
Activity of John the Baptist, 3.1-12

1: *John* resembled the OT prophets such as Elijah (cf v 4 with 2 Kings 1.8; Zech 13.4). The Christian faith understood him to fulfill Isaiah's (Isa 40.3) and Malachi's (Mal 3.1; 4.5) prophesies (see 17.10-12). Acts (Acts 18.25; 19.1-7) supported his influence outside Christianity. *In those days* indicating that, *John the Baptist* appeared while Jesus lived at Nazareth (2.23). *Gospel according to the Ebionites,* (in Epiphanius, *Against Heresies,* 30.13.6), "In the days of Herod, king of Judea, when Caiaphas was high priest, a certain man named John came baptizing with a baptism of repentance in the river Jordan. He was said to be of the family of Aaron the priest, son of Zechariah and Elizabeth, and all went out to him." *The wilderness of Judea* lay east and southeast of Jerusalem. **2:** *Repent,* literally "return," meant to come back to the way of life charted by the covenant between the LORD and Israel (Ex 19.3-6; 24.3-8; Jer 31.31-34). *Kingdom of heaven,* meaning the effective rule of God over his people, occurred 32 times in the Gospel of Matthew but not in any of the other NT writings. **3:** All three gospel writers (Mt 3.3; Mk 1.2-3; Lk 3.4-6) follow the text of Isaiah (Isa 40.3), where the prophet expected that the return of the Babylonian exiles to Palestine would be supernaturally facilitated. They connected *in the wilderness* with the *voice,* and by changing *the way of the Lord* to *his paths,* the Synoptic Gospels made *Lord* to mean "Messiah," and found biblical support for their interpretation of John as herald and forerunner of the Christ (*see* LORD). **4:** Elijah was expected to return to prepare the way for God's final work (Mal 4.5). The OT described Elijah as a hairy man, with a leather belt

---

[d] Or *my beloved Son*

around his waist but it did not include *clothing of camel's hair* (2 Kings 1.8). Several species of *locusts* are eaten today according to Jewish dietary laws. **5:** *People of Jerusalem...all Judea...all of the region along the Jordan* as people from both the rural areas and the city were *baptized by him,* or in his presence, or at his direction. Jewish baptism and probably the earliest Christian baptisms were self-administered. *Gospel according to the Ebionites,* (in Epiphanius, *Against Heresies,* 30.13.4) "John was baptizing; and Pharisees went out to him and were baptized, and all Jerusalem. Now John wore a garment of camel's hair, and a leather girdle around his waist; his food was wild honey, tasting like manna, like a cake in olive oil." **6:** John the Baptist was an important religious figure in his own right, with disciples that maintained their separate identity for a long time after his death. John called people to baptism with water, symbolizing recognition and *confession their sins* with acceptance of God's will. When a non-Jew became a Jew three things were required, the first was circumcision, as that was the mark of the covenant people. The second was to make a sacrifice for his sins, as only blood could atone for sin. The third was to be baptized and that symbolized the cleansing from the pollution of the past life.

7: The *Pharisees* (*see* Pharisees) *and Sadducees* (*see* Sadducees) each represented two major divisions within Judaism (for difference between them, see 22.23n and Acts 23.6-10). A third Jewish sect in Palestine was the Essenes (Josephus, *The History of the Jewish War,* ii.viii.2-13); their beliefs and practices were reflected in the Dead Sea Scrolls found at Qumran. *Pharisees and Sadducees coming for baptism* may be translated in other versions "to his baptism" not to be baptized but to observe what was happening. The Pharisees and Sadducees were compared to a *brood of vipers,* those low and poisonous creatures that flee in haste before the onrushing fire that swept across the wilderness. The *wrath to come* was regarding God's judgment (1 Thess 1.10). **8-10:** Just being descendants of *Abraham,* the father of Israel, was not enough, and Matthew and Luke (Lk 3.8) had John proclaim that God could reject these physical descendants and *raise up* to *Abraham* other *children* who will be obedient to God. *Fire* was a symbol of judgment (Mt 7.19; 13.40; Heb 6.7-8).

11-12: Mark expressed, *worthy to carry his sandals* as "worthy to stoop down and untie the thong of his sandals," considered the most humble of tasks (Mk 1.7). Baptism *with the Holy Spirit* would draw people into a spiritual communion with God (Acts 2.17-21; Joel 2.28-29). The Q form has "he will baptize you with fire." Mark interpreted fire to be *Holy Spirit* followed by Luke in Acts, but Matthew and Luke used *"Holy Spirit and fire"* (Mt 3.11; Lk 3.16; Lk 12.49; Acts 2.17-21; 19.1-7; 18.24-26). They used a *winnowing fork* to toss wheat, on the *threshing floor,* in the air, and the wind would blow *the chaff* away.

Jesus' baptism, 3.13-17

13-15: Unlike Mark (Mk 1.9), Matthew stated that Jesus purpose in leaving Galilee was *to be baptized* by John. Jesus recognized John's authority and identified himself with those who responded in faith to John's call. *Gospel according to the Hebrews,* (in Jerome, *Against Pelagius, 3.2)* "The mother of the Lord and his brothers said to him, 'John the Baptist baptizes for the forgiveness of sins; let us go and be baptized by him.' But he said to them, 'In what way have I sinned that I should go and be baptized by him? Unless, perhaps, what I have just said was a sin of ignorance.'" *Gospel according to the Ebionites,* (in Epiphanius, *Against Heresies,* 30.13.7-8) "After the people were baptized, Jesus also came and was baptized by John. And when Jesus came up from the water, the heavens were opened, and Jesus saw the Holy Spirit descend in the form of a dove and enter into him. And a voice from heaven said, 'You are my beloved Son; with you I am well pleased.' And again, 'Today I have begotten you.' And immediately a great light shone around the place; and John seeing it, said to Jesus, 'Who are you, Lord?' And again, a voice from heaven said to him, 'This is my beloved Son, with whom I am well pleased.' Then John, falling down before Jesus, said, 'I beseech you, Lord, baptize me!' But Jesus forbade John, saying,

'Let it be so; for thus it is fitting that all things be fulfilled.'" Other ancient authorities, from the *Itala,* read, "Then he consented; and when he was baptized a huge light shone from the water so that all who were near were frightened." *Gospel according to the Hebrews,* (in Jerome, *Commentary on Isaiah,* 11.2) "When the Lord ascended from the water, the whole fount of the Holy Spirit descended and rested upon him, and said to him, 'My son, in all the prophets I was waiting for you, that you might come, and that I might rest in you. For you are my rest; you are my firstborn son, who reigns forever.'"

16-17: This description of the certainty and self-understanding came to Jesus at his baptism. The language, akin to OT speech, portrayed a spiritual experience that words cannot adequately describe. *A voice from heaven* that combined Psalms (Ps 2.7), an ancient hymn used for a royal accession or coronation, with Isaiah (Isa 42) a part of the "servant song" of Deutero-Isaiah, "Here is my servant, whom I uphold, my chosen in whom my soul delights; he will bring forth justice to the nations" (Isa 42.1).

Chapter 3 Study Guide

1. What was John the Baptist's purpose? Was he connected with the Qumran community of the Dead Sea Scrolls?
2. Why did he call the Pharisees and Sadducees a "brood of vipers"?
3. Explain the difference between water baptism and Spirit baptism.
4. Why was Jesus baptized by John? What was the relationship between John and Jesus?
5. What do the words, "This is my Son, the Beloved" mean to you?

Chapter 4
Jesus' temptation, 4.1-11
(Mk 1.12-13; Lk 4.1-13; Heb 2.18; 4.15)

Matthew. [Q₃][Then Jesus was led up by the Spirit into the wilderness to be tempted by the devil. ²He fasted forty days and forty nights, and afterwards he was famished. ³The tempter came and said to him,

Tempter/Devil. "If you are the Son of God, command these stones to become loaves of bread."

Matthew. ⁴But he answered,

Jesus. "It is written,

Moses. (D)('One does not live by bread alone, but by every word that comes from the mouth of God.' "ª**)**

Matthew. ⁵Then the devil took him to the holy city and placed him on the pinnacle of the temple, ⁶saying to him,

Tempter/Devil. "If you are the Son of God, throw yourself down; for it is written,

Temple singer. 'He will command his angels concerning you,' ᵇ

Tempter/Devil. and

Temple singer. 'On their hands they will bear you up, so that you will not dash your foot against a stone.'" ᶜ

Matthew. ⁷Jesus said to him,

Jesus. "Again it is written,

ª Deut 8.3
ᵇ Ps 91.11
ᶜ Ps 91.12

Moses. (D)('Do not put the Lord your God to the test.'" [d])

Matthew. [8]Again, the devil took him to a very high mountain and showed him all the kingdoms of the world and their splendor; [9]and he said to him,

Tempter/Devil. "All these I will give you, if you will fall down and worship me."

Matthew. [10]Jesus said to him,

Jesus. "Away with you, Satan! for it is written,

Moses. (D)('Worship the Lord your God, and serve only him.'" [e])

Matthew. [11]Then the devil left him, and suddenly angels came and waited on him.]

Beginnings of Jesus' activity in Galilee, 4.12-25
(Mk 1.14-15; Lk 4.14-15)

Matthew. [12]Now when Jesus[f] heard that John had been arrested, he withdrew to Galilee. **(M)**([13]He left Nazareth and made his home in Capernaum by the sea, in the territory of Zebulun and Naphtali, [14]so that what had been spoken through the prophet Isaiah might be fulfilled:

Isaiah. (I)([15]"Land of Zebulun, land of Naphtali, on the road by the sea, across the Jordan, Galilee of the Gentiles - [16]the people who sat in darkness have seen a great light, and for those who sat in the region and shadow of death light has dawned." [g])

Matthew. [17]From that time) Jesus began to proclaim,

---

[d] Deut 6.16
[e] Deut 6.13
[f] Gk *he*
[g] Isa 9.1-2

Jesus. "Repent, for the kingdom of heaven has come near."[h]

Matthew. [18]As he walked by the Sea of Galilee, he saw two brothers, Simon, who is called Peter, and Andrew his brother, casting a net into the sea—for they were fishermen. [19]And he said to them,

Jesus. "Follow me, and I will make you fish for people."

Matthew. [20]Immediately they left their nets and followed him. [21]As he went from there, he saw two other brothers, James son of Zebedee and his brother John, in the boat with their father Zebedee, mending their nets, and he called them. [22]Immediately they left the boat and their father, and followed him.

[23]Jesus[i] went throughout Galilee, teaching in their synagogues and proclaiming **(M)**(the good news[j] of the kingdom and curing every disease and every sickness among the people.) [24]So his fame spread throughout all Syria, and they brought to him all the sick, those who were afflicted with various diseases and pains, demoniacs, epileptics, and paralytics, and he cured them. [25]And great crowds followed him **(M)**(from Galilee, the Decapolis,) Jerusalem, Judea, and from beyond the Jordan.

Chapter 4 Notes
Jesus' temptation, 4.1-11

1-4: The *Spirit lead* Jesus *into the wilderness* for a time of decision, and the temptation accounts illustrate Jesus' habitual refusal to allow his concern for safety or merely practical interests to influence his sense of mission. **1:** *The devil,* the *tempter* (v 3), and *Satan* (v 10) were names for evil conceived as a personal will that was actively hostile to God (Lk 13.11, 16). The rabbis taught that Satan stirred up the evil tendency (Yetser Hara) in a person (Sir 37.3), seduced him into

---

h Or *is at hand*
i Gk *He*
j Gk *gospel*

sin, denounced him before God and then punished him with death. **2:** *Forty days* in the wilderness corresponded to the forty years that Israel spent in the wilderness (Ex 24.18; 34.28) and the time Moses was on the mountain with God (Ex 34.28; 1 Kings 19.8). Mark (Mk 1.12-13) and Luke (Lk 4.1-13) have the temptations during the forty days, while Matthew placed the temptations after *he fasted forty days and forty nights.* **3:** *If you are the Son of God* applied to angels or a divine being (*see* Jesus) and a test of faith. **4:** The contrast between stone and bread is also found in 7.9. The phrase, *from the mouth of God* reads "from the mouth of the LORD" in Deuteronomy (Deut 8.3).

5: The second test was a subtle insinuation of faith centered on the promise of personal protection (Ps 91.11-12) and to see if his vocation was genuine. *The holy city* referred to Jerusalem. Maccabean coins bore the inscription "Jerusalem the Holy." The *pinnacle* mentioned in the next clause most likely overlooked the temple courts and the deep valley of the Kidron outside the temple. **6.** The temptation was to put God's promise of protection to the test, which would be a lack of faith (Ps 91.11-12). **7:** Again Jesus quoted from Deuteronomy (Deut 6.16) where the LORD was the divine (*see* LORD). **9-10:** If Jesus could obtain this secular power, he might enforce his reforms, but at the cost of denying God's power. In Deuteronomy (Deut 6.13), *Lord your God* was "LORD *your God.*"

Beginnings of Jesus' activity in Galilee, 4.12-25

12: *Now when Jesus heard that John had been arrested* was in contrast to John's report of an extensive ministry before the Baptist's arrest (Jn 3.22-30). **13:** Jesus went down from the highlands of Galilee (Nazareth is 1300 feet above sea level) to *Capernaum,* a city 686 feet below sea level (the Dead Sea is 1292 feet below sea level). Capernaum was an important toll station on the trade route from Ptolemais to Damascus. **15-16:** The point of the prophecy from Isaiah (Isa 9.1-2) was that even *Galilee of the Gentiles* would share in the coming kingdom. *The people who sat in darkness* were those who suffered most from the Assyrian invasions. **17:** *From that time* referred to after the arrest of John (v 12). *Repent,* literally "return," meant to come back to the way of life charted by the covenant between the LORD and Israel (Ex 19.3-6; 24.3-8; Jer 31.31-34). *The kingdom of heaven* was Matthew's usual way of expressing the equivalent phrase, "the kingdom of God," found in parallel accounts in the other gospels. In asserting that God's *kingdom has come near,* Jesus meant that all God's past dealings with his creation were coming to a climax and fruition. Jesus taught both the present (Lk 10.18; 11.20; 17.21) and its future realization (Mt 6.10). Jesus' message differed from that of John the Baptist in there was no great emphasis on judgment (Mk 1.15).

18-22: *Follow me,* conveyed the Jewish tradition that a disciple only followed a teacher when invited. Responding to Jesus' call, *they left their nets,* their business, their source of livelihood, and their families to go with Jesus to learn his message and to assist anyway they could. (Mk 1.16-20; Lk 5.1-11; Jn 1.25-42).

24: In ancient times, mental illness was often described as demon possession and the healing, by Jesus, took the form of exorcism (Mt 8.16, 29; 9.32; 15.22; Mk 5.15; Lk 13.11, 16). Jesus attributed physical disorders to conflict with God's purpose of salvation in his covenant with Abraham and to be the concern of his saving activity.

Chapter 4 Study Guide

1. Why was Jesus led into the wilderness to be tempted after his baptism?
2. Explain why Matthew is the only gospel writer to include this early ministry in Capernaum.
3. How did Jesus' message differ from that of John the Baptist's?
4. Reflect upon the call of the first disciples. Of all the people Jesus could have selected, why these individuals?
5. What was the crowds' response to Jesus' preaching in Galilee?

Chapter 5

The Sermon on the Mount, 5.1-7.27

Matthew. [Q₁][Jesus[a] saw the crowds, he went up the mountain; and after he sat down, his disciples came to him. ²Then he began to speak, and taught them, saying:

The Beatitudes, 5.3-12
(Lk 6.17, 20-23)

Jesus. ³"Blessed are the poor in spirit, for theirs is the kingdom of heaven.]

(**M**)(⁴"Blessed are those who mourn, for they will be comforted.)
⁵"Blessed are the meek, for they will inherit the earth.
[Q₁][⁶"Blessed are those who hunger and thirst for righteousness, for they will be filled.]
(**M**)(⁷"Blessed are the merciful, for they will receive mercy.
⁸"Blessed are the pure in heart, for they will see God.
⁹"Blessed are the peacemakers, for they will be called children of God.
¹⁰"Blessed are those who are persecuted for righteousness' sake, for theirs is the kingdom of heaven.)
[Q₂][¹¹"Blessed are you when people revile you and persecute you and utter all kinds of evil against you falsely[b] on my account. ¹²Rejoice and be glad, for your reward is great in heaven, for in the same way they persecuted the prophets who were before you."]

The witness of the disciples, 5.13-16
(Mk 9.49-50; Lk 14.34-35)

Jesus. [Q₁][¹³"You are the salt of the earth; but if salt has lost its taste, how can its saltiness be restored? It is no longer good for anything, but is thrown out and trampled under foot.]

---

[a] Gk *he*
[b] Other ancient authorities lack *falsely*

46

[14]"You are the light of the world. A city built on a hill cannot be hid. **[Q₂][**[15]No one after lighting a lamp puts it under the bushel basket, but on the lampstand, and it gives light to all in the house.**]** **(M)(**[16]In the same way, let your light shine before others, so that they may see your good works and give glory to your Father in heaven."**)**

The relation of Jesus' message to the Jewish law, 5.17-20

Jesus. (M)([17]"Do not think that I have come to abolish the law or the prophets; I have come not to abolish but to fulfill.**)** [18]For truly I tell you, until heaven and earth pass away, not one letter,[c] not one stroke of a letter, will pass from the law until all is accomplished. **(M)(**[19]Therefore, whoever breaks[d] one of the least of these commandments, and teaches others to do the same, will be called least in the kingdom of heaven; but whoever does them and teaches them will be called great in the kingdom of heaven. [20]For I tell you, unless your righteousness exceeds that of the scribes and Pharisees, you will never enter the kingdom of heaven."**)**

Illustrations of the true understanding of the law, 5.21-48

Jesus. [21]"You have heard that it was said to those of ancient times,

LORD. (J)('You shall not murder' [e]**)**

Jesus. and

LORD. (D)('whoever murders shall be liable to judgment.' [f]**)**

---

[c] Gk *one iota*
[d] Or *annuls*
[e] Ex 20.13
[f] Deut 5.17

Jesus. ²²But I say to you that if you are angry with a brother or sister,^g you will be liable to judgment; and if you insult^h a brother or sister,ⁱ you will be liable to the council; and if you say,

Crowd. 'You fool,'

Jesus. you will be liable to the hell^j of fire. ²³So when you are offering your gift at the altar, if you remember that your brother or sister^k has something against you, ²⁴leave your gift there before the altar and go; first be reconciled to your brother or sister,^l and then come and offer your gift. **[Q₂][**²⁵Come to terms quickly with your accuser while you are on the way to court^m with him, or your accuser may hand you over to the judge, and the judge to the guard, and you will be thrown into prison. ²⁶Truly I tell you, you will never get out until you have paid the last penny."]

(**M**)(²⁷"You have heard that it was said,

Lord. (J)('You shall not commit adultery.' ⁿ)

Jesus. ²⁸But I say to you that everyone who looks at a woman with lust has already committed adultery with her in his heart.) ²⁹If your right eye causes you to sin, tear it out and throw it away; it is better for you to lose one of your members than for your whole body to be thrown into hell.^o ³⁰And if your right hand causes you to sin, cut it off and throw it away; it is better for you to lose one of your members than for your whole body to go into hell.^p

---

^g Gk *a brother*; other ancient authorities add *without cause*
^h Gk *say Raca to* (an obscure term of abuse)
ⁱ Gk *a brother*
^j Gk *Gehenna*
^k Gk *your brother*
^l Gk *your brother*
^m Gk lacks *to court*
ⁿ Ex 20.14
^o Gk *Gehenna*
^p Gk *Gehenna*

(M)([31]"It was also said,

Moses. **(D)**('Whoever divorces his wife, let him give her a certificate of divorce.' [q])

Jesus. **[Q_3]**[[32]But I say to you that anyone who divorces his wife, **(M)** (except on the ground of unchastity), causes her to commit adultery; and whoever marries a divorced woman commits adultery."]

(M)([33]"Again, you have heard that it was said to those of ancient times,

Moses. **(P)**('You shall not swear falsely, but carry out the vows you have made to the LORD.' [r])

Jesus. [34]But I say to you, Do not swear at all, either by heaven, for it is the throne of God, [35]or by the earth, for it is his footstool, or by Jerusalem, for it is the city of the great King. [36]And do not swear by your head, for you cannot make one hair white or black. [37]Let your word be 'Yes, Yes' or 'No, No'; anything more than this comes from the evil one.[s]

[38]"You have heard that it was said,

LORD. **(J)**('An eye for an eye and a tooth for a tooth.'[t])

Jesus. [39]But I say to you, **(M)**(Do not resist an evildoer.) **[Q_1]**[But if anyone strikes you on the right cheek, turn the other also; **(M)** ([40]and if anyone wants to sue you) and take your coat, give your cloak as well; **(M)**([41]and if anyone forces you to go one mile, go also the second mile.) [42]Give to everyone who begs from you, and do not refuse anyone who wants to borrow from you."]

(M) ([43]"You have heard that it was said,

Moses. **(P)**('You shall love your neighbor and hate your enemy.' [u]))

---

[q] Deut 24.1-4

[r] Lev 19.12; Num 30.2

[s] Or *evil*

[t] Ex 21.24

[u] Lev 19.18

Jesus. [Q₁][[44] But I say to you, Love your enemies and pray for those who persecute you, [45]so that you may be children of your Father in heaven; for he makes his sun rise on the evil and on the good, and sends rain on the righteous and on the unrighteous. [46]For if you love those who love you, what reward do you have? Do not even the tax collectors do the same? [47]And if you greet only your brothers and sisters,[v] what more are you doing than others? Do not even the Gentiles do the same? [48]Be perfect, therefore, as your heavenly Father is perfect."]

Chapter 5 Notes
The Sermon on the Mount, 5.1-7.27

The first of five great discourses in Matthew (10.1-11.1; 13.1-52; 18.1-35; 24.1-26.2), the Sermon on the Mount (5.1-7.27) sounded the keynote of the new age that Jesus came to introduce. Internal analysis and comparison with Luke's gospel suggests that Matthew (in accord with his habit of synthesis) has inserted into this account of the Sermon portions of Jesus' teachings on other occasions. Luke's "Sermon on the Plain" (Lk 6.20-49) expresses many similar teachings of Jesus found in Matthew (Mt 5.3-7.27). Both sermons begin with beatitudes, something that was common in the OT (Ps 1.1). Both have sections on loving one's enemies and on passing judgment. Both have the parable of the healthy and the diseased trees. Both end with the parable of the two houses. Matthew's sermon was longer (107 verses) than Luke's (30 verses). Luke may have taken the sermon as it stood in Q, while Matthew expanded it.

1: Just as Moses (*see* Moses) went up the mountain to receive the Law (teaching) (Ex 19), so Jesus *went up the mountain* (17.1; 28.16). *He sat down,* as it was the custom for Jewish teachers to sit down when teaching (cf Lk 4.20-21).

---

[v] Gk *your brothers*

The Beatitudes, 5.3-12

The Hebrew verb form has no real tenses. Actions are determined by not being completed or being completed, not by the time categories of past, present and future. The Greek verb follows with the Hebrew in that the imperfect tense describes taking place or occurring while the aorist tense denotes a completed act. The English verb reflects three tenses, the past, present and future, expressed in "It was", "It is" and "It will be." These changes in the languages must be considered when asking if the kingdom of heaven is realized in the present or the future. John the Baptist and Jesus said, "The kingdom of heaven is at hand." Jesus said he would return, and his disciples believed it would be in their lifetimes, but it did not happen. The early church had to balance their faith with a delayed return. Matthew and Luke attempted to accomplish this balance in their beatitudes, as they dealt with how to live as followers of Christ (Lk 6.17, 20-23).

3-12: *Blessed,* a favorite word of Matthew, was used in Greek literature to express the highest stage of happiness and wellbeing, that which the gods enjoyed. It expressed the early church's feeling enjoyed by living in trusting obedience under God's rule. **3:** It has often been pointed out that the Hebrew word for *"poor"* came in late Judaism (Pss 9.12; 35.10) to mean "saintly" or "pious" (Isa 66.2). This interpretation seemed to be what Matthew desired to express with the phrase, *poor in spirit.* However, Luke had in mind that the *poor* were those with limited finances and possessions. Later (Lk 18.24-25) Jesus expressed that riches could constitute a barrier to the *kingdom of heaven. Theirs is the kingdom of heaven* raised the question about when God's rule might be enjoyed, now or in the future? By Jesus' time, Hebrew thought accepted both, now and in the future.

4: *Mourn* included not only those who have lost loved ones, but those who when experiencing bitter disappointments and losses, turned to God in faith for support (Isa 61.1). *Comforted* was a word that implied strengthening and consolation.

5: *Meek* referred to those who accepted life as it came, trusting in God's purpose and rule (Ps 37.11). *Inherit the earth* was more than the Promised Land, but the kingdom of God's people realizing the privileges of fellowship with God, both now and in the future.

6: *Hunger and thirst for righteousness,* just as the body hungers and thirsts for food and drink, they desire to know God's will and to be obedient followers (Isa 55.1-2; Jn 4.14; 6.48-51). *Be filled* meant they would know the joy of living in a close relationship with God.

7: Those who understood what it meant to mourn, to be meek, and to hunger, and thirst after righteousness were quick to share this knowledge with others (17.15; Lk 10.37).

8: *Pure in heart* was single mindedness or sincerity in complete loyalty to God, freedom from mixed motives; it was not synonymous with chastity, but included it (Ps 24.4; Heb 12.14). To *see God* was living a life in fellowship with God and according to his will (1 Cor 13.12; 1 Jn 3.2; Rev 22.4).

9: *Peacemakers* were those who not only worked for the absence of strife, but because of a loving, peaceful relationship with God, they wanted to live in peace with others and did not feel the need to dominate others. *Will be called children of God* meant they would be acknowledged by God.

10-11: Both Judaism and Christianity stressed that God's servants must remain faithful even in the face of danger. The later rabbis ruled that if a person was in danger of losing one's life, they might break any commandment except idolatry, chastity or murder. Yet, they taught that martyrs would be rewarded in the world to come (1 Pet 3.14; 4.14). **12:** The *great reward* of being *in heaven* was not because of being persecuted or for doing acts of kindness, rather because of the faithfulness of God (2 Chr 36.15-16; Mt 23.37; Acts 7.52). The readers were to remember God's love for *the prophets* and other faithful individuals (Heb 11.32-38) when enduring suffering and hostility.

The witness of the disciples, 5.13-16

13: *Salt* was important for food preservation and taste, and as a necessity, it was heavily taxed in ancient times and was frequently sold in an altered form that had decreased value. When it lost its effectiveness, it became useless (Mk 9.49-50; Lk 14.34-35).

14: As *the light of the world,* the disciples were to give witness to God's life changing power and goodness (Phil 2.15; Jn 8.12). **15:** *After lighting a lamp,* Matthew, Mark and Luke each placed it *on a lampstand,* rather than hide it *under a bushel basket* (a pan or container holding about eight quarts) used by Matthew, or "under the bed" in Mark, or "under a jar" as in Luke. Instead, the light was put *on the lampstand* where Matthew says, *"It gives light to all in the house,"* while Mark placed it on the lampstand with no indication where it might be located. Luke placed the *lampstand* in the vestibule of a dwelling so that "those who enter may see the light" (Mk 4.21; Lk 8.16; 11.33). **16:** Matthew shifted from the illustration about the light and clarified that the disciples were not to display their *good works* for personal honor, but to *give glory to your Father in heaven* (5.45, 48; I Pet 2.12).

The relation of Jesus' message to the Jewish law, 5.17-20

The relationship of Jesus' message to the Jewish law was a great concern for followers with a Jewish background. **17:** *The prophets* in the Hebrew Scriptures comprised the books of Joshua, Judges, Samuel, Kings, Isaiah, Jeremiah, Ezekiel, and the twelve Minor Prophets (Lk 24.27). Many Jewish peoples revered the prophets less than the Law; hence the word *or* here. **18:** *One letter* referred to the "iota," the smallest letter of the Greek alphabet that corresponded to the "yoda," the smallest part of the Hebrew letter making it different from other letters (Lk 16.17). **19:** *Breaks* can be translated "sets aside." *Teaches* implied the great responsibility of teaching the will of God and expressing it in obedience (Jas 3.1). **20:** *Righteousness* was living in a right relationship with God, something that was explained more in the following verses (Lk 18.10-14). Jesus told his disciples that *unless your righteousness exceeds that of the scribes and Pharisees, you will never enter the kingdom of heaven.* Now, since he had the disciples' attention he provided examples of what was meant by that phrase. The *scribes and Pharisees,* who were from either the school of Hillel or the school of Shammai, argued among themselves concerning interpreting God's Law (teaching). Between this verse and chapter twenty, Matthew provided many incidents where the Pharisees wanted to trap Jesus or at least gain his support on issues that divided the Pharisees. Each group from these two popular schools of Judaism believed they followed the correct path to a right relationship with God. Jesus avoided being drawn into the middle of their differences and insisted upon a higher or more difficult path to God. Finally, after showing the disciples a higher standard, they realized that no one could keep all of the laws (teachings), thus they asked, "Then who can be saved?" Jesus responded, "For mortals it is impossible, but for God all things are possible" (19.25-26). The standard for legalism had been elevated to such a level that the disciples questioned who might obtain salvation, and Jesus conveyed it was based upon grace and love.

Illustrations of the true understanding of the Law, 5.21-48

With the standard, for extreme conformity to the exact wording of each written Mosaic law (teaching) established (5.18), Matthew continued with Jesus providing several illustrations that would reveal the divine intent in the ancient law (teaching). Matthew went to great lengths to present Jesus as supportive of his Jewish heritage and scripture, and he appealed to the divine intent in the ancient law (teaching) in every conflict with the Pharisees.

21: *You have heard that it was said* (vv 21, 27, 33, 38, 43) may have implied these lessons were heard in the synagogue. The *judgment* referred to a local Jewish court established in every town or city under the command in Deuteronomy (Deut 16.18). **22:** Murder was condemned and would be punished, but anger was looked upon as the root of violence. A first century rabbi said, "He who hates his neighbor, behold he is one who belongs to the shedders of blood." *Council* means the Sanhedrin with a membership of seventy members. *You fool* identified with the Hebrew word "raca" meant "good for nothing" and those calling their *brother or sister* such would be *liable to the hell* (Gehenna) *of fire.* Gehenna, a ravine west and south of Jerusalem, where human sacrifices had once been offered, was in Jesus' day a refuse dump for Jerusalem that burned all of the time, and it became the symbol of eternal punishment. **23-24:** A person who brought an offering to the temple had to leave the offering, to bath and change clothes, to become clean. Jesus says, "You cannot enter into a right relationship with God if you are not in a right relationship with your brother or sister." **25-26:** Tomorrow may be too late to settle their differences before they have to be in *court* and be subject to the legal system (Lk 12.57-59). The emphasis here was upon reconciliation rather than justice (6.12). **26:** A *penny* was the smallest coin in circulation (Lk 12.59).

27: *Adultery* carried the death penalty, but Jesus distinguished between the act and the inward disposition that produced the act. Jesus did not discuss the social consequences of adultery, but stressed that God wanted purity of heart (Ex 20.14; Lev 20.10; Deut 5.18; 22.22). **29-30:** Unlike Matthew, Mark did not tie these verses to adultery, but they were used in a figurative manner meaning that whenever temptations to control or abuse someone arise, they were to be discarded properly and decisively (Mk 9.43-48). These verses should not be taken to support a restriction on social relations because of a fear to be involved with evil. Jesus had contact with sinners and for him the protection from evil rested in a commitment to God's will and a deep concern for the welfare of others.

31: *It was also said* (Deut 24.1-4). *A certificate of divorce,* considered by the Jews to be a step forward, allowed a woman, who as a divorcee and without protection, with a *certificate* to seek the protection of another man and would not be accused of adultery. This *certificate,* referred to in Jewish law as a "get," must be written on durable material with ink that would not fade and had to be placed in the wife's hand by the husband. Once it was delivered to the wife, it could not be retracted. Without a certificate, a woman could not remarry, and many Jews before going to war would give their wife a provisional certificate, because if the husband died without granting the certificate, the widow could not remarry. The divorced wife could not marry for ninety days, as a way of removing any question in paternity cases. A wife could take her husband to court that might compel him to grant a divorce, if he had some "loathsome" disease, if he refused to support her or to have sex with her, or when the court had ordered him to stop beating her (Deut 24.1-4). **32:** The expression *except...unchastity* occurred also in 19.9; it was absent from the accounts in Mark (Mk 10.11-12) and Luke (Lk 16.18; cf Rom 7.2-3; 1 Cor 7.10-11). It may be a later addition, because it made Jesus agree with the school of Shammai and reduced the emphasis of marriage being the purpose of God (Mk 10.11-12).

33-37: This was not a quote from the OT but rather a summary from Leviticus (Lev 19.12), Numbers (Num 30.2) and Deuteronomy (Deut 23.21). The law assumed that people would make a *vow,* which was calling upon God to confirm and judge what they said. Jesus called upon those who take a *vow* to do what you *vow* to do. Vows were binding if made on the name of God, but not by heaven or earth or by your head. **35-37:** *Do not swear,* as Jesus called upon his followers to be truthful and responsible individuals (Isa 66.1), say, *yes,* do it, or *no,* and do not do it. Matthew returned to his evasion of responsibilities again in chapter 23.16-22 (Jas 5.12). From *evil* might be what was present in the world, or from perhaps *the evil one,* who was considered the father of lies and dishonesty (Jn 8.44).

38: While the principle, an eye for an eye, was no longer literally applied in Jesus' day, it provided the foundation for their entire civil law. It was used to determine the degree of punishment administered in response to the offense (Ex 21.23-24; Lev 24.19-20; Deut 19.21). **39-42:** To strike a person on the right cheek, with the back of your hand, is still in the East considered an insulting blow. However, Jesus here was not speaking of an insult, but was concerned with the persecution and dishonor that would arise because of discipleship. We need not only to resist the usual impulse to strike back, but to overcome evil with good (Isa 50.5; Lk 6.29-30; Rom 12.17; 1 Cor 6.7;

1 Pet 2.19; 3.9). **40:** To give the *cloak,* a long outer garment, was a proof of greater self-denial than to give the *coat* (an inner tunic of a short-sleeved garment that was knee length and held in at the waist by a girdle). **41:** Soldiers could compel civilians to carry their baggage; to go *a second mile* relieved another from the burden.

44-48: The command to *love your enemies* was the hardest of the commandments, but it was put into proper prospective that *your Father in heaven, for he makes his sun rise on the evil and the good, and sends rain on the righteous and on the unrighteous* (Lk 6.27-28, 32-36). **45:** To be *children of* God was to pattern one's attitudes after God. These words, *children of,* commonly meant persons who showed the quality named or trait of character implied (see 23.31n; Lk 6.35; 10.6; Jn 8.39-47). **48:** Disciples were first to "give glory to your Father in heaven" (v 16), then by keeping the law (teaching) to be "children of your Father in heaven", to be *perfect* in love to all *as your heavenly Father is perfect* (Col 3.14; I Jn 4.19).

Chapter 5 Study Guide

1. Do you agree that the Sermon on the Mount (Mt 5-7) is an obedience-ethic like what is found in the OT? If not, why not?
2. If it is not possible to fulfill the Sermon on the Mount, what is the intent of Jesus' teachings?
3. Explain the difference between the Sermon on the Mount and Luke's Sermon on the Plain (Lk 6.17-49). Who was the audience? Who were the poor?
4. What does the fact that Jesus called his disciples, those viewed as being weak and having little faith at times, "the light of the world" convey to you? Compare this with Jesus saying, "I am the light of the world" (Jn 8.12).

Chapter 6

Teachings in practical piety, 6.1-34

Jesus. (M)("Beware of practicing your piety before others in order to be seen by them; for then you have no reward from your Father in heaven."

[2]"So whenever you give alms, do not sound a trumpet before you, as the hypocrites do in the synagogues and in the streets, so that they may be praised by others. Truly I tell you, they have received their reward. [3]But when you give alms, do not let your left hand know what your right hand is doing, [4]so that your alms may be done in secret; and your Father who sees in secret will reward you.[a]"

[5]"And whenever you pray, do not be like the hypocrites; for they love to stand and pray in the synagogues and at the street corners, so that they may be seen by others. Truly I tell you, they have received their reward. [6]But whenever you pray, go into your room and shut the door and pray to your Father who is in secret; and your Father who sees in secret will reward you.[b]"

[7]"When you are praying, do not heap up empty phrases as the Gentiles do; for they think that they will be heard because of their many words. [8]Do not be like them, for your Father knows what you need before you ask him.)

[Q₁][[9]"Pray then in this way:

Our Father **(M)**(in heaven,) hallowed be your name.

[10] Your kingdom come. **(M)**(Your will be done, on earth as it is in heaven.)

[11] Give us this day our daily bread.[c]

[12] And forgive us our debts, as we also have forgiven our debtors.

[13] And do not bring us to the time of trial,[d]] **(M)**(but rescue us from the evil one.[e])

---

[a] Other ancient authorities add *openly*

[b] Other ancient authorities add *openly*

[c] Or *our bread for tomorrow*

[d] Or *us into temptation*

[e] Or *from evil*. Other ancient authorities add, in some form, *For the kingdom and the power and the glory are yours forever. Amen.*

¹⁴For if you forgive others their trespasses, your heavenly Father will also forgive you; (**M**)(¹⁵but if you do not forgive others, neither will your Father forgive your trespasses."

¹⁶"And whenever you fast, do not look dismal, like the hypocrites, for they disfigure their faces so as to show others that they are fasting. Truly I tell you, they have received their reward. ¹⁷But when you fast, put oil on your head and wash your face, ¹⁸so that your fasting may be seen not by others but by your Father who is in secret; and your Father who sees in secret will reward you.ᶠ)

[**Q₁**][¹⁹"Do not store up for yourselves treasures on earth, where moth and rustᵍ consume and where thieves break in and steal; ²⁰but store up for yourselves treasures in heaven, where neither moth nor rustʰ consumes and where thieves do not break in and steal. ²¹For where your treasure is, there your heart will be also."]

[**Q₂**][²²"The eye is the lamp of the body. So, if your eye is healthy, your whole body will be full of light; ²³ but if your eye is unhealthy, your whole body will be full of darkness. If then the light in you is darkness, how great is the darkness!"]

[**Q₂**][²⁴"No one can serve two masters; for a slave will either hate the one and love the other, or be devoted to the one and despise the other. You cannot serve God and wealth.ⁱ"]

[**Q₁**][²⁵"Therefore I tell you, do not worry about your life, what you will eat or what you will drink,ʲ or about your body, what you will wear. Is not life more than food, and the body more than clothing? ²⁶Look at the birds of the air; they neither sow nor reap nor gather into barns, and yet your heavenly Father feeds them. Are you not of more value than they? ²⁷And can any of you by worrying add a single hour to your span of life?ᵏ ²⁸And why do you worry about clothing? Consider the lilies of the field, how they grow; they neither toil nor spin, ²⁹yet I tell you, even Solomon in all his glory was not

---

ᶠ Other ancient authorities add *openly*
ᵍ Gk *eating*
ʰ Gk *eating*
ⁱ Gk *mammon*
ʲ Other ancient authorities lack *or what you will drink*
ᵏ Or *add one cubit to your height*

clothed like one of these. [30]But if God so clothes the grass of the field, which is alive today and tomorrow is thrown into the oven, will he not much more clothe you—you of little faith? [31]Therefore do not worry, saying,

Crowd. 'What will we eat?'

Jesus. or

Crowd. 'What will we drink?'

Jesus. or

Crowd. 'What will we wear?'

Jesus. [32]For it is the Gentiles who strive for all these things; and indeed your heavenly Father knows that you need all these things. [33]But strive first for the kingdom of God[l] and his[m]righteousness, and all these things will be given to you as well."]

(**M**)([34]"So do not worry about tomorrow, for tomorrow will bring worries of its own. Today's trouble is enough for today.")

Chapter 6 Notes
Teachings in practical piety, 6.1-34

The first part of this chapter dealt with the practices of piety, almsgiving, prayer, and fasting, all-important aspects of religious life. The angel Raphael told Tobit and his son, Tobias, "Bless God and acknowledge him in the presence of all the living for the good things he has done for you. Bless and sing praise to his name. With fitting honor, declare to all people the deeds of God. Do not be slow to acknowledge him. It is good to conceal the secret of a king, but to acknowledge and reveal the works of God, and with fitting

---

[l] Other ancient authorities lack *of God*
[m] Or *its*

honor to acknowledge him. Do good and evil will not overtake you. Prayer with fasting is good, but better than both is almsgiving with righteousness. A little with righteousness is better than wealth with wrongdoing. It is better to give alms than to lay up gold. For almsgiving saves from death and purges away every sin. Those who give alms will enjoy a full life" (Tobit 12.6-9). Jesus' disciples must be the light to the world, and the world should see their good works, but it should not be done to seek honor for self, rather to "give glory to your Father in heaven" (Mt 5.14-17).

1: *Father in heaven* did not mean that God was absent from human life on earth, but expressed his majesty and transcendent nature (6.9). **2:** Giving *alms* (relief of the poor) was considered by Judaism to be the foremost act of piety. Jesus considered it a private matter. **3:** The *left hand* being unaware of *what the right hand is doing* was a metaphor of secrecy, with the assurance that the Father in heaven would be aware of what you are doing.

5: *Have received their reward* meant those acts done to obtain the praise of others should not expect any reward beyond that (Lk 18.10-14). **7:** *Do not heap up empty phrases* when read in the Greek meant to "babble" *as the Gentiles do.* The prayers of the pagans (non-Jews) were often long because they believed it was important to address the correct god. Therefore, all the gods were mentioned, in order to not offend any, or to exclude the correct one. **8:** God does not need to be informed, he already knows. However, Jesus did teach persistence in prayer (7.11; Lk 18.1-7).

9-13: The Lord's Prayer in Luke (Lk 11.2-4) appeared closer to the original. Matthew's version may have been developed out of the seven-fold form designed for public worship. The prayer fell into two parts: after the opening invocation, there were three petitions concerning God's glory, followed by those concerning human needs. *Our Father* probably reflected its usage in the synagogue services by Jewish Christians, since it was not the custom of individual Jews to refer to God as his Father (Isa 63.16). *In heaven,* see 6.1. *Your kingdom come* as in the Kaddish, that God would establish his *kingdom* in the world he created. The phrase, *on earth as it is in heaven* (v 10),

61

belonged to each of the first three petition. The word translated *daily* was not found in Greek writings other than in Christian literature, except for one place, and its meaning has never been satisfactorily explained. It might mean "bread for tomorrow." *Debts* were a Jewish term used for "sins" (18.23-35). *As we also* meaning we cannot ask for ourselves what we deny to others. *Time of trial* or temptation was usually taken as a request for God to remove the occasions for sin or evil or the evil one (2 Thess 3.3; Jas 1.13). Based on David's prayer (1 Chr 29.11-13), the early church added an appropriate concluding doxology, "For the kingdom and the power and the glory are yours forever, Amen." **14-15:** The forgiving of others was again (v 12) made a condition for God's forgiveness of our sins (18.35; Mk 11.25-26; Eph 4.32; Col 3.13).

16-18: Jesus was not against fasting (Isa 58.5), but he rejected its use to win a reputation of piety. Pious Jews used to fast twice a week, on Mondays and Thursdays (Lk 18.12). By the second century, zealous Christians had adopted the practice, but changed the days to Wednesday and Fridays (*Didache,* 8.1). *Disfigure their faces* probably meant they left them unwashed (cf *Testament of Joseph,* 3.4). **19-21:** The folly was in trusting in possessions (Lk 12.33; Jas 5.2-3). In antiquity, a large part of riches often consisted of costly garments especially liable to destruction by a *moth.* The word for *rust* may mean "worm" and Jesus could have meant *where moth and* worm *consume* garments and woven things. *Thieves break in and steal,* since they could dig through the mud walls of a house and rob the owners.

22-23: *If your eye is unhealthy* described the person who had a selfish character (20.15). *The light in you* in ancient times was believed to be the function of the heart. "Conscience" appeared to have been introduced into the Christian faith by Paul. Jesus told the disciples "You are the light of the world" (5.14; Lk 11.34-26). **24:** Devotion to God and devotion to money are incompatible loyalties (Lk 16.13). *No one can serve two masters,* even though a slave might be the legal property of two owners, he would soon favor one.

25-33: To worry about life showed you lacked trust in God. *The birds of the air* were examples of freedom from anxiety. Worry did not serve any purpose and could not *add a single hour to your span of life.* God lavished his care on even the lowest forms of life. *Lilies* are still a general term used by the Arabs for wild flowers. *They neither toil nor spin,* they performed neither men's nor women's work. Do not be distracted about the little things (Lk 10.41; 12.11; Phil 4.6). **29:** Even the splendor of *Solomon in all his glory* did not match the royal robes of the lilies (1 Kings 10.4-7). **30:** *You of little faith* meant unwilling to rest in the assurance that God cared about your lives (8.26; 14.31; 16.8). **32:** *For it is* characteristic of pagans, *the Gentiles,* to worry about material things. Knowledge that these things came from the Father as gifts to his children was based upon his knowledge of their needs and his love for his children (Lk 12.22-31). **33:** *But, strive first for the kingdom of God* that was to ask for the heavenly things and the earthly things shall be *given to you as well* (Mk 10.29-30; Lk 18.29-30).

Chapter 6 Study Guide

1. What is your understanding of "your Father" or "our Father" being in heaven?
2. How do you explain that you are to be a light to the world, showing them what to do and yet your prayers and gifts are to be done mostly in private?
3. Is "do not bring us to the time of trial" more accurate than "lead us not into temptation" in light of James (Jas 1.13-14), where it is stated "God cannot be tempted by evil and he himself tempts no one"?
4. Given our current economic conditions, how can you not be concerned about money?
5. How do you stop worrying about those close to you?

Chapter 7

Illustrations of the practical meaning of Jesus' message, 7.1-29

Jesus. [Q₁]["Do not judge, so that you may not be judged. ²For with the judgment you make you will be judged, and the measure you give will be the measure you get. ³Why do you see the speck in your neighbor's[a] eye, but do not notice the log in your own eye? ⁴Or how can you say to your neighbor,[b] 'Let me take the speck out of your eye,' while the log is in your own eye? ⁵You hypocrite, first take the log out of your own eye, and then you will see clearly to take the speck out of your neighbor's[c] eye."**]**

(M)(⁶"Do not give what is holy to dogs; and do not throw your pearls before swine, or they will trample them under foot and turn and maul you."**)**

[Q₁][⁷"Ask, and it will be given you; search, and you will find; knock, and the door will be opened for you. ⁸For everyone who asks receives, and everyone who searches finds, and for everyone who knocks, the door will be opened. ⁹Is there anyone among you who, if your child asks for bread, will give a stone? ¹⁰Or if the child asks for a fish, will give a snake? ¹¹If you then, who are evil, know how to give good gifts to your children, how much more will your Father in heaven give good things to those who ask him!"

¹²"In everything do to others as you would have them do to you;**] (M)(**for this is the law and the prophets."**)**

[Q₂][¹³"Enter through the narrow gate; **(M)(**for the gate is wide and the road is easy[d] that leads to destruction, and there are many who take it. ¹⁴For the gate is narrow and the road is hard that leads to life,**)** and there are few who find it."**]**

(M)(¹⁵"Beware of false prophets, who come to you in sheep's clothing but inwardly are ravenous wolves. ¹⁶You will know them by their fruits.**) [Q₁][**Are grapes gathered from thorns, or figs from

---

[a] Gk *brother's*
[b] Gk *brother*
[c] Gk *brother's*
[d] Other ancient authorities read *for the road is wide and easy*

thistles?] [17]In the same way, every good tree bears good fruit, but the bad tree bears bad fruit. **[Q₁][**[18]A good tree cannot bear bad fruit, nor can a bad tree bear good fruit.**]** **(M)(**[19]Every tree that does not bear good fruit is cut down and thrown into the fire.**)** [20]Thus you will know them by their fruits."

[21]"Not everyone who says to me,

Scoffer. 'Lord, Lord,'

Jesus. (M)(will enter the kingdom of heaven, but only the one who does the will of my Father in heaven. [22]On that day many will say to me,

Scoffer. 'Lord, Lord, did we not prophesy in your name, and cast out demons in your name, and do many deeds of power in your name?'**)**

Jesus. [23]Then I will declare to them, 'I never knew you; go away from me, you evildoers.'"

[Q₁][[24]"Everyone then who hears these words of mine and acts on them will be like a wise man who built his house on rock. [25]The rain fell, the floods came, and the winds blew and beat on that house, but it did not fall, because it had been founded on rock. [26]And everyone who hears these words of mine and does not act on them will be like a foolish man who built his house on sand. **(M)(**[27]The rain fell, and the floods came, and the winds blew and beat against that house), and it fell—and great was its fall!"**]**

Matthew. [Q₂][[28]Now when Jesus had finished saying these things,**]** the crowds were astounded at his teaching, [29]for he taught them as one having authority, and not as their scribes.

Chapter 7 Notes

Illustrations of the practical meaning of Jesus' message, 7.1-29

1-5: Of course, the disciples and readers must discriminate between the appropriate or incorrect course of action. However, we are not to sit in judgment of our neighbors, or to determine their status before God. Only God can do that (Lk 6.37-38, 41-42; Mk 4.24; Rom 2.1; 14.10). **3:** The saying about the *speck* and the *log* revealed the humor of Christ while presenting the principle of self-examination. A *hypocrite* was someone who quickly saw the faults in others but was slow to recognize them in self. Nothing was more repulsive than someone who wanted to improve others but would not improve self.

6: The Gentiles were called *"dogs"* or *"swine"*, because they were the enemies of Israel. *What is holy* meant the flesh of Jewish sacrifices. This verse appealed to those who found comfort in it during times of controversy. Still Jesus went out among the outcasts, and he did not withhold his teaching for fear of a hostile response (10.13-14; 22.8-10).

7-8: *Ask, search,* and *knock* were three parts to prayer. Jesus proclaimed that prayer would be answered while leaving the "ifs" and "buts" to the commentators. True petitionary prayer was seeking to discover God's will and then submitting to it (Lk 11.9-10). **9-10:** That round *stone* looked like a loaf of *bread* and a dried *fish* resembled a *snake.*

12: All major world religions have some variation of the Golden Rule. Many have formulated a negative Golden Rule that urged inaction. "And what you hate, do not do to anyone" (Tobit 4.15). The positive form here required active contribution to the welfare and happiness of others. Matthew differed from Luke's (Lk 6.31) in adding, *"For this is the law and the prophets."*

13-14: The two contrasting ways were commonly used in the OT, "See, I am setting before you the way of life and the way of death" (Jer 21.8). The path of goodness and sacrifice remains the more difficult to follow.

15-20: The *false prophets* were not the Pharisees or Sadducees, because they did not claim to prophesy. Rather, they might refer to the false teachers or the fringe edges of the church and reflect problems that existed in Matthew's time (Lk 6.43-45). **15:** It was predicted that they would appear in the last days (Mt 24.11, 24; Ezek 23.27; 1 Jn 10.12). *Sheep* often symbolized a group of followers in a religious sense (Ezek 34.1-24; Lk 12.32). **16:** 3.8; 12.33-35; Lk 6.43-45. **19:** In order to stress the urgency of the matter, Matthew brought in the teaching of John the Baptist with a reference to the destruction of an unproductive tree (Mt 3.10; Lk 13.6-9; Jas 3.10-12).

22: *That day* meant the beginning of the messianic age or the world to come (Isa 2.11, 17; Zech 14.6) or the day of judgment. Jesus spoke as the divine judge who with authority would have the final word.

24-27: *These words of mine* referred to all that was contained in the Sermon on the Mount (chs 5-7; Lk 6.47-49; Jas 1.22-25). The illustration of the wise and the foolish man reflected the climate conditions in Palestine. Most of the year there was no heavy rain, but in the rainy season, the water rushed down the valleys flooding the level places. The *wise man* would build to withstand the waters of the rainy season by building *on rock*. The *foolish man* built on the sandy soil and as a result, the house fell. Only a life built on the rock of faithful obedience would be able to withstand the trials of life.

28: *When Jesus had finished saying these things,* this (or a similar) formula marked the conclusion of each of the five main discourses in the gospel (see Introduction and 11.1; 13.53; 19.1; 26.1). **29:** *Not as their scribes,* Jesus spoke on his own responsibility without appealing to traditional authority (Mk 1.22; 11.18; Lk 4.32).

Chapter 7 Study Guide

1. What does it mean, "Do not judge"? Does this mean you are not to have an opinion or encourage cultural standards?
2. Interpret the phrase, "do not throw you pearls before swine." Give some examples of how this might apply to your life.

3. If you do not get what you request in prayer, what is the problem?
4. Explain the golden rule in your own words.
5. Is it enough to hear the word of God?

Chapter 8
Events in Galilee, 8.1-9.38
(Mk 1.40-44; Lk 5.12-14)

Matthew. (M)(When Jesus[a] had come down from the mountain, great crowds followed him); [2]and there was a leper[b] who came to him and knelt before him, saying,

Leper. "Lord, if you choose, you can make me clean."

Matthew. [3]He stretched out his hand and touched him, saying,

Jesus. "I do choose. Be made clean!"

Matthew. Immediately his leprosy[c] was cleansed. [4] Then Jesus said to him,

Jesus. "See that you say nothing to anyone; but go, show yourself to the priest, and offer the gift that Moses commanded, as a testimony to them."

Matthew. [Q₂]][5]When he entered Capernaum, a centurion came to him, appealing to him [6]and saying,

Centurion. "Lord, my servant is lying at home paralyzed, in terrible distress."

Matthew. [7]And he said to him,

---

a Gk *he*
b The terms *leper* and *leprosy* can refer to several diseases
c The terms *leper* and *leprosy* can refer to several diseases

Jesus. "I will come and cure him."

Matthew. And the centurion answered and said,

Centurion. [8]"Lord, I am not worthy to have you come under my roof; but only speak the word, and my servant will be healed. [9]For I also am a man under authority, with soldiers under me; and I say to one, 'Go,' and he goes, and to another, 'Come,' and he comes, and to my slave, 'Do this,' and the slave does it."

Matthew. [10]When Jesus heard him, he was amazed and said to those who followed him,

Jesus. "Truly I tell you, in no one[d] in Israel have I found such faith.] [11]I tell you, many will come from east and west and will eat with Abraham and Isaac and Jacob in the kingdom of heaven, [12]while the heirs of the kingdom will be thrown into the outer darkness, where there will be weeping and gnashing of teeth."

Matthew. [Q₂][[13]And to the centurion Jesus said,

Jesus. "Go; let it be done for you according to your faith."

Matthew. And the servant was healed in that hour.]
    [14]When Jesus entered Peter's house, he saw his mother-in-law lying in bed with a fever; [15]he touched her hand, and the fever left her, and she got up and began to serve him. [16]That evening they brought to him many who were possessed with demons; and he cast out the spirits with a word, and cured all who were sick. **(M)**([17]This was to fulfill what had been spoken through the prophet Isaiah,

Isaiah. (D-I)("He took our infirmities and bore our diseases." [e]))

---

[d] Other ancient authorities read *Truly I tell you, not even*

[e] Isa 53.4

Matthew. (M)([18]Now when Jesus saw great crowds around him, he gave orders to go over to the other side.**)** **[Q₂][**[19]A scribe then approached and said,

Scribe. "Teacher, I will follow you wherever you go."

Matthew. [20]And Jesus said to him,

Jesus. "Foxes have holes, and birds of the air have nests; but the Son of Man has nowhere to lay his head."

Matthew. [21]And another of his disciples said to him,

Disciple (Another). "Lord, first let me go and bury my father."

Matthew. [22]But Jesus said to him,

Jesus. "Follow me, and let the dead bury their own dead."]

Matthew. [23]And when he got into the boat, **(M)(**his disciples followed him.**)** [24]A windstorm arose on the sea, so great that the boat was being swamped by the waves; but he was asleep. [25]And they went and woke him up, saying,

Disciples. "Lord, **(M)(**save us!**)** We are perishing!"

Matthew. (M)([26]And he said to them,

Jesus. "Why are you afraid, you of little faith?"**)**

Matthew. Then he got up and rebuked the winds and the sea; and there was a dead calm. [27]They were amazed, saying,

Disciples. "What sort of man is this, that even the winds and the sea obey him?"

Matthew. [28]When he came to the other side, to the country of the Gadarenes,[f] two demoniacs coming out of the tombs met him. They were so fierce that no one could pass that way. [29]Suddenly they shouted,

Demoniacs. "What have you to do with us, Son of God? Have you come here to torment us before the time?"

Matthew. [30]Now a large herd of swine was feeding at some distance from them. [31]The demons begged him,

Demoniacs. (M)("If you cast us out), send us into the herd of swine."

Matthew. [32]And he said to them,

Jesus. "Go!"

Matthew. So they came out and entered the swine; and suddenly, the whole herd rushed down the steep bank into the sea and perished in the water. [33]The swineherds ran off, and on going into the town, **(M)** (they told the whole story about what had happened to the demoniacs.) [34]Then the whole town came out to meet Jesus; and **(M)**(when they saw him,) they begged him to leave their neighborhood.

Chapter 8 Notes
Events in Galilee, 8.1-9.38

1-3: Leprosy was a term that covered a variety of ulcerous diseases, some of which were curable. The leper was expected to separate himself and to cry, "Unclean, unclean" as a warning to others of his condition (Lev 13.45-46). It would have been unlawful for a leper to approach anyone, yet Matthew and Mark (Mk 1.40-44) recorded the *leper* came to Jesus *and knelt before him* while Luke (Lk 5.12-14) implied that Jesus might have been passing by the leper.

---

[f] Other ancient authorities read *Gergesenes*; others, *Gerasenes*

71

If you choose, you can make me clean, the leper not only wanted to be healed, but the freedom to rejoin the Jewish community. Only when a priest had pronounced him "clean" and he had made the prescribed offering could he be readmitted to society (Lev 14.1-32). **4:** Mark (Mk 1.41) had Jesus being moved with pity as he touched him saying, *"I do choose. Be made clean!"* Jesus in Mark's gospel goes from having pity for the leper to "sternly" warning him to tell no one; yet to show himself to the priest (Mk 1.43). In other translations the word "sternly" is translated "strictly" because "sternly" in the Greek meant being very angry with him. Luke corrected this difficult account as Jesus ordered the leper, while Matthew just told the healed leper to *say nothing to anyone,* but he was to go and *show* himself *to the priest,* and make an offering as *Moses commanded* according to religious rite and legal custom (Lev 14.2-32). While Matthew and Luke do not continue the account, Mark had the leper instead of going to the priest, going out and telling others how Jesus healed him (Mk 1.45). Cf: *Egerton Papyrus 2,* "A person with leprosy came up to Jesus and said, 'Master Jesus, journeying with leprous people and eating with them in the inn, I also became leprous. If, therefore, you will, I can be made clean.' Then the Lord answered, 'I will; be clean.' And immediately the leprosy departed; and the Lord said, 'Go and show yourself to the priests.'"

5-13: Matthew and Luke (Lk 7.1-10) had the incident with the centurion taking place in *Capernaum,* while John (Jn 4.46-53) had the meeting take place in Cana, but the ill son was in Capernaum. The *centurion, (see* Centurion), a non-Jewish commander, was convinced that diseases were as obedient to Jesus as soldiers were to him. **7:** *I will come and cure him* was probably presented as a question, "Shall I, a Jew, come and heal him in a Gentile home?" In the gospels, Jesus did not heal anyone in a Gentile home, it was always accomplished at a distance. The centurion understood this and said, *"I am not worthy to have you come under my roof; but only speak the word, and my servant will be healed,"* even from a distance. He was quite familiar with *authority* and implied that God had delegated his authority to Jesus as a healer. **10:** *Faith* referred to the centurion's trust and recognition of Jesus' power. **11-12:** These verses are found in another context in Luke (Lk 13.28-29) in reference to the great banquet. The idea that many Gentiles will be accepted was found in Isaiah (Isa 45.6; 49.12) and Malachi (Mal 1.11). *Heirs of the kingdom* were the Jewish people who by their ancestry and privilege expected to share in the final kingdom, and they *will be thrown into the outer darkness.* John the Baptist gave the same warning to the Pharisees (3.9). *Weeping and gnashing of teeth* was a common expression of disappointment and pain expressed six times in Matthew, but did not necessarily mean physical punishment. **13:** While there was a command in Matthew, Luke just explained that when the friends returned to the centurion's house, they found the slave in good health.

14-17: Paul confirmed that Peter was a married man (1 Cor 9.5). Jesus entered the home of Peter and his *mother-in-law* was *with a fever.* Jesus *touched her hand, and the fever left her and she got up and began to serve him,* which was not the Jewish tradition to have women wait on the tables of men (Acts 6.2). **16:** In ancient times, mental illness was often described in terms of demon possession therefore, the healing, by Jesus, took the form of exorcism. **17:** In typical manner, Matthew added a text from the prophet Isaiah (Isa 53.4).

18: *The other side* was the eastern shore of the Sea of Galilee. **22:** *Follow me,* Jesus implied that obedience to his call must take precedence over every other duty or love (cf 10.37). *Let the dead,* meaning the spiritually dead, those who were not alive to the greater demands of the kingdom of God, *bury their own dead.*

23-27: Nature miracles formed a small group in the gospels. Mark and Luke understood the incident of calming the sea as a display of his supernatural powers. Sudden windstorms were common occurrences on the Sea of Galilee. *Faith* here meant trusting in the providence of God. Luke followed a similar pattern when the disciples and the people witness one of Jesus' miracles, they were *afraid* and amazed. Matthew softened Mark's (Mk 4.35-41) picture of the disciples by saying, *"Lord, save us! We are perishing!"* And later Jesus' words, "Have you still no faith" became, *"Why are you afraid, you of little* *faith?"* As they sensed God's presence and power in Jesus, they asked, *what sort of man is this?*

28: *Gadarenes* were the inhabitants of the city or of the surrounding district of Gadara, the capital of Perea. Here Jesus cured, not one (Mk 5.1-20; Lk 8.26-39) but two demoniacs, who lived in *the tombs* and *were so fierce that no one could pass that way.* **29:** *Torment us before the time* reflected the popular beliefs that demons were destined to be overthrown by God and his helpers as a prelude to the renewal of the world (*Testament of Asher,* 1.9; 6.2; *Testament of Benjamin,* 5.2; *Testament of Daniel,* 1.6-7; *Testament of Issachar,* 4.4; *Testament of Judah,* 13.3; 14.2; *Testament of Levi,* 19.1; *Testament of Naphtali,* 2.6; 3.1). **30-32:** Rather than being tormented, they *begged* to enter a herd of swine. Because they could only exist in human or animal bodies, the demons' requests were granted, but then *the whole herd rushed down the steep bank into the sea and perished in the water.* **33-34:** The *swineherds* who lost the swine *ran off and told* what happened in the *town* inhabited with a predominantly non-Jewish population, who had no problems raising swine. When the people *came out to meet Jesus,* they *begged him to leave their neighborhood,* not because of the financial loss, but because they did not know what to do with this man with such power. Luke added that the people "were seized with great fear" to explain their reason for requesting Jesus to go away.

Chapter 8 Study Guide

1. Why was it inappropriate for the leper to approach Jesus? Is there a connection with the status of the leper and the centurion?
2. Why does Matthew include the account of the impulsive and reluctant followers?
3. State the purpose for Jesus calming the sea.
4. Why did Jesus send the demon into a herd of swine?
5. Why did the people want Jesus to leave their neighborhood?

Chapter 9

Matthew. ¹And after getting into a boat he crossed the sea and came to his own town.

²And just then some people were carrying a paralyzed man lying on a bed. When Jesus saw their faith, he said to the paralytic,

Jesus. "Take heart, son; your sins are forgiven."

Matthew. ³Then some of the scribes said to themselves,

Scribes. "This man is blaspheming."

Matthew. ⁴But Jesus, perceiving their thoughts, said,

Jesus. "Why do you think evil in your hearts? ⁵For which is easier, to say, 'Your sins are forgiven,' or to say, 'Stand up and walk'? ⁶But so that you may know that the Son of Man has authority on earth to forgive sins"—

Matthew. he then said to the paralytic—

Jesus. "Stand up, take your bed and go to your home."

Matthew. ⁷And he stood up and went to his home. ⁸When the crowds saw it, they were filled with awe, and they glorified God, who had given such authority to human beings.

Matthew. ⁹As Jesus was walking along, he saw a man called Matthew sitting at the tax booth; and he said to him,

Jesus. "Follow me."

Matthew. And he got up and followed him.

[10]And as he sat at dinner[a] in the house, many tax collectors and sinners came and were sitting[b] with him and his disciples. [11]When the Pharisees saw this, they said to his disciples,

Pharisees. "Why does your teacher eat with tax collectors and sinners?"

Matthew. [12]But when he heard this, he said,

Jesus. "Those who are well have no need of a physician, but those who are sick. **(M)**([13]Go and learn what this means,

LORD. (Je)('I desire mercy, not sacrifice.' [c]))

Jesus. For I have come to call not the righteous but sinners."

Matthew. [14]Then the disciples of John came to him, saying,

Disciples. (John the Baptist's) "Why do we and the Pharisees fast often,[d] but your disciples do not fast?"

Matthew. [15]And Jesus said to them,

Jesus. "The wedding guests cannot mourn as long as the bridegroom is with them, can they? The days will come when the bridegroom is taken away from them, and then they will fast. [16]No one sews a piece of unshrunk cloth on an old cloak, for the patch pulls away from the cloak, and a worse tear is made. [17]Neither is new wine put into old wineskins; otherwise, the skins burst, and the wine is spilled, and the skins are destroyed; but new wine is put into fresh wineskins, and so both are preserved."

---

[a] Gk *reclined*
[b] Gk *were reclining*
[c] Hos 6.6
[d] Other ancient authorities lack *often*

Matthew. (M)([18]While he was saying these things to them,**)** suddenly a leader of the synagogue[e] came in and knelt before him, saying,

Jairus. "My daughter has just died; but come and lay your hand on her, and she will live."

Matthew. [19]And Jesus got up and followed him, with his disciples. [20]Then suddenly a woman who had been suffering from hemorrhages for twelve years came up behind him and touched the fringe of his cloak, [21]for she said to herself,

Woman. "If I only touch his cloak, I will be made well."

Matthew. [22]Jesus turned, and seeing her he said,

Jesus. (M)("Take heart,**)** daughter; your faith has made you well."

Matthew. And **(M)(**instantly**)** the woman was made well. [23]When Jesus came to the leader's house and saw **(M)(**the flute players and**)** the crowd making a commotion, [24]he said,

Jesus. "Go away; for the girl is not dead but sleeping."

Matthew. And they laughed at him. [25]But when the crowd had been put outside, he went in and took her by the hand, and the girl got up. **(M)(**[26]And the report of this spread throughout that district.**)**
[27]As Jesus went on from there, two blind men followed him, crying loudly,

Blind. "Have mercy on us, Son of David!"

Matthew. [28]When he entered the house, the blind men came to him; and Jesus said to them,

Jesus. "Do you believe that I am able to do this?"

---

[e] Gk lacks *of the synagogue*

Matthew. They said to him,

Blind. "Yes, Lord."

Matthew. [29]Then he touched their eyes and said,

Jesus. "According to your faith let it be done to you."

Matthew. [30]And their eyes were opened. **(M)**(Then Jesus sternly ordered them,

Jesus. "See that no one knows of this."

Matthew. [31]But they went away and spread the news about him throughout that district.)
   [Q2][[32]After they had gone away, a demoniac who was mute was brought to him. [33]And when the demon had been cast out, the one who had been mute spoke; and the crowds were amazed and said,

Crowds. "Never has anything like this been seen in Israel."

Matthew. [34]But the Pharisees said,

Pharisees. "By the ruler of the demons he casts out the demons."[f]]

Matthew. [35]Then Jesus went about all the cities and villages, teaching **(M)**(in their synagogues, and proclaiming the good news of the kingdom, and curing every disease and every sickness.) [36]When he saw the crowds, he had compassion for them, because they were **(M)** (harassed and helpless,) like sheep without a shepherd. [Q1][[37]Then he said to his disciples,

Jesus. "The harvest is plentiful, but the laborers are few; [38]therefore ask the Lord of the harvest to send out laborers into his harvest."]

---

[f]   Other ancient authorities lack this verse

Chapter 9 Notes

1: Jesus returned to *his own town,* Capernaum. Matthew implied that the paralyzed man was brought to Jesus as he arrived in the land. Mark (Mk 2.1-12) and Luke (Lk 5.17-26) had this event-taking place in a house.

2-3: The *bed* would have been more like a rug or stretcher. There was no reason to deny that the paralytic had *faith,* but Mark stressed the *faith* of his helpers. When Jesus said, *"Your sins are forgiven,"* he claimed a divine right, as did the apostles and the church after him. Clearly, the early church taught that baptism marked the annulment of past sins and the beginning of a new life (6.9-15; 2 Cor 2.5-11). **3:** This differed from the OT and rabbinical tradition where it was only a divine prerogative to proclaim forgiveness of sins (Ex 34.6-7; Isa 43.25-26; 44.22). The difference here was that Jesus pronounced the forgiveness of a person's sin independent of the prescribed sin offering or the Day of Atonement offering, or any evidence of his repentance (Lev 4-7; 16). No one can forgive sins except God, not even the Messiah, according to the rabbis. **4:** With spiritual insight, he knew *their thoughts.* Later rabbinic teaching held that blasphemy, or wrong speech, concerning God was punishable by death (*Mishnah Sanhedrin,* 7.5). **5:** It would be *easier* to say, *"Your sins are forgiven* than *stand up and walk,* because no one but God could tell if the pronouncement was correct. **6:** The messianic title, *Son of Man,* only occurred in the gospels from the lips of Jesus. The Son of Man embodied the belief that the Messiah would come from the clouds as God's Messiah and put an end to the present age. Jesus was the first to unite the Suffering Servant (Isa 53) with the Son of Man to describe the role of the Messiah. Jesus told the paralyzed man to *stand up, take your bed and go to your home.* **7:** The cure was verified by the patient's response to the *awe* of the people, *and they glorified God, who had given such authority to human beings.*

9: A tax collector, better described as an enforcer, had the right to collect a Roman tax (*see* Tax collector). Mark identified *Levi* as "the son of Alphaeus" (Mk 2.13). All of the Synoptic Gospels included James "the son of Alphaeus" in the list of the disciples, but there was no Levi. Matthew did have a similar story about a tax collector by the name of Matthew, who was included as a member of the inner circle. The importance was not the name, but the fact that Jesus sought to draw in (call) the outcasts that the Pharisees excluded from society. **10:** Matthew gave a dinner for Jesus *and his disciples*, and invited a large group of his *tax collector* friends and others. *The house* was presumed to be Matthew's house (see v 9; Lk 7.34; 15.1-2). **11:** Matthew had the Pharisees raise the question to Jesus' disciples, Mark had the scribes of the Pharisees and Luke has both the Pharisees and their scribes. The rabbis concluded that sharing a meal with those who did not observe the law was among those "things that shame a pupil of the scribes." For Luke, the issue may have been Judaism's charge that Gentiles and other riffraff were being welcomed into the membership of the early Christian church. *Sinners* here meant Jewish people who do not observe the dietary and other laws. The hostilities between the tax collectors and the Pharisees was explained in a remark of *R. Akiba* (132 CE), "When I was a tax collector I used to say, 'If I could get hold of one of the scholars I would bite him like an ass.' 'You mean, like a dog,' said his disciples. 'No,' said Akiba, 'an ass's bite breaks bones.'" **13:** When Jesus said, *"Go and learn,"* he implied that the Pharisees did not understand the Scriptures (Hos 6.6; Mt 12.7). Jesus used a biblical quotation to challenge a conventional religious idea.

14: The Day of Atonement was the only day when fasting was required. Special fasts were proclaimed in times of emergencies, such as a drought. The disciples of John and the Pharisees as a special act of devotion fasted on Mondays and Thursdays. **15:** Some wondered why Jesus' disciples did not follow the example of John's disciples and the disciples of the Pharisees. The implication was that Jesus came as a *bridegroom* for his followers (the bride). Fasting was inappropriate at a wedding and therefore it was not appropriate for his disciples. John the Baptist refused to share in his disciples' concern and affirmed that he was only the friend of the bridegroom, leading Israel, the bride, to Jesus, the bridegroom (Jn 3.27-29). Matthew included Mark's shadow of the Cross with his words *when the bridegroom is taken from them.* Jesus recognized the principle of fasting, but denied that it fit the circumstances of his life. The gospels make it clear that neither Jesus nor his disciples practiced fasting on a regular basis. However, the Didache, an early second-century Christian catechism, indicated that the early church did: "Do not fast with the hypocrites, for they fast on the second and fifth days of the week (i.e., Mondays and Thursdays); but you should fast on the fourth day and on the day of Preparation (i.e., Wednesdays and Fridays)" (*Didache,* 8.1). Matthew may have used this reference to *the bridegroom* to justify the lack of fasts by the disciples and to approve the later practice of fasting by the early church. Cf *Gospel of Thomas,* Logion 27 and 104b, "Jesus said, 'If you do not fast from the world you will not find the kingdom; if you do not keep the sabbath as sabbath you will not see the Father.'" "When the bridegroom comes out of the bridal chamber, then let them fast and let them pray." **16:** Mark and Matthew stated that a patch of *unshrunk cloth* would shrink after it had been sewed on an *old cloak,* leaving a tear that was worse than before (Mk 2.21). Luke (Lk 5.36) placed a different emphasis when he stated that no one tears a piece from a new garment that was ruining a new garment, to patch an old one since the piece from the new will not match the old. *New wine* meant unfermented wine. *Old wineskins* became hard and dry and therefore, they would *burst* when the fermentation occurred. These parables taught that you should not mix the new with the old, but they did not pass judgment on the merits of the one to the other. In their application they pointed out that the new Christian message and the old forms of Judaism were incompatible, and more specifically that the new gospel had nothing to do with the old ritual of fasting.

18: Mark (5.22) and Luke (Lk 8.41) identified Jairus as the *leader of the synagogue,* where Jairus asked Jesus to heal his daughter who was dying. Matthew related that the daughter *has just died,* but he wanted Jesus to *come and lay* his *hand on her, and she will live.* **19-21:** On the way to Jairus' house Jesus encountered a woman who for *twelve years* had suffered from *hemorrhages,* and she touched Jesus, *the fringe of his cloak* from behind. *The fringe,* or sacred tassel, was

the early church (Mk 6.34; Mt 14.14; 15.32; Num 27.17; Ezek 34.1-6; Zech 10.2).

Chapter 9 Study Guide

1. Is God the only one that can forgive sins? If not God, then who has received this power?
2. Explain Matthew's use of the crowd in this chapter.
3. What is your reaction to "those who are well have no need of a physician"?
4. Can the old endure the new in patterns of religion and culture?
5. Explain why Jairus could believe that Jesus could heal, but not raise his daughter from the dead.
6. Explain why the healed man was sternly ordered to tell no one of his healing.

Chapter 10
Commissioning and instruction of the Twelve, 10.1-11.1
(Mk 6.7; 3.13-19; Lk 9.1; 6.12-16)

Matthew. Then Jesus[a] summoned his twelve disciples and gave them authority over unclean spirits, to cast them out, and to cure every disease and every sickness. **(M)**(²These are the names of the twelve apostles: first,) Simon, also known as Peter, and his brother Andrew; James son of Zebedee, and his brother John; ³Philip and Bartholomew; Thomas and Matthew the tax collector; James son of Alphaeus, and Thaddaeus;[b] ⁴Simon the Cananaean, and Judas Iscariot, the one who betrayed him.

⁵These twelve Jesus sent out **(M)**(with the following instructions:

Jesus. "Go nowhere among the Gentiles, and enter no town of the Samaritans, ⁶but go rather to the lost sheep of the house of Israel.)

---

a Gk *he*
b Other ancient authorities read *Lebbaeus,* or *Lebbaeus called Thaddaeus*

[**Q₁**][⁷As you go, proclaim the good news, 'The kingdom of heaven has come near.'ᶜ ⁸Cure the sick, (**M**)(raise the dead, cleanse the lepers,ᵈ cast out demons. You received without payment; give without payment. ⁹Take no gold, or silver, or copper in your belts,) ¹⁰no bag for your journey, or two tunics, or sandals, or a staff; for laborers deserve their food. ¹¹Whatever town or village you enter, (**M**)(find out who in it is worthy,) and stay there until you leave. ¹²As you enter the house, greet it. ¹³If the house is worthy, let your peace come upon it; but if it is not worthy, let your peace return to you. ¹⁴If anyone will not welcome you or listen to your words, shake off the dust from your feet as you leave that house or town. ¹⁵Truly I tell you, it will be more tolerable for the land of Sodom and Gomorrah] (**M**)(on the day of judgment than for that town.)

[**Q₁**][¹⁶"See, I am sending you out like sheep into the midst of wolves;] (**M**)(so be wise as serpents and innocent as doves.) ¹⁷Beware of them, for they will hand you over to councils and flog you in their synagogues; ¹⁸and you will be dragged before governors and kings because of me, as a testimony to them and the Gentiles. [**Q₂**][¹⁹When they hand you over, do not worry about how you are to speak or what you are to say; for what you are to say will be given to you at that time;] ²⁰for it is not you who speak, but the Spirit (**M**)(of your Father speaking through you.) ²¹Brother will betray brother to death, and a father his child, and children will rise against parents and have them put to death; ²²and you will be hated by all because of my name. But the one who endures to the end will be saved. (**M**)(²³When they persecute you in one town, flee to the next; for truly I tell you, you will not have gone through all the towns of Israel before the Son of Man comes.)

[**Q₁**][²⁴"A disciple is not above the teacher, nor a slave above the master; ²⁵it is enough for the disciple to be like the teacher,] (**M**)(and the slave like the master. If they have called the master of the house Beelzebul, how much more will they malign those of his household!")

ᶜ Or *is at hand*
ᵈ The terms *leper* and *leprosy* can refer to several diseases

(M)(²⁶"So have no fear of them;) **[Q₁]**[for nothing is covered up that will not be uncovered, and nothing secret that will not become known. ²⁷What I say to you in the dark, tell in the light; and what you hear whispered, proclaim from the housetops. ²⁸Do not fear those who kill the body but cannot kill the soul; rather fear him who can destroy both soul and body in hell.ᵉ ²⁹Are not two sparrows sold for a penny? Yet not one of them will fall to the ground apart from your Father. ³⁰And even the hairs of your head are all counted. ³¹So do not be afraid; you are of more value than many sparrows."]

[Q₂][³²"Everyone therefore who acknowledges me before others, I also will acknowledge before my Father in heaven; ³³but whoever denies me before others, I also will deny before my Father in heaven."

³⁴"Do not think that I have come to bring peace to the earth; I have not come to bring peace, but a sword.

³⁵For I have come to set a man against his father, and a daughter against her mother, and a daughter-in-law against her mother-in-law;] **(M)**(³⁶and one's foes will be members of one's own household.)

[Q₁][³⁷Whoever loves father or mother more than me **(M)** (is not worthy of me; and whoever loves son or daughter more than me is not worthy of me;) ³⁸and whoever does not take up the cross and follow me is not worthy of me. ³⁹Those who find their life will lose it, and those who lose their life **(M)**(for my sake) will find it."]

[Q₂][⁴⁰"Whoever welcomes you welcomes me, and whoever welcomes me welcomes the one who sent me.] **(M)**(⁴¹Whoever welcomes a prophet in the name of a prophet will receive a prophet's reward; and whoever welcomes a righteous person in the name of a righteous person will receive the reward of the righteous;) ⁴²and whoever gives even a cup of cold water **(M)**(to one of these little ones) in the name of a disciple—truly I tell you, none of these will lose their reward."

ᵉ Gk *Gehenna*
ᶠ Mic 7.6

Chapter 10 Notes
Commissioning and instruction of the Twelve, 10.1-11.1

The second of the five great discourses in Matthew (5.1-7.27; 13.1-52; 18.1-35; 24.1-26.2) dealt with empowering and instructing the Twelve to carry out God's mission. He gave the disciples authority over unclean spirits and the power to cure every disease and sickness. He instructed them what should be said and how they should act.

1: The gospels reflected a widespread dread of demons with a feeling of helplessness regarding their activity. Jesus was portrayed as one who delivered people from demonic oppression and from Satan himself (Mk 1.23; 12.22; Lk 4.31-37; 7.33; 13.16). **2:** Only here did Matthew use the word *"apostles,"* meaning "those sent." The word applied to not only the Twelve disciples but also others sent with a commission to proclaim the good news of God's love through Christ. The Twelve sent out by Jesus were sent out with an emphasis upon healing. *Simon* (*see* Peter) was usually listed first among the disciples. His name in Greek was Peter and in Aramaic translated "rock" (Gal 1.18; 1 Cor 1.12; Jn 1.42). **3:** *Philip* (*see* Philip) was a Greek name meaning "lover of horses." The bar in *Bartholomew* usually meant "son of" but the rest of the name was uncertain. *Thomas* was often identified as "the twin" and may be from the Aramaic word for twin (Jn 11.16; 20.24). *Matthew* (*see* Matthew) was identified as *the tax collector* (9.9). *James* was identified as the *son of Alphaeus* to distinguish him from James, the son of Zebedee (Mk 2.14). *Thaddaeus* in some manuscripts was called "Lebbaeus" which may indicate the early church was not sure about his identity. **4:** *Simeon the Cananaean* identified Simon as a zealot that came from the Aramaic word *Cananaean* (Lk 6.15; Acts 1.13). *Judas* was always listed last and with a note, he betrayed Jesus. *Iscariot* may come from the Aramaic word meaning "the false" or from a place in Judea, and if so he would have been the only non-Galilean among the disciples (*see* Judas Iscariot).

5-6: Matthew's gospel was usually described as being more limited to the Jewish or Jewish-Christian in scope than Mark or

Luke. He was the only gospel writer who gave instructions to the disciples to *go nowhere among the Gentiles, and enter no town of the Samaritans, but go rather* to the *house of Israel.* Yet, later on they were to bear witness to the Gentiles (v 18) and to proclaim the good news of the kingdom "throughout the world" (24.14). The context of sending the Twelve out must be placed in the previous chapter (9.35-38) where Jesus went about in all the villages, teaching in the synagogues, proclaiming the good news, and curing every disease and sickness. He had compassion and looked upon them as sheep without a shepherd. Jesus told the disciples that the harvest was ripe that the conditions were right, while the laborers were few. It was in response to these conditions that he sent out the disciples on their first mission, where they would be encouraged by a measure of success, and where a transformed Israel would be the instrument to transform the world (15.21-28; Lk 9.52; Jn 4.9). **7:** The disciples' primary message was *the kingdom of heaven has come near,* or was actually present (see 4.17n). **8:** The powers of the disciples were clearly described: to *cure the sick, raise the dead, cleanse the lepers,* and *cast out demons.* The disciples received the power to heal without pay or deserving it, so they must share this gift without charge to others. **9:** The disciples were to travel lightly and to let their listeners care for their needs (Lk 22.35-36). **10:** Take no *bag,* which was probably used for food. *Tunic* was a short-sleeved garment of knee-length, held in at the waist by a girdle (Mk 1.6). *For labors deserve their food* was a Jewish principle (1 Cor 9.3-14; *Aboth,* 4.5). **12-13:** *Greet it,* the usual form was "Peace be to this house" and the one receiving the greeting would respond in similar fashion, then the blessing would take effect, if not the blessing returned to the disciple. **14:** When the Jews, returned from the heathen territory, they would shake *the dust from their feet* in order to keep the holy land clean. An unfriendly house was to be treated as heathen (Neh 5.13; Acts 18.6). **15:** Life and death depended on one's response to God's kingdom. *Sodom and Gomorrah* were examples of wicked cities that abused their guests. The rabbis debated if the people of Sodom would be resurrected and judged *on the day of judgment* (Gen 18.16-33; ch 19).

Matthew was the only one who added the element of *judgment than for that town.*

16-25: While this section did not address the concerns of a swift preaching and healing tour among the Jewish people, it spoke to the issues of the early church. The passages referred to the dangers faced by all the apostles while continuing the mission of Christ. **16:** *I am sending you out like sheep into the midst of wolves* were also found in Luke (Lk 10.3), but the proverb about being *wise as serpents and innocent as doves* was only in Matthew. **17:** *Councils and flog you in their synagogues* was probably regarding the local Sanhedrin, comprising twenty-three members, that existed in Jewish cities outside Jerusalem. Flogging was usually done by synagogue attendants and was limited to thirty-nine lashes (Deut 25.1-3; Acts 22.19). **18:** *Governors* may have been Roman officials like Pilate, and *kings* could include rulers like Herod Antipas or Herod Agrippa (Acts 12.1). **20:** *Spirit of your Father,* meant the Holy Spirit, would speak in and through them (Jn 16.7-11). **21:** Even more difficult than official persecutions would be family divisions that resulted in their being handed over to the officials or mobs that put them *to death* (10.35-36; Lk 12.52-53). **22:** *Because of my name* was "because of me and my cause." **23:** These words stressed the urgency of the disciples' task. They may have also been regarding the flight of the Jewish Christians from Jerusalem to Pella in Transjordan during the war in 66-70 CE. **24:** The *disciple* should expect to receive the same treatment that Christ did and to suffer as he suffered (Lk 6.40; Jn 13.16; 15.20; Mt 9.34; 12.24; Mk 3.22). **25:** Just as Jesus was called *Beelzebul,* the prince of demons, so might his disciples (12.24).

26: *Have no fear,* or some variation of this phrase, was repeated three times in these verses (28, 31). *Oxyrhynchus Papyrus,* 654, Logion 4. "Jesus said, 'Everything that is not before you, and what is hidden from you will be revealed to you. For there is nothing hidden that will not be revealed, nor buried, that will not be raised.'" *Gospel of Thomas,* Logion 5 and 6, [5]"Jesus said, 'Know what is in your sight, and what is hidden from you will be revealed to you. For there is nothing hidden that will not be manifest.'" [6]"There is nothing hidden that will not be revealed, and there is nothing covered that will remain without being uncovered." **27:** *Proclaim from the housetops,* unlike the Rabbis who often *whispered* to their disciple's secret doctrines such as interpreting Ezekiel (Ezek 1.28) "I heard the voice of someone speaking." Compare 1 Kings 19.12 where the divine presence was presented as "a sound of sheer silence" or "a soft murmuring sound" (NJPS). **28:** While it was believed that evil and Satan could tempt someone and lead him or her to destruction, yet, God alone had power over life and death, to bring people to *hell* (Gehenna, see 5.22n) and back again (Wisd of Sol 16.13-15; 4 Macc 13.14-15; Jas 4.12; Heb 10.31). **29-31:** God cared for even a *sparrow* that was sold for a half penny. And he cared more for you than he did for a sparrow that fell on the ground (6.26-33; see Lk 12.21-31n).

32-33: Matthew had Jesus mediating before the Father while Luke had the confession being done before the angels of God (Lk 12.8-9).

34-36: The rabbis and apocalyptic writers believed that the days of the Messiah would be ushered in by wars and family strife. The Jewish *daughter-in-law* was expected to obey the *mother-in-law* (Mic 7.6). While Christ's ultimate purpose was to reconcile humanity with God and to one another, it was understood that in the establishment of the kingdom, there would be differences (vv 16-25) and even families would be divided. **37:** *Whoever loves father and mother more than me* made the condition of discipleship different from Luke who says, "Whoever comes to me and does not hate father and mother more than me." Wife and brothers and sisters were also in Luke's version, along with "even life itself" (16.24-25; Mk 8.34-35; Lk 9.23-24; 14.26-27; 17.33). **38:** The *cross,* a Roman means of execution, was carried by the condemned to the scene of death. A condemned person had to take his *cross* (the main beam) and carry it to the place of execution, and then the crossbeam would be fixed to it before it was placed in the ground. Jesus saw that the acceptance of his message, with its promise, also brought seeming destruction (v 34). Only those who in faith accept the threat of destruction would find life (v 39; 5.11-12; 16.24; Mk 8.34-35; 10.29-31; Lk 9.24-25; 14.27; 17.33; Jn 12.25). **39:**

Those who risked their lives by handing it over to God, even if it meant death, would gain their real self, a life in union with God. **41:** *In the name of a prophet* would be out of respect for the office and work of the prophet. **42:** *Even a cup of water to one of these little ones in the name of a disciple,* meant that in doing what may seemed to be an unimportant and simple, became a real service to Christ and they would not *lose their reward.*

Chapter 10 Study Guide

1. Why did Matthew use the name "apostles" instead of "disciples" in verse 1?
2. To who were, the apostles sent? Why did Jesus instruct them against sharing the message with the Gentiles?
3. What message was carried by the disciples?
4. Why are verses 17-23 only found in the Gospel of Matthew?
5. What did Jesus mean when he says, "I have not come to bring peace, but a sword"?

Chapter 11

Matthew. (M)(Now when Jesus had finished instructing his twelve disciples, he went on from there to teach and proclaim his message in their cities.)

Narratives illustrating the authority claimed by Jesus, 11.2-12.50

Matthew. [Q₂][[2When John heard in prison what the Messiah[a] was doing, he sent word by his[b]disciples [3]and said to him,

Disciples. (John the Baptist's) "Are you the one who is to come, or are we to wait for another?"

---

[a] Or *the Christ*
[b] Other ancient authorities read *two of his*

Matthew. [4]Jesus answered them,

Jesus. "Go and tell John what you hear and see:

Messenger. (I)([5]the blind receive their sight, the lame walk, the lepers[c] are cleansed, the deaf hear, the dead are raised, and the poor have good news brought to them. [d])

Jesus. [6]And blessed is anyone who takes no offense at me."]

Matthew. [Q₂][[7]As they went away, Jesus began to speak to the crowds about John:

Jesus. "What did you go out into the wilderness to look at? A reed shaken by the wind? [8]What then did you go out to see? Someone[e] dressed in soft robes? Look, those who wear soft robes are in royal palaces. [9]What then did you go out to see? A prophet?[f] Yes, I tell you, and more than a prophet. [10]This is the one about whom it is written,

Lord. 'See, I am sending my messenger ahead of you, who will prepare your way before you.' [g]

Jesus. [11]Truly I tell you, among those born of women no one has arisen greater than John the Baptist; yet the least in the kingdom of heaven is greater than he.] **[Q₃]**[[12]From the days of John the Baptist until now the kingdom of heaven has suffered violence,[h] and the violent take it by force. [13]For all the prophets and the law prophesied until John came;] **(M)**([14]and if you are willing to accept it, he is Elijah who is to come.) [15]Let anyone with ears[i] listen!"

---

[c] The terms *leper* and *leprosy* can refer to several diseases
[d] Isa 35.5-6; 61.1
[e] Or *Why then did you go out? To see someone*
[f] Other ancient authorities read *Why then did you go out? To see a prophet?*
[g] Mal 3.1
[h] Or *has been coming violently*
[i] Other ancient authorities add *to hear*

[Q₂][¹⁶"But to what will I compare this generation? It is like children sitting in the marketplaces and calling to one another,

Children. ¹⁷'We played the flute for you, and you did not dance;

Children. (other) we wailed, and you did not mourn.'

Jesus. ¹⁸For John came neither eating nor drinking, and they say,

People. 'He has a demon';

Jesus. ¹⁹the Son of Man came eating and drinking, and they say,

People. 'Look, a glutton and a drunkard, a friend of tax collectors and sinners!'

Jesus. Yet wisdom is vindicated by her deeds."ʲ]

Matthew. (M)(²⁰Then he began to reproach the cities in which most of his deeds of power had been done, because they did not repent.)

Jesus. [Q₂][²¹"Woe to you, Chorazin! Woe to you, Bethsaida! For if the deeds of power done in you had been done in Tyre and Sidon, they would have repented long ago in sackcloth and ashes. ²²But I tell you, on the day of judgment it will be more tolerable for Tyre and Sidon than for you. ²³And you, Capernaum, will you be exalted to heaven? No, you will be brought down to Hades.]

(**M)(**For if the deeds of power done in you had been done in Sodom, it would have remained until this day.) **[Q₂][**²⁴But I tell you that on the day of judgment it will be more tolerable for the land of Sodom than for you."]

Matthew. [Q₂][²⁵At that time Jesus said,

ʲ Other ancient authorities read *children*

Jesus. "I thank[k] you, Father, Lord of heaven and earth, because you have hidden these things from the wise and the intelligent and have revealed them to infants; [26]yes, Father, for such was your gracious will.[l] [27]All things have been handed over to me by my Father; and no one knows the Son except the Father, and no one knows the Father except the Son and anyone to whom the Son chooses to reveal him."]

(M)([28]"Come to me, all you that are weary and are carrying heavy burdens, and I will give you rest. [29]Take my yoke upon you, and learn from me; for I am gentle and humble in heart, and you will find rest for your souls. [30]For my yoke is easy, and my burden is light.")

Chapter 11 Notes

1: *When Jesus had finished instructing,* this (or a similar) formula marked the conclusion of each of the five main discourses in the gospel (5.1-7.28; 13.53; 19.1; 26.1). After instructing and sending out the Twelve, Jesus continued his own ministry in Jewish cities.

Narratives illustrating the authority claimed by Jesus, 11.2-12.50

2-19: Among the early Christians, there must have been interest about what John the Baptist thought of Jesus. Acts (Acts 19.1-5) presented an account of disciples in Ephesus who had known only "the baptism of John." There was evidence that some followers of John the Baptist remained independent of the Christian church for a hundred years or more and at times were in competition with it.

Luke in his birth narrative had Jesus related to John by blood. However, Matthew and Luke in their versions of the baptism story assumed that John knew of Jesus' messianic mission. Now both gospel writers included material where John questioned if Jesus was the Messiah or not (Lk 7.20). Based upon John's possible relationship with the Qumran community, the continuing differences between

---

[k] Or *praise*

[l] Or *for so it was well-pleasing in your sight*

[a] Hos 6.6

John's disciples and the early church, and Jesus' response, it was probable that Jesus was just not fulfilling the messianic role expected by John. **2:** *In prison,* at Machaerus, a fortified place about five miles east of the Dead Sea. **4-5:** Jesus' indirect responses were from Isaiah (Isa 35.5-6; Isa 61.1), with the addition of *lepers are cleansed* and *the dead are raised.* Jesus in effect was saying, the signs of the new age, foretold by the OT prophet were in evidence, now you draw your own conclusion. **6:** Jesus avoided being identified as the Messiah, which was in keeping with all of the gospels outside of the passion narrative. He said that his teachings and works were not to be ignored, but to have faith in the evidence.

7-15: *As* John's disciples *went away, Jesus began to* share with *the crowds* his thoughts of John. Matthew had Jesus identify John the Baptist as Elijah revisited (Mt 11.13-14). Jesus asked the people what they expected to find when they went to listen to John, out into the wilderness. If they expected to find a polished preacher, they encountered instead a *prophet.* However, John was *more than a prophet.* **10:** What followed was an adaptation of the LORD's proclaimation in Malachi (Mal 3.1); "See, I am sending my messenger ahead of you, who will prepare your way before you" (*see* LORD). The change in the personal pronouns made this quotation refer to the herald of the Messiah. **12:** *The violent* are eager, ardent multitudes. **14:** Biblical prophecy depended on human acceptance of the LORD's terms for fulfillment. Had John's message been accepted, his activity would have been foretold in Elijah's name. Jesus did not seem to expect the literal return of *Elijah* (17.10-13; Mal 4.5; Mk 9.9-13; Lk 1.17).

18: *John* was criticized because he did not eat bread nor drink wine, and Jesus was criticized as a glutton and drunkard and a friend to the outcasts in society (Lk 7.33). **19:** Divine *wisdom is vindicated* by its results, and it could use agents of different types to achieve it.

20: This verse was an editorial introduction of Matthew 11.20-24. **21:** *Chorazin,* only mentioned here and in Luke (Lk 10.13), was believed to be the ruins known as "Kerazeh," two or three miles northeast of Capernaum. Jesus worked in the area of *Bethsaida* but never in the center, linked with the cities of *Tyre and Sidon,* long associated in Jewish circles as paganism at its worst (Ex 26-28; Isa 23). A separate warning was devoted to *Capernaum,* modeled on a post exile pronouncement against Nebuchadnezzar (Isa 14.13-15). The city was to be punished for its unwarranted pride, perhaps because it had been the center of a large part of Jesus' ministry (Isa 14.13, 15).

25: *The wise and the intelligent* were assumed to be scribes and Pharisees, while the *infants* were the disciples and common people. The meaning of this saying of Jesus remains unclear because Jesus had not spoken before of God being hidden from human knowledge and his truth revealed to only the chosen few. Its understanding might reflect the conflict between the Jewish rabbis and the early church (9.13; 10.42; 16.17; Lk 10.21-22; 24.16). **27:** Jesus claimed a special relationship to God, which he could share with others (Jn 3.35; 13.3).

28: Jesus invited the *weary* and those *carrying heavy burdens* to come to him and be refreshed, granting them *rest.* **29-30:** The rest should not be considered idleness or inaction as the *yoke* implied a task. The rabbis spoke of the *yoke* of the Law that was to be learned and fulfilled. The yoke Jesus placed on his followers included learning God's will and obeying it in active service. This yoke of active service was promised to be *easy, and* the *burden* of it *light* because those who bore it would receive the blessings of God through Christ.

Chapter 11 Study Guide

1. Was John the Baptist outside the kingdom because he rejected Jesus?
2. Explain the difference perceived as the kingdom by John the Baptist and Jesus.
3. Was John the Baptist the destined Elijah (Mal 4.5)?
4. Explain the judgment on the unrepentant cities.
5. Why is the yoke of Christ easy to bear?

Chapter 12
Jesus and sabbath laws, 12.1-14
(Mk 2.23-3.6; Lk 6.1-11)

Matthew. At that time Jesus went through the grainfields on the sabbath; his disciples were hungry, and they began to pluck heads of grain and to eat. **(M)(**²When the Pharisees saw it,**)** they said to him,

Pharisees. "Look, your disciples are doing what is not lawful to do on the sabbath."

Matthew. He said to them,

Jesus. ³"Have you not read what David did when he and his companions were hungry? ⁴He entered the house of God and ate the bread of the Presence, which it was not lawful for him or his companions to eat, but only for the priests. **(M)(**⁵Or have you not read in the law that on the sabbath the priests in the temple break the sabbath and yet are guiltless?**)** ⁶I tell you, **(M)(**something greater than the temple is here. ⁷But if you had known what this means,

Lord. (Je)('I desire mercy and not sacrifice,' ᵃ**)**

Jesus. you would not have condemned the guiltless.**)** ⁸For the Son of Man is lord of the sabbath."

Matthew. ⁹He left that place and entered their synagogue; ¹⁰a man was there with a withered hand, and they asked him,

Pharisees. "Is it lawful to cure on the sabbath?"

Matthew. so that they might accuse him. ¹¹He said to them,

Jesus. "Suppose one of you has only one sheep and it falls into a pit on the sabbath; will you not lay hold of it and lift it out? **(M)(**¹²How

---

ᵃ Hos 6.6

much more valuable is a human being than a sheep!**)** So it is lawful to do good on the sabbath."

Matthew. [13]Then he said to the man,

Jesus. "Stretch out your hand."

Matthew. He stretched it out, and it was restored, **(M)(**as sound as the other.**)** [14]But the Pharisees went out and conspired against him, how to destroy him.

Work of healing, 12.15-21
(Mk 3.7-12; Lk 6.17-19; 4.40)

Matthew. [15]When Jesus became aware of this, he departed. Many crowds[b] followed him, and he cured all of them, [16]and he ordered them not to make him known. **(M)(**[17]This was to fulfill what had been spoken through the prophet Isaiah:

Lord. (D-I)([18]"Here is my servant, whom I have chosen, my beloved, with whom my soul is well pleased. I will put my Spirit upon him, and he will proclaim justice to the Gentiles. [19]He will not wrangle or cry aloud, nor will anyone hear his voice in the streets. [20]He will not break a bruised reed or quench a smoldering wick until he brings justice to victory. [21]And in his name the Gentiles will hope." [c]**))**

Sources of Jesus' power, 12.22-37
(Mk 3.20-30; Lk 11.14-23, 12.10)

Matthew. [22]Then they brought to him a demoniac who was blind and mute; and he cured him, so that the one who had been mute could speak and see. [23]All the crowds were amazed and said,

Crowds. (M)("Can this be the Son of David?"**"")**

---

[b] Other ancient authorities lack *crowds*
[c] Isa 42.1-4

Matthew, [24]But when the Pharisees heard it, they said,

Pharisees. "It is only by Beelzebul, the ruler of the demons, that this fellow casts out the demons."

Matthew. [25]He knew what they were thinking and said to them,

Jesus. [Q₂]["Every kingdom divided against itself is laid waste, and no city or house divided against itself will stand. [26]If Satan **(M)**(casts out Satan), he is divided against himself; how then will his kingdom stand? [27]If I cast out demons by Beelzebul, by whom do your own exorcists[d] cast them out? Therefore they will be your judges. [28]But if it is by the Spirit of God that I cast out demons, then the kingdom of God has come to you. [29]Or how can one enter a strong man's house and plunder his property, without first tying up the strong man? Then indeed the house can be plundered. [30]Whoever is not with me is against me, and whoever does not gather with me scatters.] [31]Therefore I tell you, people will be forgiven for every sin and blasphemy, **(M)** (but blasphemy against the Spirit will not be forgiven). [32]Whoever speaks a word against the Son of Man will be forgiven, but whoever speaks against the Holy Spirit will not be forgiven, **(M)**(either in this age or in the age to come").

[33]"Either make the tree good, and its fruit good; or make the tree bad, and its fruit bad; **[Q₁]**[for the tree is known by its fruit.] **(M)** ([34]You brood of vipers! How can you speak good things, when you are evil? For out of the abundance of the heart the mouth speaks.) **[Q₁]** [[35]The good person brings good things out of a good treasure, and the evil person brings evil things out of an evil treasure.] **(M)**([36]I tell you, on the day of judgment you will have to give an account for every careless word you utter; [37]for by your words you will be justified, and by your words you will be condemned.")

---

[d] Gk *sons*

Request for a sign, 12.38-42
(Lk 11.16, 29-32)

Matthew. [Q₂][³⁸Then some of the scribes and Pharisees said to him,

Pharisees and Scribes. "Teacher, we wish to see a sign from you."

Matthew. ³⁹But he answered them,

Jesus. "An evil and adulterous generation asks for a sign, but no sign will be given to it except the sign of the prophet Jonah. ⁴⁰For just as Jonah was three days and three nights in the belly of the sea monster, so **(M)**(for three days and three nights) the Son of Man will be in the heart of the earth. ⁴¹The people of Nineveh will rise up at the judgment with this generation and condemn it, because they repented at the proclamation of Jonah, and see, something greater than Jonah is here! ⁴²The queen of the South will rise up at the judgment with this generation and condemn it, because she came from the ends of the earth to listen to the wisdom of Solomon, and see, something greater than Solomon is here!"]

The return of unclean spirit, 12.43-45
(Lk 11.24-26)

Jesus. [Q₂][⁴³"When the unclean spirit has gone out of a person, it wanders through waterless regions looking for a resting place, but it finds none. ⁴⁴Then it says,

Demon. 'I will return to my house from which I came.'

Jesus. When it comes, it finds it empty, swept, and put in order. ⁴⁵Then it goes and brings along seven other spirits more evil than itself, and they enter and live there; and the last state of that person is worse than the first.] **(M)**(So will it be also with this evil generation.")

Jesus' true family, 12.46-50
(Mk 3.31-35; Lk 8.19-21)

Matthew. (M)(⁴⁶While he was still speaking to the crowds), his mother and his brothers were standing outside, wanting to speak to him. ⁴⁷Someone told him,

Messenger. "Look, your mother and your brothers are standing outside, wanting to speak to you."ᵉ

Matthew. (M)(⁴⁸But to the one who had told him this), Jesusᶠ replied,

Jesus. "Who is my mother, and who are my brothers?"

Matthew. ⁴⁹And pointing to his disciples, he said,

Jesus. "Here are my mother and my brothers! ⁵⁰For whoever does the will of my Father **(M)(**in heaven) is my brother and sister and mother."

Chapter 12 Notes
Jesus and the sabbath laws, 12.1-14

1: It remains unclear why or when the "Sabbath" in the OT became *sabbath* in the NT, other than to reduce its importance and to increase the meaning of "the Lord's Day" to celebrate the resurrection of Jesus. Rabbinical tradition added to the OT prohibition of Sabbath labor thirty-nine "major occupations" including harvesting and threshing (*Mishnah Sabbath*, 7.2). To pluck heads of grain in a neighbor's field was not considered stealing (Deut 23.25), but to do it on the sabbath was considered to be "harvesting" and was breaking the Law. **3-5:** Jesus defended the disciples' actions by referring to David's action *when he and his companions were hungry* (1 Sam 21.1-6). Human

---

ᵉ Other ancient authorities lack verse 47

ᶠ Gk *he*

needs could override the letter of the Law. Matthew and Luke omit Mark's mistaken reference to Abiathar, instead of Ahimelech as high priest (Mk 2.26). **4:** *The bread of the Presence* was twelve cakes placed each sabbath on a "table of pure gold" in the sanctuary and only eaten by priests (Lev 24.5-9). **6:** Since no penalty was exacted from those who set aside provisions of the Law for the sake of some human need or some more significant service to God, Jesus' disciples ate because of their need and served him who was greater than the institutions of the Law (see vs 41-42). **7:** Matthew for the second time had Jesus use a biblical quotation from Hosea (Hos 6.6; Mt 9.13), where the LORD proclaimed, "I desire steadfast love and not sacrifice," to challenge a conventional religious idea. **8:** No doubt, the early church found this argument useful in its controversy with the Jews over the celebration of the Christian Sunday as all three of the synoptic writers declared *the Son of Man is lord of the sabbath.* Jesus claimed by virtue of his mission as the Messiah, authority over another's obedience to God (11.27; Jn 5.1-18). Cf *Gospel of Thomas,* Logion 27b, "Jesus said, 'If you do not keep the sabbath as sabbath you will not see the Father.'"

9: Nothing was said about the man in the synagogue except that he *had a withered hand.* Luke (Lk 6.6) added that it was his *right hand.* In the *Gospel according to the Hebrews,* Jerome, described the man as a mason, who depended on the use of his hands. He pleaded for Jesus to heal him with the following words: "I was a mason, earning a living with my hands; I beg you, Jesus, restore my health to me, so that I need not beg for my food in shame." **10:** Mark (Mk 3.2) and Luke (Lk 6.7) have the Pharisees watching to see if Jesus would cure him on the sabbath, but Matthew had the Pharisees ask Jesus, *"Is it lawful to cure on the sabbath,"* in order to accuse him. **11-12:** The rabbis agreed with the principle of attending to accidental injury and danger on the sabbath, but they thought that chronic conditions should wait (Lk 13.14). For Jesus it was important to restore a person to useful life. **12:** *A human being* is *more valuable* than *a sheep* (10.31). **14:** The Pharisees *conspired,* not as to how they might heal on the sabbath, rather *how to destroy* Jesus.

Work of healing, 12.15-21

15-21: These verses are a summary of Mark (Mk 3.7-12). *Became aware of this,* meant that while the Pharisees were plotting on how to destroy him, *he departed* because he did not want to attract the kind of publicity that might hinder the continuation of God's plan, and he added the quote from Isaiah (Isa 42.1-4). **18-21:** Matthew understood Jesus to be the *servant* that had been *chosen* by God and in whom he *was well pleased.* In his dealings with the Gentiles, he must *not wrangle or cry aloud,* but be gentle and patient, so as to *not break a bruised reed or quench a smoldering wick.* **20:** *Smoldering wick* was in reference to a lamp wick whose flame has almost gone out.

Sources of Jesus' power, 12.22-37

22-24: To state an individual was connected with the forces of evil was a dangerous one in a superstitious age. Mark had this claim made by the "scribes" (Mk 3.22) and in Matthew, it was by *"the Pharisees."* Luke (Lk 11.15) had "some in the crowd" that probably represented Q. *Beelzebul* was derived from the Hebrew text of 2 Kings (2 Kings 1.2-3), where Baalzebub (lord of flies) was a mocking distortion of Baalzebul (lord of the temple), the name for the god of Ekron. In Aramaic, Beelzebul was interpreted as "lord of dung." None of these forms are found in Jewish literature as a name for Satan. The biblical writers spoke of either curing the victim or casting out the demon (v 24; 9.32-33; Lk 11.14-15). **23:** *Son of David* was a title of the Messiah (21.9). **27:** *Your own exorcists* were in reference to the Pharisee's exorcists (cf 1 Pet 5.13). Exorcising demons was not limited to Jesus and his followers (7.22-23; Mk 9.38; Acts 19.13-19). **28:** Jesus claimed to cast out demons by the *Spirit of God,* and it was a sign that the *kingdom of God has come to you* (Lk 4.18-20). **29-30:** How could *a strong man's house* be entered unless someone who was stronger tied *up the strong man?* If the man became blind and mute by Beelzebul, then to be healed by the Spirit of God in Jesus meant he was stronger than Beelzebul. **31-32:** *Blasphemy against the Spirit,* the unforgivable sin, was the complete rebellion against God that denied him as the doer of his own acts (Mk 3.28-30; Lk 12.10). *Either in this age or in the age to come* was only found in Matthew's gospel and may reflect his position of extremes.

33-36: Matthew placed this saying about the tree and its fruit in response to the claim that Jesus was acting on behalf of Beelzebul. A *tree* would produce its own kind of *fruit,* and the true nature of their lives would be revealed by their words and actions (7.16-20; Lk 6.43-45). *Brood of vipers* (3.7; 23.33) was their evil nature, and they could not *speak good things.* **36:** *Careless,* or useless, may be barren in James (Jas 2.20). **37:** Cf Rom 2.6.

Request for a sign, 12.38-42

38: The request *to see a sign* was often asked of a Jewish teacher to determine if his teaching was true. However, this request from Jesus seemed strange because the healing of the demoniac who was blind and mute was a sign that the kingdom of God had come (vv 22-28). **39-41:** *Adulterous* was a term used by OT prophets to describe Israel's turning away from God (Jer 3.8; Ezek 23.37; Hos 2.2-10). The *sign* offered was Jonah's preaching of repentance, as no other sign would be given to the Ninevites (Jon 3.5; Mt 11.20-24; 12.6). **42:** *The queen of the South* was in reference to the queen of Sheba (1 Kings 10.1; 2 Chr 9.1-0).

The return of the unclean spirit, 12.43-45

43: *Unclean spirit* was one of the Jewish terms used to describe a demon. **44:** *My house* was the person previously possessed by the demons. *Empty,* meant that though evil had been temporarily expelled nothing good had been put in its place. **45:** So the demon returned with *seven other spirits* making the situation worse than it was before.

Jesus' true family, 12.46-50

46-50: Mark (Mk 3.31-35) and Luke (Lk 8.19-21) have similar sayings where bonds of the spirit bind the family of God. According to Mark's account, Jesus' family was disturbed by the rumor that he was a lunatic, and they had come to take him home. In Luke's version, all of this disappeared and those who hear the word of God and do it are identified as members of his family. Matthew had the membership based upon *whoever does the will of my Father in heaven.* There is no reason to believe that the *brothers* here were not his brothers in the usual sense of the word.

Chapter 12 Study Guide

1. Explain both sides of what was lawful on the sabbath.
2. Contrast the attitude of Jesus reflected in verses 15-20 with the attitude reflected in Matthew 10.5-15.
3. What did Isaiah (Isa 42.1-4) say about relating to those who have differing beliefs?
4. Why did Matthew promote gentleness and patience with Gentiles but harshness for the Pharisees?
5. What did the parable of the return of the unclean spirit mean to you?

Chapter 13
Teaching in parables, 13.1-52
(Mk 4.1-34; Lk 8.4-18; 13.18-21)

Matthew. That same day Jesus **(M)** (went out of the house and) sat beside the sea. [2]Such great crowds gathered around him that he got into a boat and sat there, while the whole crowd stood on the beach. [3]And he told them many things in parables, saying:

The sower, 13.3b-8

Jesus. "Listen! A sower went out to sow. ⁴And as he sowed, some seeds fell on the path, and the birds came and ate them up. ⁵Other seeds fell on rocky ground, where they did not have much soil, and they sprang up quickly, since they had no depth of soil. ⁶But when the sun rose, they were scorched; and since they had no root, they withered away. ⁷Other seeds fell among thorns, and the thorns grew up and choked them. ⁸Other seeds fell on good soil and brought forth grain, some a hundredfold, some sixty, some thirty. ⁹Let anyone with ears[a] listen!"

Matthew. ¹⁰Then the disciples came and asked him,

Disciples. "Why do you speak to them in parables?"

Matthew. ¹¹He answered,

Jesus. "To you it has been given to know the secrets[b] of the kingdom of heaven, but to them it has not been given. ¹²For to those who have, more will be given, **(M)**(and they will have an abundance;) but from those who have nothing, even what they have will be taken away. ¹³The reason I speak to them in parables is that 'seeing they do not perceive, and hearing they do not listen, nor do they understand.' **(M)**(¹⁴With them indeed is fulfilled the prophecy of Isaiah that says:

Lord. (D-I)('You will indeed listen, but never understand, and you will indeed look, but never perceive. ¹⁵For this people's heart has grown dull, and their ears are hard of hearing, and they have shut their eyes; so that they might not look with their eyes, and listen with their ears, and understand with their heart) and turn—and I would heal them.' [c]))

---

[a] Other ancient authorities add *to hear*
[b] Or *mysteries*
[c] Isa 6.9-10

Jesus. [Q₂][[16]But blessed are your eyes, for they see, and your ears, for they hear. [17]Truly I tell you, many prophets and righteous people longed to see what you see, but did not see it, and to hear what you hear, but did not hear it.]

[18]"Hear then the parable of the sower. [19]When anyone hears **(M)** (the word of the kingdom and does not understand it), the evil one comes and snatches away what is sown in the heart; **(M)**(this is what was sown on the path.) [20]As for what was sown on rocky ground, this is the one who hears the word and immediately receives it with joy; [21]yet such a person has no root, but endures only for a while, and when trouble or persecution arises on account of the word, that person immediately falls away.[d] [22]As for what was sown among thorns, this is the one who hears the word, but the cares of the world and the lure of wealth choke the word, and it yields nothing. [23]But as for what was sown on good soil, this is the one who hears the word and understands it, who indeed bears fruit and yields, in one case a hundredfold, in another sixty, and in another thirty."

Weeds in the wheat, 13.24-30

Matthew. (M)([24]He put before them another parable:

Jesus. "The kingdom of heaven may be compared to someone who sowed good seed in his field; [25]but while everybody was asleep, an enemy came and sowed weeds among the wheat, and then went away. [26]So when the plants came up and bore grain, then the weeds appeared as well. [27]And the slaves of the householder came and said to him,

Slaves. 'Master, did you not sow good seed in your field? Where, then, did these weeds come from?'

Jesus. [28]He answered them,

---

[d] Gk *stumbles*

Homeowner. 'An enemy has done this.'

Jesus. The slaves said to him,

Slaves. 'Then do you want us to go and gather them?'

Jesus. ²⁹But he replied,

Homeowner. 'No; for in gathering the weeds you would uproot the wheat along with them. ³⁰Let both of them grow together until the harvest; and at harvest time I will tell the reapers, Collect the weeds first and bind them in bundles to be burned, but gather the wheat into my barn.'")

The mustard seed, 13.31-32
(Lk 13.18, 19)

Matthew. (M)(³¹He put before them another parable:)

Jesus. [Q₁]["The kingdom of heaven is like a mustard seed that someone took and sowed in his field; ³²it is the smallest of all the seeds, but when it has grown it is the greatest of shrubs and becomes a tree, so that the birds of the air come and make nests in its branches."]

Yeast, 13.33-43
(Lk 13.20-21)

Matthew. (M)(³³He told them another parable:)

Jesus. [Q₁]["The kingdom of heaven is like yeast that a woman took and mixed in withᵉ three measures of flour until all of it was leavened."]

ᵉ Gk *hid in*

Matthew. [34]Jesus told the crowds all these things in parables; without a parable he told them nothing. **(M)(**[35]This was to fulfill what had been spoken through the prophet:[f]

Asaph singer. "I will open my mouth to speak in parables; I will proclaim what has been hidden from the foundation of the world."[g][h]

Matthew. (M)([36]Then he left the crowds and went into the house. And his disciples approached him, saying,

Disciples. "Explain to us the parable of the weeds of the field."

Matthew. [37]He answered,

Jesus. "The one who sows the good seed is the Son of Man; [38]the field is the world, and the good seed are the children of the kingdom; the weeds are the children of the evil one, [39]and the enemy who sowed them is the devil; the harvest is the end of the age, and the reapers are angels. [40]Just as the weeds are collected and burned up with fire, so will it be at the end of the age. [41]The Son of Man will send his angels, and they will collect out of his kingdom all causes of sin and all evildoers, [42]and they will throw them into the furnace of fire, where there will be weeping and gnashing of teeth.) [43]Then the righteous will shine like the sun in the kingdom of their Father. Let anyone with ears[i] listen!"

Hidden treasure and the pearl of great value, 13.44-46

Jesus. (M)([44]"The kingdom of heaven is like treasure hidden in a field, which someone found and hid; then in his joy he goes and sells all that he has and buys that field."

---

[f] Other ancient authorities read *the prophet Isaiah*
[g] Other ancient authorities lack *of the world*
[h] Ps 78.2
[i] Other ancient authorities add *to hear*

[45]"Again, the kingdom of heaven is like a merchant in search of fine pearls; [46]on finding one pearl of great value, he went and sold all that he had and bought it.")

The dragnet, 13.47-52

Jesus. (M)([47]"Again, the kingdom of heaven is like a net that was thrown into the sea and caught fish of every kind; [48]when it was full, they drew it ashore, sat down, and put the good into baskets but threw out the bad. [49]So it will be at the end of the age. The angels will come out and separate the evil from the righteous [50]and throw them into the furnace of fire,) where there will be weeping and gnashing of teeth."

(**M)(**[51]"Have you understood all this?"

Matthew. They answered,

Disciples. "Yes."

Matthew. [52]And he said to them,

Jesus. "Therefore every scribe who has been trained for the kingdom of heaven is like the master of a household who brings out of his treasure what is new and what is old.")

Events of decisive acceptance or rejection of Jesus, 13.53-17.27
Rejection at home, 13.53-58

Matthew. (M)([53]When Jesus had finished these parables, he left that place.)

[54]He came to his hometown and began to teach the people[j] in their synagogue, so that they were astounded and said,

Synagogue members. "Where did this man get this wisdom and these deeds of power? [55]Is not this the carpenter's son? Is not his mother called Mary? And are not his brothers James and Joseph and

---

[j] Gk *them*

Simon and Judas? ⁵⁶And are not all his sisters with us? **(M)**(Where then did this man get all this?")

Matthew. ⁵⁷And they took offense at him. But Jesus said to them,

Jesus. "Prophets are not without honor except in their own country and in their own house."

Matthew. ⁵⁸And he did not do many deeds of power there, because of their unbelief.

Chapter 13 Notes
Teaching in parables, 13.1-52

The material in the last two chapters enabled Matthew to use material from Mark and other sources to develop a discourse on the acceptance and rejection of the kingdom of heaven. In this chapter Matthew presented the third of his great five discourses (5.1-7.27; 10.1-11.1; 18.1-35; 24.1-26.2) with Jesus using parables to teach about the kingdom of heaven to the crowd in a public manner and to his chosen Twelve privately. *Parables* are stories describing situations in everyday life, which, as Jesus used them, convey a spiritual meaning. In general the teaching of each parable related to a single point, and apart from this the details may, or may not, have a particular meaning. Jesus used this method of teaching because; (*a*) it gave vivid, memorable expression to his teachings: (*b*) it led those who heard to reflect on his words and bear responsibility for their decision to accept or oppose his claim; (*c*) it probably reduced specific grounds for contention by hostile listeners; (*d*) so people could retell it.

1: *The Sea* was Galilee. Matthew, like Mark (Mk 4.1-9), placed the parable of the sower after the question about Jesus' family, in fact he had Jesus leaving the house and sitting beside the sea. **2:** Because of the crowd of people, identified by Luke (Lk 8.4) as being from town after town, Jesus *got into a boat* to teach.

The sower, 13.3b-23

3: Matthew and Mark (Mk 4.3) have Jesus starting to teach with the word *"listen,"* that suggested the urgency of the message, "Hear, O Israel" (Deut 6.4), and for the hearer to exercise a degree of understanding. *Gospel of Thomas,* Logion 109 began the parable with "Whoever has ears to hear, let him hear" instead of ending the parable with those words. **4:** Mark (Mk 4.4) and Matthew's seed that *"fell on the path"* was expanded by Luke (Lk 8.5), "and was trampled on," before the *birds came and ate them up.* **5:** Matthew and Mark (Mk 4.5) have other *seeds fall on rocky ground* that does *not have much soil,* but Luke (Lk 8.6) has the seed fell on "rock" where it "withered because of a lack of moisture." **6:** All of the gospel writers have the seeds that *fell among* the *thorns* being *choked* after they grew up. **8:** It was the seed that fell on the *good soil* that yields *"thirty," "sixty,"* and a *"hundredfold"* per Matthew and Mark (Mk 4.8) while Luke (Lk 8.8) has a hundredfold.

10: Matthew assumed the *disciples* asked Jesus why he spoke *to them in parables* when the crowd was absent, but Mark (Mk 4.10) still had them present. In Mark and Luke (Lk 8.9), the disciples asked Jesus to interpret the parable of the sower for them. **11:** But before Jesus answered the question, he told the disciples they are different because to them had *been given the secrets of the kingdom of heaven.* Jesus' response to the disciples was difficult to understand since the subject of the parables was the kingdom. **12-13:** Matthew added those who have been given the ability to understand would be given even greater insights, while *those who have nothing,* even that *will be taken away.* **14:** Jesus used the quote from Isaiah (Isa 6.9-10) to explain why he spoke to the crowds in parables. In Isaiah, the LORD (*see* LORD) told the prophet that the stubborn people would not heed his message that had to be presented by the prophet. Matthew used this to predict that the Jewish people would not understand or hear the message that Jesus taught. All of the gospel writers affirmed they heard, but did not comprehend the truth. Matthew said it was because their hearts had grown dull, their ears were plugged and their eyes were shut. **16-17:** In contrast to the crowd's inability to comprehend, the disciples were able to see and hear. In Matthew and Luke (Lk 10.23-24), Jesus continued to tell the disciples that in the days of the prophets, those who lived in hope and desired in vain to see the kingdom of God realized. The disciples should be grateful because they were living in the dramatic days of the fulfillment of God's kingdom (Lk 10.23-24). **17:** *See* and *hear* were Jesus' messages about God's kingdom.

18-23: It was not clear if these words were those of Jesus or those of someone in the early church. It was not the custom for Jesus to explain his parables in allegorical detail. The interpretation seemed to refer to times after the resurrection when the Christian message was proclaimed to those in danger of losing their zeal for the faith.

The sower sowed the message, which here was be taken to be the message about Christ. Now the parable took on a description of four different types of hearers. The first was the unresponsive hearer where the word did not receive any understanding. The *evil one*, Satan, or Devil, was usually pictured as a serpent (Rev 12.9), or a dragon (Rev 13.3), but not usually as a bird. The intent here was that he blocked the acceptance of the gospel and took away the unresponsive hearer's opportunity to receive it. The second hearer was a shallow hearer, one that lacked deep roots. He understood that the message was important, but his faith and commitment lacked depth and persistence. The third hearer let concern for material matters crowd out his loyalty to God. His life was cluttered up with material concerns and worries as he tried to serve God and the world. The fourth hearer heard the word, accepted it and God's will on his life and received the joy of living a life of obedience to God. There appeared to be no blame or punishment attached to the lesser harvests, only that good soil, properly cultivated would yield a richer harvest.

Weeds in the wheat, 13.24-30

24-30: This parable about the kingdom of heaven where the weeds in the wheat grew together was only contained in Matthew's gospel. **25:** The point was not that *everyone was asleep,* but that the weeds were sowed among the wheat in secrecy and were not noticed until the plants were grown. The poisonous weed mentioned was a bearded darnel that grew about the same height as wheat and was regarded by the rabbis a perverted kind of wheat (*Mishnah Kilayim,* 1.1). **27-28:** *The slaves* wondered where *the weeds* came *from* and offered to go out and *gather them,* which really meant to pull them up. **29-30:** The response was *let both of them grow together until the harvest* and then the *reapers* would do the separation. Then the weeds and the wheat could be safely separated without doing damage to the wheat placed in the *barn.* The obvious point of the parable was that God's judgment was better than human judgment.

The mustard seed, 13.31-32

31: Judeans sowed *mustard seed* in *fields,* but it was forbidden by the rabbis to sow it in a garden *(Mishnah Kilayim,* 3.2), and therefore Matthew was preferred over Luke (Lk 13.19). Mustard was cultivated for its seed and as a vegetable. The *mustard seed* was the smallest seed, but it produced a large plant of ten feet in height. The parable stressed though the beginnings of God's kingdom were small, it would grow to its intended end, startlingly different in size from its beginning. **32:** *So that the birds of the air come and make nests in its branches* was a reference to Daniel (Dan 4.21) where Nebuchadnezzar's kingdom appeared in a vision as a great tree whose top reached to heaven, "under which animals of the fields lived, and in whose branches the bird of the air had nests." It is possible that this verse was added by the early church. *Gospel of Thomas,* Logion 20, "The disciples said to Jesus, 'Tell us what the kingdom of heaven is like.' Jesus said to them, 'It is like a mustard seed, smaller than all seeds. But when it falls on the tilled ground, it produces a large branch and becomes a shelter for the birds of heaven.'"

Yeast, 13.33-43

33: Although *yeast* was usually used in the Scriptures as a symbol of evil influence, Jesus did not hesitate to use it to express God's rule that was working in a hidden way and would pervade one's life, giving it a new quality. *Three measures* would be a very large amount.

34-35: Most of Jesus' teachings were direct and clear and the statement that he only spoke to the crowds in parables was an exaggeration perhaps by the early church. Or it may have been Matthew's way of dealing with why the message of Jesus was not always accepted. *The prophet* was probably Asaph the seer (2 Chr 29.30; Ps 78.2) who commented on the past dealings with Israel. Matthew here revealed that Jesus used parables to *proclaim what has been hidden from the foundation of the world.*

36-43: Matthew interpreted the parable as an allegory. *Into the house* was where the disciples could speak to him in private. **38-42:** For Matthew, the missionary *field is the world.* The *good seeds* were those who accepted Jesus' teaching and the *weeds* were those who accepted the *evil one's* teaching. *The harvest is the end of the age and the reapers are angels* who carried out the command of *the Son of Man.* All evil conditions and evil people that hindered good living (Zeph 1.3) would be removed from *his kingdom* and *they will throw them in the furnace of fire* that was the fires of Gehenna. *Weeping and gnashing of teeth* indicated their continued existence and miserable lot. **43:** Then *the righteous* without the presence of evil would *shine like the sun in the final kingdom of their Father* (Dan 12.3). The hearers were warned to *listen* to the teachings of Jesus and not to be confused by their present circumstances where evil appeared strong and in control.

Hidden treasure and the pearl of great value, 13.44-46

These two parables taught the kingdom of heaven was of value greater than anything else. **44:** There was no intent to deal with the character of the person who would conceal the real value of the field, but that the *kingdom of heaven* was so desirable that out of sheer *joy he goes and sells all that he has* to obtain it. *Gospel of Thomas,* Logion 109, "Jesus said, 'The kingdom is like a man who had a treasure hidden in his field, and did not know it. And when he died, he left it to his son, who know nothing about it, and accepted the field, and sold it. And the buyer went, and while he was plowing, he found the treasure. And he began to lend at interest to whoever he wished.'" **45-46:** The second parable about the *pearl of great value* made the same point. This parable did not imply that anyone could purchase or earn it, but taught the value of God's kingdom. *Gospel of Thomas,* Logion 76, "Jesus said, 'The kingdom of the Father is like a merchant who possessed merchandise and found a pearl. That merchant was prudent. He sold the merchandise and bought the pearl alone for himself. You, too, are to seek for the treasure that does not fail, that endures, where no moth comes near to devour and where no worm destroys.'"

The dragnet, 13.47-52

47: The dragnet was familiar to the hearers who lived by the sea and knew that the net between two boats or a boat and the shore would catch *fish of every kind,* the point of the parable. The *bad* would be the fish that had no scales or fins (Lev 11.9-12), and they could not be eaten by the Jewish people. At the end of the age, *the angels* would do the separating with the same refrain as in verse 42.

51: Matthew insisted that although the disciples asked for the meaning of the parables (13.36) that they understood this. **52:** Each disciple should be as the *scribe* who *has been trained for the kingdom of heaven is like the master of the household who brings out of his* *treasure,* knowledge about *what is new and what is old,* that was from their heritage.

Events of decisive acceptance or rejection of Jesus, 13.53-17.27
Rejection at home, 13.53-58

53: *When Jesus had finished saying these parables,* this (or a similar) formula marked the conclusion of each of the five main discourses in the gospel (see Introduction and 7.28; 11.1; 19.1; 26.1). **54:** *His hometown* would be his ancestral home. **55-56:** It was an insult to be called the son of his mother instead of his father. Matthew may have stated it both ways to avoid any conflict about his birth. *Mother...brothers...sisters,* the latter terms may refer to relatives other than siblings (see also 12.46; Mk 3.31-32; 6.3; Lk 8.19-20; Jn 2.12; 7.3, 5; 1 Cor 9.5; Gal 1.19). There was no evidence that the brothers, identified as James, Joses, Judas and Simon (Mk 6.3), believed in Jesus during his ministry, but became early leaders in the church (Acts 1.14). **58:** Jesus required faith by those who sought healing for themselves or for others (occasional apparent exceptions occurred, such as in Jn 5.13).

Chapter 13 Study Guide

1. Explain why the people did not hear, see or understand what Jesus taught them. How does one's heart grow dull?
2. Explain the parable of the sower.
3. From the parables of the weeds in the wheat, the mustard seed, the yeast, the hidden treasure and pearl of great price, and the dragnet, what picture of the kingdom of heaven did you receive?
4. Why were the people in his hometown unwilling to accept Jesus' teaching?
5. What message did Matthew convey in this chapter?

Chapter 14
Death of John, 14.1-12
(Mk 6.14-29; Lk 9.7-9)

Matthew. At that time Herod the ruler[a] heard reports about Jesus; [2] and he said to his servants,

Herod. "This is John the Baptist; he has been raised from the dead, and for this reason these powers are at work in him."

Matthew. [3] For Herod had arrested John, bound him, and put him in prison on account of Herodias, his brother Philip's wife,[b] [4] because John had been telling him,

John the Baptist. "It is not lawful for you to have her."

Matthew. [5] Though Herod[c] wanted to put him to death, he feared the crowd, because they regarded him as a prophet. [6] But when Herod's birthday came, the daughter of Herodias danced before the company, and she pleased Herod [7] so much that he promised **(M)**(on oath) to grant her whatever she might ask. [8] Prompted by her mother, she said,

Salome. "Give me the head of John the Baptist here on a platter."

Matthew. [9] The king was grieved, yet out of regard for his oaths and for the guests, he commanded it to be given; [10] he sent and had John beheaded in the prison. [11] The head was brought on a platter and given to the girl, who brought it to her mother. [12] His disciples came and took the body and buried it; **(M)**(then they went and told Jesus.)

---

[a] Gk *tetrarch*
[b] Other ancient authorities read *his brother's wife*
[c] Gk *he*

Five thousand fed, 14.13-21
(Mk 6.30-44; Lk 9.10-17; Jn 6.1-13)

Matthew. (M)([13]Now when Jesus heard this,**)** he withdrew from there in a boat to a deserted place by himself. But when the crowds heard it, they followed him on foot from the towns. [14]When he went ashore, he saw a great crowd; and he had compassion for them and cured their sick. [15]When it was evening, the disciples came to him and said,

Disciples. "This is a deserted place, and the hour is now late; send the crowds away so that they may go into the villages and buy food for themselves."

Matthew. [16]Jesus said to them,

Jesus. "They need not go away; you give them something to eat."

Matthew. [17]They replied,

Disciples. "We have **(M)(**nothing here but**)** five loaves and two fish."

Matthew. [18]And he said,

Jesus. "Bring them here to me."

Matthew. [19]Then he ordered the crowds to sit down on the grass. Taking the five loaves and the two fish, he looked up to heaven, and blessed and broke the loaves, and gave them to the disciples, and the disciples gave them to the crowds. [20]And all ate and were filled; and they took up what was left over of the broken pieces, twelve baskets full. [21]And those who ate were about five thousand men, **(M)(**besides women and children.**)**

Jesus walks on water, 14.22-36
(Mk 6.45-52; Jn 6.15-21)

Matthew. ²²Immediately he made the disciples get into the boat and go on ahead to the other side, while he dismissed the crowds. ²³And after he had dismissed the crowds, he went up the mountain by himself to pray. When evening came, **(M)**(he was there alone,) ²⁴but by this time the boat, battered by the waves, was far from the land,[d] for the wind was against them. ²⁵And early in the morning he came walking toward them on the sea. ²⁶ But when the disciples saw him walking on the sea, they were terrified, saying,

Disciples. "It is a ghost!"

Matthew. And they cried out in fear. ²⁷But immediately Jesus spoke to them and said,

Jesus. "Take heart, it is I; do not be afraid."

Matthew. (M)(²⁸Peter answered him,

Peter. "Lord, if it is you, command me to come to you on the water."

Matthew. ²⁹He said,

Jesus. "Come."

Matthew. So Peter got out of the boat, started walking on the water, and came toward Jesus. ³⁰But when he noticed the strong wind,[e] he became frightened, and beginning to sink, he cried out,

Peter. "Lord, save me!"

---

d   Other ancient authorities read *was out on the sea*
e   Other ancient authorities read *the wind*

Matthew. [31]Jesus immediately reached out his hand and caught him, saying to him,

Jesus. "You of little faith, why did you doubt?")

Matthew. [32]When they got into the boat, the wind ceased. [33]And those in the boat worshiped him, **(M)**(saying,

Disciples. "Truly you are the Son of God.")

Matthew. [34]When they had crossed over, they came to land at Gennesaret. [35]After the people of that place recognized him, they sent word throughout the region and brought all who were sick to him, [36]and 1 begged him that they might touch even the fringe of his cloak; and all who touched it were healed.

Chapter 14 Notes
Death of John, 14.1-12

1-2: *Herod* Antipas (*see* Herod), son of Herod the *Great* was tetrarch or prince of Galilee and Perea (Transjordan). His mother was a Samaritan named Malthace and he governed until his death in 39 CE. Herod *heard reports about Jesus* and he thought he was *John the Baptist* raised *from the dead* suggesting that the ministries of Jesus and John did not overlap. Although John did not perform the miracles that Jesus did, Herod, who must have believed John to be a holy person, thought that Jesus was John who *had been raised from the dead.* **3-4:** *Philip* was not the ruler mentioned in Luke (Lk 3.1), but a half-brother of *Herod* Antipas. Herod divorced his first wife, the daughter of Aretas, to marry Herodias. While the Law allowed the divorce it was against the Law to marry his brother's wife while his brother was alive (Lev 18.16; 20.21). **5:** Josephus said that Herod arrested John because he was jealous of his influence over the *crowd* and *because they regarded him as a prophet.* Mark identified Herodias as the enemy of John and that Herod liked to "listen to him" (Mk 6.19-20). **6:** *The daughter* was Salome (Josephus, *Jewish Antiquities,* X.Viii.5.4). **10:** According to Josephus (*The History of the Jewish War,* 7, 6, 2), John was imprisoned at Machaerus, a fortress near the Dead Sea, and was beheaded there. Later Herod's army was destroyed by Aretas, and it was considered by the people to be just punishment for what he had done to John the Baptist. It was against Jewish law to execute a person without a trial, and execution by beheading was not permitted, but it was in accordance with Roman and Greek customs. **12:** Matthew had John's disciples telling Jesus about his death after they buried his body.

Five thousand fed, 14.13-21

Each of the gospel writers had their own version of this story (Mk 6.30-44; Lk 9.10-17; Jn 6.1-13). John drew upon both the feeding of the five thousand and the four thousand along with the writings of Mark and Matthew. His barley loaves (Jn 6.9) remind the reader of Elisha's stories (2 Kings 4.42-44) and if combined with 1 Kings (1 Kings 17.9-16), may provide a pattern for the gospel stories. The Jewish Talmud contained a miracle story of a similar nature.

13: After John's death Jesus' life was redirected (cf his reaction to John's imprisonment, Mk 1.14-15). In Mark's gospel Jesus and the disciples went away in the boat to a deserted place for a needed rest and not because of John's death (Mk 6.32). **14:** *When he went ashore,* Jesus was moved with compassion to heal *their sick.* **15:** Since the hour for the evening meal was passed, *the disciples* wanted Jesus to dismiss the crowd in order that they might *go into the village and buy food for themselves.* **16-17:** All of the synoptic writers report that Jesus responded, *"You give them something to eat"* with the disciples protesting in Mark, "are we to go and buy two hundred denarii (two denarius was a day's wage for labor) worth of bread?" (Cf Elisha's feeding of a hundred prophets, 2 Kings 4.42-43). Luke said, "Unless we are to go and buy food for all these people." Each gospel writer reported there were *five loaves and two fish.* **19:** Mark had the *crowd to sit down* on green *grass* indicating it was spring. *Blessed and broke* suggested the prayer of praise and blessing spoken at the Last Supper (26.26) and at the beginning of a Jewish meal, "Praise to you, O LORD our God, King of the Universe, you bring forth bread from the earth." **20:** *Baskets* were in reference to the little food baskets that the Jewish carried so they could only eat food prepared according to the dietary laws. *Twelve* indicated that each of twelve disciples carried one to collect the left over *broken pieces.* **21:** Matthew added *besides women and children* conveying the custom that they would stand or sit separate from the men and it increased the number.

Jesus walks on the water, 14.22-36

22: *Made the disciples* seemed to imply the disciples did not want to separate themselves from the excitement of the feeding of the five thousand. **23:** As was his custom, Jesus went *up the mountain by himself to pray* (1.35; 3.13) in order to remain focused upon his purpose (4.1-11). **24:** *Was far from the land,* or as the Greek was translated literally "was many stadia from the land"; a stadion was about one-eighth of a mile. **25:** *Early in the morning,* Greek translated literally "in the fourth watch of the night" (the fourth watch was from 3 to 6 a.m.). The Jewish divided the night into three watches. **26:** *Ghosts* in the OT was the belief that *ghosts* or shades were lifeless creatures without any power to do good or evil. However, the popular belief in the Near East was that the shades of the dead could rise from the nether world to inflict harm upon the living, if they had been neglected by their family, or failed to receive the last rites of burial (Prov 21.16; Isa 19.3; 29.4). **28-33:** Matthew was the only one that told of Peter's unsuccessful attempt to walk *on the water.* Some have used this incident to explain Peter's career, pride, fall, rescue and restoration. Matthew had three miracles occurring in this account: Jesus walked on the water; so did Peter temporarily; and the wind ceased. These were not the acts of a mere human, but the Son of God (Mk 6.51-52).

34-36: *Gennesaret* was a district on the northwestern shore of the Sea of Galilee, which was also called the Lake of Gennesaret.

This fertile plain was densely populated. *The fringe of his cloak,* or sacred tassel, was tied by a blue thread to each of the four corners of the outer cloak (Num 15.38-39; Duet 22.12), that served as clothes during the day and as a blanket at night. The tassels were intended to remind the Israelites of their obligations to the Law (9.19-21). Peter's lack of faith to walk on the water was contrasted with those who were sick and believed they would be healed, if *they might touch even the fringe of his cloak.*

Chapter 14 Study Guide

1. Why did Herod think that Jesus was John the Baptist raised from the dead?
2. Is keeping your word more important than killing someone?
3. What is your understanding of the feeding of the five thousand, plus women and children?
4. Explain the disciples' belief in ghosts but not in the ability for Jesus to walk on water.
5. How would you respond to Jesus' invitation to get out of the boat?

Chapter 15
Tradition of the elders, 15.1-20
(Mk 7.1-23)

Matthew. Then Pharisees and scribes came to Jesus **(M)**(from Jerusalem) and said,

Pharisees and Scribes. ²"Why do your disciples break the tradition of the elders? For they do not wash their hands before they eat."

Matthew. ³He answered them,

Jesus. "And why do you break the commandment of God for the sake of your tradition? [4]For God said,[a]

Lord. (J)('Honor your father and your mother,' [b])

Jesus. and,

Lord. (J)('Whoever speaks evil of father or mother must surely die.' [c])

Jesus. [5]But you say that whoever tells father or mother,

Pharisees and Scribes. 'Whatever support you might have had from me is given to God,'[d]

Jesus. then that person need not honor the father.[e] [6]So, for the sake of your tradition, you make void the word[f] of God. **(M)**('You hypocrites! Isaiah prophesied rightly about you when he said:

Lord. (I)([8]'This people honors me with their lips, but their hearts are far from me; [9]in vain do they worship me, teaching human precepts as doctrines.'" [g]))

Matthew. [10]Then he called the crowd to him and said to them,

Jesus. "Listen and understand: [11]it is not what goes into the mouth that defiles a person, but it is what comes out of the mouth that defiles."

Matthew. (M)([12]Then the disciples approached and said to him,

---

[a] Other ancient authorities read *commanded, saying*
[b] Ex 20.12; Deut 5.16
[c] Ex 21.17; Lev 20.9
[d] Or *is an offering*
[e] Other ancient authorities add *or the mother*
[f] Other ancient authorities read *law*; others, *commandment*
[g] Isa 29.13

Disciples. "Do you know that the Pharisees took offense when they heard what you said?"

Matthew. [13]He answered,

Jesus. "Every plant that my heavenly Father has not planted will be uprooted.) [Q₁][[14]Let them alone; they are blind guides of the blind.[h] And if one blind person guides another, both will fall into a pit."]

Matthew. [15]But Peter said to him,

Peter. "Explain this parable to us."

Matthew. [16]Then he said,

Jesus. "Are you also still without understanding? [17]Do you not see that whatever goes into the mouth enters the stomach, and goes out into the sewer? [18]But what comes out of the mouth **(M)**(proceeds from the heart, and this) is what defiles. [19]For out of the heart come evil intentions, murder, adultery, **(M)** (fornication, theft,) false witness, slander. [20]These are what defile a person, **(M)**(but to eat with unwashed hands does not defile.")

The Canaanite woman, 15.21-28
(Mk 7.24-30)

Matthew. [21]Jesus left that place and went away to the district of Tyre and Sidon. [22]Just then a Canaanite woman **(M)**(from that region came out and) started shouting,

Woman. **(M)**("Have mercy on me, Lord, Son of David;) my daughter is tormented by a demon."

---

[h] Other ancient authorities lack *of the blind*

Matthew. (M)([23]But he did not answer her at all. And his disciples came and urged him, saying,

Disciples. "Send her away, for she keeps shouting after us."

Matthew. [24]He answered,

Jesus. "I was sent only to the lost sheep of the house of Israel."

Matthew. [25]But she came and knelt before him, saying,

Woman. "Lord, help me.")

Matthew. [26]He answered,

Jesus. "It is not fair to take the children's food and throw it to the dogs."

Matthew. [27]She said,

Woman. "Yes, Lord, yet even the dogs eat the crumbs that fall from their masters' table."

Matthew.[28]Then Jesus answered her,

Jesus. "Woman, great is your faith! Let it be done for you as you wish."

Matthew. And her daughter was healed instantly.

Healings, 15.29-31
(Mk 7.31-37)

Matthew. [29]After Jesus had left that place, he passed along the Sea of Galilee, **(M)**(and he went up the mountain, where he sat down.) [30]Great crowds came to him, bringing with them the lame, the maimed, the blind, the mute, and many others. They put them at his feet, and he cured them, ³¹so that the crowd was amazed when they saw the mute speaking, **(M)**(the maimed whole, the lame walking, and the blind seeing. And they praised the God of Israel.)

Four thousand fed, 15.32-39
(Mk 8.1-10)

Matthew. ³²Then Jesus called his disciples to him and said,

Jesus. "I have compassion for the crowd, because they have been with me now for three days and have nothing to eat; and I do not want to send them away hungry, for they might faint on the way."

Matthew. ³³The disciples said to him,

Disciples. "Where are we **(M)**(to get enough bread in the desert) to feed so great a crowd?"

Matthew. ³⁴Jesus asked them,

Jesus. "How many loaves have you?"

Matthew. They said,

Disciples. "Seven, **(M)**(and a few small fish.")

Matthew. ³⁵Then ordering the crowd to sit down on the ground, ³⁶he took the seven loaves **(M)**(and the fish;) and after giving thanks he broke them and gave them to the disciples, and the disciples gave them to the crowds. ³⁷And all of them ate and were filled; and they took up the broken pieces **(M)**(left over,) seven baskets full. ³⁸Those who had eaten were four thousand men, **(M)**(besides women and children.) ³⁹After sending away the crowds, he got into the boat and went to the region of Magadan.[i]

---

[i] Other ancient authorities read *Magdala* or *Magdalan*

Chapter 15 Notes
Tradition of the elders, 15.1-20

At the climax of Jesus' ministry in Galilee, Matthew presented a series of conflicts with the Pharisees and scribes. This followed the rejection of others, including those from his hometown, and even his disciples did not seem to understand. Three issues were presented: unwashed hands (1-2), and the Corban vow (3-9) that was directed to the Pharisees, while the last issue, ritual uncleanness (10-11), was directed to the crowd.

1: Some *Pharisees and scribes* from *Jerusalem* came to Galilee either to find fault with Jesus or to spread their beliefs into Galilee, which was to become an important center of rabbinic Judaism in the next century. **2:** The prohibition of eating without washing the hands was a requirement for temple priests before participating in the sacrifices (Lev 22.1-16). However, it was not a general requirement before 100 CE, when the practice was extended to the laity as they tried to build a fence around the Law *(Mishnah Avot, 1.1)*. The rational was "if it is good for the priests to be holy, it is appropriate for all the Holy People." *Tradition of the elders* was the oral law or tradition that became part of the Mishnah in about 300 BCE. The Pharisees believed that the oral traditions were received by Moses on Sinai and were equal to the Torah, a position held even today by Orthodox Jews. Since this was one of the differences between the Pharisees and the Sadducees, the statement all of the Jews would be inaccurate. While modern conservative and reform Jews believe some kind of oral law was necessary to make the Torah comprehensible and workable, they reject the belief that most of the Talmud (613 commandments) was received by Moses. For them the Talmud and the oral law become more of an evolving process, the result of debates over generations on how to incorporate the Torah within their lives. These modern conservative and reform Jews, might agree with Jesus and feel freer than the orthodox (Pharisees) to ignore, modify or change the oral law. **3:** Jesus' response to the Pharisees question as to why the disciples *do not wash their hands before they eat* was that they abandoned *the commandment of God* to hold to human tradition, which leads to the second issue, the Coban vow. **5-6:** Matthew omitted the word "Coban" (Mk 7.11) that meant "gift" or "temple offering." Property that might be used to help a person's *father* or *mother* could be called a Coban, that was designated for the temple and thereby releasing him from the obligation of caring for his parents. This vow in Jesus' time was changed by the rabbis by 100 CE where "Honor your father and your mother" (Ex 20.12) took precedence over a number of Jewish laws. (*Gospel of the Nazaraeans,* 12), "The Jewish gospel has: Corban is what you should gain from us." **7:** The Pharisees were called *hypocrites* because they pretended to follow God, but followed men, their religious leaders (Mt 23.13, 15, 23, 25, 27, 29). **8-9:** These verses showed how far Jesus and the Pharisees were from each other as he used the LORD's (*see* LORD) complaint concerning Jerusalem's leaders in Isaiah (Isa 29.13).

10-11: In response to the issue, concerning ritual uncleanness, Jesus addressed *the crowd* (*see* Crowd) expressing that it was what came out of a person that defiled a person, not what went in. *Defiles* meant a person would be unclean or unfit to share in the public ritual (Acts 10.14-15; 1 Tim 4.3). If these words of Jesus had been accepted by all the followers of Jesus, there would have been no problems later (Acts 10.1-29; Gal 3.19-29). **12:** The disciples were worried about the hostile reaction from the Pharisees to Jesus' teaching. **13-14:** The response was that the Pharisees were blind leaders who cannot lead others, unless they *both will fall into a pit.* **15-20:** Jesus had to explain the parable (v 11) to the disciples because they were *still without understanding,* and he was concerned with what came from the *mouth* and from the *heart.* Matthew may have used the list from Mark's gospel, a list that may have been an addition to his gospel, because they were characteristic of Hellenistic rather than Jewish teachings, as they are found in Romans (Rom 1.29-31) and Galatians (Gal 5.19-23).

The Canaanite woman, 15.21-28

21: The meaning of this section remains unclear, but it seemed that Jesus was willing to extend his healing ministry to the Gentiles at *Tyre and Sidon.* This came directly after his conflict with the Pharisees, leading some to believe that it reflected the attitudes of the early church and Paul, "To the Jew first and also to the Greeks" (Rom 1.16). Matthew did not help when he inserted, "I was only sent to the lost sheep of the house of Israel" (v 24). **22:** The woman was *a Canaanite,* a Phoenician and not a Jewess, but she identified Jesus as the Messiah (*see* Jesus), *Lord, Son of David.* The Canaanites were often spoken of in the OT with reproach (Gen 24.3; Ezra 9.1; Zech 14.21). **26-27:** *The children* were Judeans (cf Hos 1.10), and the *dogs,* the Gentiles. *The dogs* seemed like some harsh words from Jesus, but in this account, they should be understood as the common prejudices during this period, reflecting both that of the Judeans and Christians. Matthew seemed to believe that Jesus was only testing the woman's faith (v 24). **27:** The woman's response in Mark was that the dogs eat the children's crumbs, however in Matthew it read, *"Even the dogs eat the crumbs that fall from their master's table."* **28:** Her *faith* was recognized and *her daughter was healed instantly.*

Healings, 15.29-31

29-31: Jesus returned to the area around *the Sea of Galilee, and went up the mountain* where the reader might expect Jesus to pray or teach, but where he received and cured *the lame, the maimed, the blind, the mute, and many others.*

Four thousand fed, 15.32-39

32-39: There were several common points between the feeding of the five thousand (Mt 14.13-21) and the feeding of the four thousand: a deserted place; little food except for a few *loaves* and *fish;* the crowd sitting down to eat; the thanks and breaking of bread; and the food left over. However, there were several differences, beginning here with Jesus *not* wanting *to send them away hungry;* the *seven baskets* full of leftovers, and *four thousand men besides women and children.* Jesus' motives in this account were clearly stated, one of sympathy, and fearing that they *might faint on the way,* if he sent them away. Jesus was moved to feed them rather than to tell the disciples to do so (Mt 14.16; Mk 6.37; Lk 9.13). **39:** *Magadan* was apparently on the west side of the Sea of Galilee.

Chapter 15 Study Guide

1. What did you make of the conflict between Jesus and the Pharisees over the tradition of the elders?
2. How did the account of the Canaanite woman change if you omit those portions of the account only in Matthew?
3. What was your understanding of Jesus' statement, "I was sent only to the lost sheep of the house of Israel"?
4. Why did Jesus heal and feed all when he resisted this temptation in the wilderness?
5. Explain the attitudes of the Pharisees and the crowds in this chapter.

Chapter 16
Demand for signs, 16.1-4
(Mk 8.11-21; Lk 11.16, 29; 12.54-56)

Matthew. The Pharisees **(M)**(and Sadducees) came, and to test Jesus[a] they asked him to show them a sign from heaven. [2]He answered them,

Jesus. [Q$_2$]["When it is evening, you say,

Pharisees and Sadducees. 'It will be fair weather, for the sky is red.'

---
[a] Gk *him*

Jesus. ³And in the morning,

Pharisees and Sadducees. 'It will be stormy today, for the sky is red and threatening.'

Jesus. You know how to interpret the appearance of the sky, but you cannot interpret the signs of the times.ᵇ] ⁴An evil **(M)** (and adulterous) generation asks for a sign, but no sign will be given to it except the sign of Jonah."

Matthew. Then he left them and went away.

Yeast of the Pharisees, 16.5-12
(Mk 8.14-21; Lk 12.1)

Matthew. ⁵When the disciples reached the other side, they had forgotten to bring any bread. ⁶Jesus said to them,

Jesus. "Watch out, and beware of the yeast of the Pharisees and Sadducees."

Matthew. ⁷They said to one another,

Disciples. "It is because we have brought no bread."

Matthew. ⁸And becoming aware of it, Jesus said,

Jesus. (M)("You of little faith,) why are you talking about having no bread? ⁹Do you still not perceive? Do you not remember the five loaves for the five thousand, and how many baskets you gathered? ¹⁰Or the seven loaves for the four thousand, and how many baskets you gathered? ¹¹How could you fail to perceive that I was not speaking about bread? **(M)**(Beware of the yeast of the Pharisees and Sadducees!"

ᵇ Other ancient authorities lack ²*When it is . . . of the times*

Matthew. [12]Then they understood that he had not told them to beware of the yeast of bread, but of the teaching of the Pharisees and Sadducees.)

Peter's confession, 16.13-23
(Mk 8.27-33; Lk 9.18-22)

Matthew. [13]Now when Jesus came into the district of Caesarea Philippi, he asked his disciples,

Jesus. "Who do people say that the Son of Man is?"

Matthew. [14]And they said,

Disciples. "Some say John the Baptist, but others Elijah, and still others Jeremiah or one of the prophets."

Matthew. [15]He said to them,

Jesus. "But who do you say that I am?"

Matthew. [16]Simon Peter answered,

Peter. "You are the Messiah,[c] the Son of the living God."

Matthew. (M)([17]And Jesus answered him,

Jesus. "Blessed are you, Simon son of Jonah! For flesh and blood has not revealed this to you, but my Father in heaven. [18]And I tell you, you are Peter,[d] and on this rock[e] I will build my church, and the gates of Hades will not prevail against it. [19]I will give you the keys of the kingdom of heaven, and whatever you bind on earth will be bound in heaven, and whatever you loose on earth will be loosed in heaven.")

---

[c] Or *the Christ*
[d] Gk *Petros*
[e] Gk *petra*

133

Matthew. [20]Then he sternly ordered the disciples not to tell anyone that he was[f] the Messiah.[g]

[21]From that time on, Jesus began to show his disciples that he must **(M)**(go to Jerusalem and) undergo great suffering at the hands of the elders and chief priests and scribes, and be killed, and on the third day be raised. [22]And Peter took him aside and began to rebuke him, **(M)**(saying,

Peter. "God forbid it, Lord! This must never happen to you.")

Matthew. [23]But he turned and said to Peter,

Jesus. "Get behind me, Satan! **(M)**(You are a stumbling block to me;) for you are setting your mind not on divine things but on human things."

On discipleship, 16.24-28
(Mk 8.34-9.1; Lk 9.23-27)

Matthew. [24]Then Jesus told his disciples,

Jesus. "If any want to become my followers, let them deny themselves and take up their cross and follow me. [25]For those who want to save their life will lose it, and those who lose their life for my sake will find it. [26]For what will it profit them if they gain the whole world but forfeit their life? Or what will they give in return for their life?

[27]"For the Son of Man is to come with his angels in the glory of his Father, **(M)**(and then he will repay everyone for what has been done.) [28]Truly I tell you, there are some standing here who will not taste death before they see the Son of Man coming in his kingdom."

---

[f] Other ancient authorities add *Jesus*
[g] Or *the Christ*

Chapter 16 Notes
Demand for signs, 16.1-4

1: Jesus gave an almost identical response to a similar demand earlier (12.38-39). While Mark (Mt 8.11) and Luke (Lk 11.29) did not mention the *Sadducees,* Matthew added them for the first time since 3.7. Both groups, the Sadducees and Pharisees, were not concerned with the miracles of healing or any of the wonders that Jesus performed, they wanted a visible or audible *sign from heaven.* It was the custom to request such a *sign* from a rabbi to prove that his teaching was true (Jn 2.18). The rabbinic commentary (*Pesikta Rabbati,* 1, 641), taught that when the Messiah came he would stand on the roof of the temple, and those doubting would see a light from heaven streaming over him. **2-3:** They considered themselves experts in predicting the weather, but they were not able to understand the spiritual warnings of *the times.* **4:** Mark said that "no sign will be given to this generation." Luke added, because it is "an evil generation", while Matthew identified them to be *an evil and adulterous generation,* and they would only be given *the sign of Jonah.* Jonah preached to the Ninevites, "Forty days more, and Nineveh shall be overthrown!" And the people of Nineveh believed God and God changed his mind about the calamity (Jon 3.4-10). Matthew and Mark indicated that *he left them* that meant the Pharisees and Sadducees, and *went away.*

Yeast of the Pharisees, 16.5-12

5: *The other side* was in reference to the eastern shore of the Sea of Galilee. While in the boat, it was discovered that the disciples *had forgotten to bring any bread.* Mark said that they only had one loaf (Mk 8.14). Jesus used the situation to warn the disciples against the yeast of the Pharisees and Sadducees. Yeast was a symbol of the evil impulse or wicked ways of humans. Before celebrating the seder at the Passover, all care was taken to remove all leaven bread from the house, as the power of yeast infected the new dough and spread it (Ex 12.15; 13.7). Jesus used yeast as a symbol of the kingdom of

God (Mt 13.33; Lk 13.20-21) to suggest that the kingdom's influence was greater than evil. **7:** The disciples took the reference to yeast to mean because *we have brought no bread.* **8-12:** Jesus reminded the disciples of the feeding of the five thousand and the four thousand, and wondered how they could fail *to perceive* that he was not talking about bread, but the *teaching of the Pharisees and Sadducees.*

Peter's confession, 16.13-23

This section marked the second half of the Gospel where Jesus revealed the secret that the Son of Man must suffer, and where his ministry turned toward the cross. **13:** Matthew had Jesus inquire of the disciples, *who do people say that the Son of Man is,* as they were on their way to *villages of Caesarea Philippi.* Caesarea Philippi was at the foot of Mount Hermon where the god Pan was worshipped along with the emperor cult. The setting for Luke was after the disciples reported to Jesus about their missionary journey and the crowd had left following the feeding of the five thousand. It was usual for the students to ask questions of the teacher in rabbinical dialogues, but here Jesus took the initiative (2.8-9' 3.4; 12.35). **14:** The disciples responded with the same rumors told to Herod. *Elijah* was believed by the Judeans to be a forerunner of the Messiah. **15:** Jesus in turn asked the disciples their opinion of him, *"Who do you say that I am?"* Mark reported that *Peter,* the spokesperson for the disciples, identified Jesus as *"the Messiah"* (Mk 8.29). Luke added, "of God" (Lk 19.20) while Matthew added, *"Son of the living God"* to mark his unique nature and relationship with God. **16:** Peter asserted that Jesus was the Messiah, not merely one of the prophets (v 14). He identified Jesus with the figure of Malachi (Mal 3.1-4; cf Mk 1.2; Mt 1.16; Jn 1.49; 11.27). The Davidic Messiah was expected to be a king of human origin who would establish the political supremacy of Israel over the world. A reign that would usher in a new period of righteousness and peace, and even if it was established by God, it was believed that it would not be achieved without struggle and war. **17-19:** Found only in Matthew's gospel, these verses seem to speak of a church that was separate from Judaism, a church that along with Peter received complete authority, something not supported in any of the other gospels or the Book of Acts. Yet, Peter could have been praised because he expressed, with a degree of understanding, the messianic role of Jesus. **17:** *Flesh and blood* was often used in Jewish writings to mean "humanity" rather than the divine (1 Cor 15.50; Gal 1.16; Eph 6.12). **18:** The Greek text involved a play on two words, "Petros" ("Peter") and "petra" ("rock"). Palestinian Aramaic, which Jesus usually spoke, used the same word for both proper name and common noun: 'You are 'Kepha' [Cephas; cf 1 Cor 15.5; Gal 2.9], and on this 'kepha' [rock] I will build...". The word *church* had OT roots that meant a congregation within Israel that represented what all Israel should be and sought to become. *The gates of Hades* were the power of death would not be able to destroy this church. **19:** The master gave *the keys* in trust to the servant. *Bind* and *loose* did not refer to excluding from or admitting into the kingdom as it was later understood by the early church (18.18; Jn 20.23), but its original meaning was to teach what was forbidden and permitted. **20:** Jesus accepted Peter's confession, but *he sternly ordered them,* meaning Peter and the disciples, *not to* make it public until he had a chance to reinterpret it in terms of service, suffering and sacrifice. If the people had been told that Jesus was the Christ, it would have raised false nationalistic hopes. **21:** *From that time,* Jesus began to teach the disciples about the kingdom of heaven, the cross and to define the messianic promise in terms of the Suffering Servant of Deutero Isaiah. Matthew and Luke had *"on the third day be raised"* instead of Mark's "after three days rise again." **22-23:** Peter rebuked Jesus. And Jesus rebuked Peter while teaching about *divine things* rather than *human things.* Peter's rebuke expressed the common Jewish outlook that expected a Messiah to triumph easily and completely. While Peter took Jesus *aside and began to rebuke him,* Jesus probably said loud enough for the other disciples to hear, *"Get behind me, Satan!"* I want nothing to do with you when you talk like that, as Jesus heard the temptation to avoid the cross.

On discipleship, 16.24-28

24: After the prediction of his death, resurrection and the rebuke of Peter, Jesus began to teach the disciples about the cost of discipleship. His followers must *deny themselves and take up their cross,* meaning they were to be willing to do away with self-concern and to be ready for self-sacrifice, even to death. **25:** To run the risk of losing physical comfort and life, if necessary, would lead to a true life with God. **26:** Here *life* was not merely physical existence, but the higher or spiritual life, the real self (cf Lk 9.25; 12.15). These words were written for a martyr church where its members, like Jesus, would be ready to face death, if they refused to renounce Christ.

On July 18, 64 CE, a fire began in Rome and continued for a week, destroying nearly two-thirds of the city, and leaving half the population homeless. The Emperor Nero fretted (not "fiddled") while Rome burned and began a program to rebuild the city with straight, broad streets and wide squares, including a fifty acre palace, leading many Romans to believe he deliberately set the fire to clear a site for the palace. Nero blamed the Christians for starting the fire, leading to the crucifixion of the apostle Peter and other Christians being torn apart by dogs or burned at the stake.

27: What does it profit someone to have material success and to die without enjoying it? Cf the story of the rich fool (Lk 12.15-20). The apostate who renounced the faith may gain a longer life, and even some temporary benefits, but he would lose his life eventually and what would he say when he stood before the Son of Man (see Mk 9.1n; 1 Cor 16.22; 1 Thess 4.15-18; Jas 5.7; Rev 1.7)? **28:** This prediction was not fulfilled and later Christians found it necessary to explain that it had been fulfilled at Pentecost. This issue might be addressed in terms of a preliminary kingdom in contrast to the full or entire kingdom. The point was not the delay, but the necessity of being prepared for it at all times.

Chapter 16 Study Guide

1. Why did Jesus not give a sign to the Pharisees and Sadducees?
2. What is your understanding of the "yeast of the Pharisees"?
3. Who do you say that the Son of Man is?
4. What kind of Messiah do you expect?
5. Explain the meaning of the statement, "Get behind me Satan."

Chapter 17

The transfiguration, 17.1-8
(Mk 9.2-8; Lk 9.28-36)

Matthew. Six days later, Jesus took with him Peter and James and his brother John and led them up a high mountain, by themselves. ²And he was transfigured before them, and his face shone like the sun, and his clothes became dazzling white. ³Suddenly there appeared to them Moses and Elijah, talking with him. ⁴Then Peter said to Jesus,

Peter. "Lord, it is good for us to be here; if you wish, I[a] will make three dwellings[b] here, one for you, one for Moses, and one for Elijah."

Matthew. ⁵While he was still speaking, suddenly a bright cloud overshadowed them, and from the cloud a voice said,

God. "This is my Son, the Beloved;[c] with him I am well pleased; listen to him!"

Matthew. (M)(⁶When the disciples heard this, they fell to the ground and were overcome by fear. ⁷But Jesus came and touched them, saying,

Jesus. "Get up and do not be afraid.")

---

[a] Other ancient authorities read *we*
[b] Or *tents*
[c] Or *my beloved Son*

Matthew. ⁸And when they looked up, they saw no one except Jesus himself alone.

Prophecies about Elijah, 17.9-13
(Mk 9.9-13)

Matthew. ⁹As they were coming down the mountain, Jesus ordered them,

Jesus. "Tell no one about the vision until after the Son of Man has been raised from the dead."

Matthew. ¹⁰And the disciples asked him,

Disciples. "Why, then, do the scribes say that Elijah must come first?"

Matthew. ¹¹He replied,

Jesus. "Elijah is indeed coming and will restore all things; ¹²but I tell you that Elijah has already come, **(M)**(and they did not recognize him,) but they did to him whatever they pleased. **(M)**(So also the Son of Man is about to suffer at their hands."

Matthew. ¹³Then the disciples understood that he was speaking to them about John the Baptist.)

An epileptic child healed, 17.14-21
(Mk 9.14-29; Lk 9.37-42)

Matthew. ¹⁴When they came to the crowd, a man came to him, **(M)** (knelt before him,) ¹⁵and said,

Father. "Lord, have mercy on my son, for he is an epileptic **(M)**(and he suffers terribly; he often falls into the fire and often into the water.) ¹⁶And I brought him to your disciples, but they could not cure him."

Matthew. [17]Jesus answered,

Jesus. "You faithless and perverse generation, how much longer must I be with you? How much longer must I put up with you? Bring him here to me."

Matthew. [18]And Jesus rebuked the demon,[d] and it[e]came out of him, and the boy was cured instantly. [19]Then the disciples came to Jesus privately and said,

Disciples. "Why could we not cast it out?"

Matthew. [20]He said to them,

Jesus. "Because of your little faith. For truly I tell you, [**Q₂**] [if you have faith the size of a[f] mustard seed, you will say to this mountain,

Disciples. 'Move from here to there,'

Jesus. and it will move; and nothing will be impossible for you."[g]]

The Passion foretold a second time, 17.22-23
(Mk 9.30-32; Lk 9.43-45)

Matthew. [22]As they were gathering[h] in Galilee, Jesus said to them,

Jesus. "The Son of Man is going to be betrayed into human hands, [23]and they will kill him, and on the third day he will be raised."

Matthew. And they were greatly distressed.

---

d   Gk *it* or *him*
e   Gk *the demon*
f   Gk *faith as a grain of*
g   Other ancient authorities add verse 21, *But this kind does not come out except by prayer and fasting*
h   Other ancient authorities read *living*

Money for the temple, 17.24-27

Matthew. (M)([24]When they reached Capernaum, the collectors of the temple tax[i] came to Peter and said,

Temple tax collectors. "Does your teacher not pay the temple tax?"[j]

Matthew. [25]He said,

Peter. "Yes, he does."

Matthew. And when he came home, Jesus spoke of it first, asking,

Jesus. "What do you think, Simon? From whom do kings of the earth take toll or tribute? From their children or from others?"

Matthew. [26k]When Peter said,

Peter. "From others,"

Matthew. Jesus said to him,

Jesus. "Then the children are free. [27]However, so that we do not give offense to them, go to the sea and cast a hook; take the first fish that comes up; and when you open its mouth, you will find a coin;[l] take that and give it to them for you and me.")

Chapter 17 Notes
The transfiguration, 17.1-8

After the resurrection, all Christians understood that Jesus was the Messiah, but during Jesus' lifetime only a few of his followers

---

[i] Gk *didrachma*
[j] Gk *didrachma*
[k] Gk *he*
[l] Gk *stater*; the stater was worth two didrachmas

were permitted a glimpse of what was to come with an event that began with prayer and grew into an intense religious experience.

1: Matthew and Mark placed this event *six days* after Peter's confession (Mk 16.16; Mk 8.29), while Luke placed it "about eight days after these sayings" (Lk 9.20). Moses went up the mountain with Aaron, Nadab and Abihu and the seventy elders. Later Moses went up alone and for six days, the cloud covered the mountain (Ex 24.9-18). *Peter and James and his brother John* were the three who seemed to be the closest to Jesus. The *high mountain* was not identified, but it probably was Mount Hermon located near Caesarea Philippi and stood about nine thousand feet high. Luke added they went up the mountain *to pray.* **2:** Matthew expanded Luke's comment that the appearance of his face was changed to say it *shone like the sun* making it similar to Moses' when he conversed with God (Ex 34.29-35). **3:** *Moses* was the prototype (Deut 18.15) and *Elijah* the forerunner (Mal 4.5) of the Messiah and according to Deuteronomy (Deut 34.6) and 2 Kings (2 Kings 2.11), both went directly into the heavens. Moses and Elijah were equated with the Law and the Prophets. Only Luke revealed that their conversation covered Jesus' departure, that he was about to accomplish at Jerusalem, which could be translated from the Greek "the fate that awaited him." Only Luke (Lk 9.32) reported the disciples were having a difficult time staying awake. **4:** Peter may have wanted to prolong a rewarding experience, and if it was out of fear (Mk 9.6), as Mark stated, then the comment, "Rabbi, it is good for us to be here" seemed out of place. *Three dwellings* should be translated "three tents" to maintain reference to the Feast of Booths, "On the fifteenth day of this seventh month, and lasting seven days, there shall be the festival of booths...so that your generation may know that I made the people of Israel live in booths when I brought them out of the land of Egypt" (Lev 23.33-44). The Feast of Booths, a kind of Jewish thanksgiving, was one of three pilgrim festivals or holidays where Jewish males would make pilgrimages to the temple in Jerusalem with an offering. The booth or tent, by design was to be a temporary shelter and a reminder of the hardships endured during the years in the wilderness. The booth was a firm link between the spiritual and material world, constructed so that one might look through the roof at night and see the stars and to recall one's reliance on the will of God in a hostile world. It was a joyful response to a special event, *"Lord, it is good for us to be here."* **5:** Jesus did not answer, but a *bright cloud,* the traditional symbol of God's presence *overshadowed them. From the cloud* came *a voice* that affirmed what Peter thought about Jesus as the Messiah and they are to *listen to him* (3.17). **6-8:** It was then that the disciples *were overcome* with *fear.*

Prophecies about Elijah, 17.9-13

9: This event was not made public by the disciples until after the resurrection because Jesus wanted his messiahship to be a secret until his entry into Jerusalem. Matthew omits Mark's statement, "So they kept the matter to themselves, questioning what this rising from the dead could mean," to avoid showing the disciples lack of understanding about the resurrection. **10-12:** Elijah had a role in the final events at the end of history but the scribes failed to recognize that *Elijah has already come* in the person of John the Baptist. **13:** This verse was an editorial comment commonly used by Matthew to expand upon Mark.

An epileptic child healed, 17.14-21

14: Matthew alone recorded that the father came up to Jesus and *knelt before him.* **15:** To be *epileptic* was attributed to the baleful influences of the moon, a demonic force (cf Ps 121.6). Luke (Lk 9.38) added, "He is my only child" for additional sympathy. **16:** The failure of the disciples to heal raised the question about the power of God granted to them when they were sent out to heal and preach (Mt 9.1-2). **17:** Jesus' response expressed a mood of weariness that was not easy to understand, and a *faithless and perverse generation* (Deut 32.5) included more than the disciples. Facing his own death, Jesus may have been concerned if the disciples were ready to proclaim the kingdom of God. Jesus rebuked the demon, healed the boy, and gave him back to his father. **20:** *Little faith* was distinguished from unbelief (Mt 13.58). Jesus' saying was in figurative language: faith was concerned with God's will, not with moving mountains (cf 21.21-22; Mk 11.22-23; Lk 17.6; 1 Cor 13.2; Jas 1.6).

The Passion foretold a second time, 17.22-23

All three gospel writers reported that Jesus told the disciples for a second time *the Son of Man is going to be betrayed into human hands* (cf Mt 16.21; 20.17-19). **22:** Matthew has this warning while they *were gathering,* for the pilgrimage to Jerusalem for the Passover, while in Mark (Mk 9.30) they were on their way to Jerusalem. Luke (Lk 9.44) placed an emphasis upon the words of Jesus as he told the disciples to "let the words sink into your ears," in other words, "pay attention to what I am saying." Luke implied the comment was not understood because the Messiah's death was not a part of the disciples' Jewish faith, a spiritual truth not yet revealed to them. **23:** After the second prediction of the Passion, Matthew said *they were greatly distressed,* and Mark and Luke added that they "were afraid to ask him," about his death. Luke did not include in his prediction any comment about his death and resurrection.

Money for the temple, 17.24-27

24: Jewish males paid the half-shekel tax annually in March for the upkeep of the temple. On the value see Mt 26.15n (Ex 30.13; 38.26). **27:** The *coin* (Greek "stater") was exactly enough (two drachmas) to pay for both of them.

Chapter 17 Study Guide

1. What was the significance of the transfiguration event?
2. Why did Peter want to make three dwellings (booths)?

3. If the end of time was so near, was it not too late for Elijah's preparatory ministry?
4. Explain the disciple's inability to heal the epileptic boy.
5. Why did Jesus only pay the temple tax for Peter and himself and not for the rest of the disciples?

Chapter 18

Sayings on humility and forgiveness, 18.1-35
True greatness, 18.1-5
(Mk 9.33-37; Lk 9.46-48)

Matthew. At that time the disciples came to Jesus and asked,

Disciples. "Who is the greatest **(M)**(in the kingdom of heaven?")

Matthew. ²He called a child, whom he put among them, ³and said,

Jesus. "Truly I tell you, unless you change and become like children, you will never enter the kingdom of heaven. ⁴Whoever becomes humble like this child is the greatest in the kingdom of heaven. ⁵Whoever welcomes one such child in my name welcomes me.

Warnings of hell, 18.6-9
(Mk 9.42-48; Lk 17.1-2)

Jesus. [Q₂][⁶"If any of you put a stumbling block before one of these little ones who believe in me, it would be better for you if a great millstone were fastened around your neck and you were drowned in the depth of the sea.

(**M**)(⁷Woe to the world because of stumbling blocks!) Occasions for stumbling are bound to come, but woe to the one by whom the stumbling block comes!"]

⁸"If your hand or your foot causes you to stumble, cut it off and throw it away; it is better for you to enter life maimed or lame than to have two hands or two feet and to be thrown into the eternal fire.

[9]And if your eye causes you to stumble, **(M)**(tear it out and) throw it away; it is better for you to enter life with one eye than to have two eyes and to be thrown into the hell[a] of fire."

The lost sheep, 18.10-14
(Lk 15.3-7)

Jesus. (M)([10]"Take care that you do not despise one of these little ones; for, I tell you, in heaven their angels continually see the face of my Father in heaven.[b]**) [Q₂][**[12]What do you think? If a shepherd has a hundred sheep, and one of them has gone astray, does he not leave the ninety-nine on the mountains and go in search of the one that went astray? [13]And if he finds it, truly I tell you, he rejoices over it] **(M)**(more than over the ninety-nine that never went astray.) [14]So it is not the will of your[c] Father in heaven **(M)**(that one of these little ones should be lost.)

Discipline among followers, 18.15-20
(Lk 17.3)

Jesus. [Q₂][[15] "If another member of the church[d] sins against you,[e] go and point out the fault when the two of you are alone. If the member listens to you, you have regained that one.[f]**] (M)(**[16]But if you are not listened to, take one or two others along with you, so that every word may be confirmed by the evidence of two or three witnesses. [17]If the member refuses to listen to them, tell it to the church; and if the offender refuses to listen even to the church, let such a one be to you as a Gentile and a tax collector. [18]Truly I tell you, whatever you bind on earth will be bound in heaven, and whatever you loose on earth will be loosed in heaven. [19]Again, truly I tell you, if two of you agree on earth about anything you ask, it will be done for you by my

---

[a] Gk *Gehenna*
[b] Other ancient authorities add verse 11, *For the Son of Man came to save the lost*
[c] Other ancient authorities read *my*
[d] Gk *If your brother*
[e] Other ancient authorities lack *against you*
[f] Gk *the brother*

Father in heaven. [20]For where two or three are gathered in my name, I am there among them.")

Forgiveness, 18.21-35

Matthew. (M)([21]Then Peter came and said to him,

Peter. [Q₂]["Lord,) if another member of the church[g] sins against me, how often should I forgive? As many as seven times?"]

Matthew. [22]Jesus said to him,

Jesus. (M)("Not seven times, but, I tell you, seventy-seven[h] times.
[23]"For this reason the kingdom of heaven may be compared to a king who wished to settle accounts with his slaves. [24]When he began the reckoning, one who owed him ten thousand talents[i] was brought to him; [25]and, as he could not pay, his lord ordered him to be sold, together with his wife and children and all his possessions, and payment to be made. [26]So the slave fell on his knees before him, saying,

Slave. 'Have patience with me, and I will pay you everything.'

Jesus. [27]And out of pity for him, the lord of that slave released him and forgave him the debt. [28]But that same slave, as he went out, came upon one of his fellow slaves who owed him a hundred denarii;[j] and seizing him by the throat, he said,

Slave. 'Pay what you owe.'

Jesus. [29]Then his fellow slave fell down and pleaded with him,

Slave. (fellow) 'Have patience with me, and I will pay you.'

---

[g] Gk *if my brother*
[h] Or *seventy times seven*
[i] A talent was worth more than fifteen years' wages of a laborer
[j] The denarius was the usual day's wage for a laborer

Jesus. ³⁰But he refused; then he went and threw him into prison until he would pay the debt. ³¹When his fellow slaves saw what had happened, they were greatly distressed, and they went and reported to their lord all that had taken place. ³²Then his lord summoned him and said to him,

King. 'You wicked slave! I forgave you all that debt because you pleaded with me. ³³Should you not have had mercy on your fellow slave, as I had mercy on you?'

Jesus. ³⁴And in anger his lord handed him over to be tortured until he would pay his entire debt. ³⁵So my heavenly Father will also do to every one of you,) if you do not forgive your brother or sister^k from your heart."

Chapter 18 Notes
Sayings on humility and forgiveness, 18.1-35

Matthew presented the fourth of his five great discourses (5.1-7.27; 10.1-11.1; 13.1-52; 24.1-26.2), and this one dealt with disputes that might arise within the community. He compiled the teachings of Jesus that conveyed every effort should be made to keep the weak from stumbling or deserting the fellowship (18.5-7), and when the church was confronted with decisions (18.15-20) it should be done in the spirit of Christ (18.21-35).

True greatness, 18.1-5

Whenever Jesus spoke of the kingdom of God, people and the disciples thought of their role in it. Jesus reminded the disciples they should be thinking of and seeking opportunities for service to God's little ones (Mk 9.33-37; Lk 9.46-48). **3:** To *change* their disposition and habits meant *become like children,* turn away from self-chosen

---

^k Gk *brother*

goals and relate oneself to God as to a father. (*Acts of Philip,* 34) "Unless you change your 'down' to 'up' (and 'up' to 'down' and 'right' to left') and 'left' to 'right', you will not enter my kingdom (of heaven)." **5:** The pagan world did not place the same value upon children as Jesus. Hilarion, an Egyptian laborer, wrote to his wife concerning their unborn child, "When the child is born, she should rear it if it is a boy, but if it is a girl, she should allow it to die." Jesus stressed that children were objects of God's love, and this belief was communicated to the early church (Mt 10.40-42; 25.31-46). Childlike relationships to a parent, not childish behavior, were in view (Mk 10.15; Lk 18.17; 1 Pet 2.2). When the disciples did something *in my name,* they would be doing it "at my command" or "for my sake."

Warnings of hell, 18.6-9

6: *Little ones,* while Luke may have meant this message was addressed to the disciples or a special group among them, Matthew and Mark added, *"who believe in me"* (Mk 9.42-48; Lk 17.1-2). A *millstone* was a heavy stone that could only be turned by using an animal, and if *fastened around your neck,* you would surely drown, if thrown into *the sea.* **7:** *Occasions for stumbling* were bound to occur, but for those who wanted to cause others to stumble, it would be better for them to be born *maimed or lame.* **8-9:** These verses were used in a figurative manner meaning that whenever temptations to control or abuse someone arose, they were to be discarded properly and decisively (Mk 9.43-48; Mt 5.29-30), nor should they be taken to support a restriction on social relationships because of a fear to be involved with evil. Jesus had contact with sinners and for him the protection from evil rested in a commitment to God's will and a deep concern for the welfare of others. *Hell of fire* compares the Greek phrase: "Gehenna of fire."

The lost sheep, 18.10-14

10: This verse was only found in Matthew. *Little ones* were probably the same ones referred to in verse 6. During the period following the Jewish exile in Babylon (586-538 BCE) the belief in *angels* emerged, mostly from the Persian religions (*see* Angels). So, by the time of Daniel (168 BCE), it was believed that nations had guardian angels and that Michael had been assigned to Israel. It was also believed that each child had a guarding angel, so in the verse it could be understood that, no matter how little or insignificant a believer might be in the eyes of humanity, in the eyes of God that person was important enough to have a guardian angel in heaven. This belief provided the background that introduced three parables that described God's love for the individual. Luke assumed that Jesus must have spoken these beliefs to the Pharisees and scribes in response to their complaints about his ministry to the tax collectors and sinners (Lk 17.24-27). The virtues of repentance were praised in rabbinical literature, but the direct searching for, and appeal to, the sinner was new and important for the early church. The good shepherd searched for the lost sheep, reclaimed it, and rejoiced over it. This parable continued to play a positive role in the moral and religious development in the world. The parable illustrated God's concern for those who lacked the ability to find him. He sought them. **11:** *For the Son of Man came to save the lost* was added by other ancient authorities. **12-13:** Matthew addressed the parable of the lost sheep to the disciples while Luke's audience was the Pharisees and scribes. *A hundred sheep* would be a large flock in Jesus' day. The loss of even one animal would be a serious one. The phrase, "until he finds it," was in harmony with Luke's universalism (Lk 15.4), and it contrasted with the *"if"* in Matthew.

Discipline among followers, 18.15-20

Within some of the Dead Sea writings, there were accounts on some of the differences within the religious community (*The*

Community Rule or *The Manual of Discipline,* V.24-vi.1). Rabbinical Judaism revealed a similar practice, presented by Matthew, within Judaism until the second century, when it was abandoned for fear of sitting in judgment of our neighbors or determining their status before God (cf Mt 7.1-5). Paul used the principle of excommunication based on two or three witnesses (1 Cor 5.3-5; 9-13; 2 Cor 13.1-3), and it must have been practiced within many Jewish Christian churches (Acts 5.1-11). These verses also revealed that within the local congregations no one official had full disciplinary authority.

15: This chapter was the only place in Matthew's gospel where the word *church* was used other than in connection with Peter's confession (Mt 16.18). *Alone* meant to be given solitary reproof would be more gracious than to receive it in public. Some manuscripts omit *against you.* **16:** *Take one or two others along* was a quote from Deuteronomy (Deut 19.15) where the rule of two or three witness was practiced. **17:** The expelled *member* was treated *as a Gentile and a tax collector,* an expression that seemed to belong to Jewish Christian tradition rather than from the lips of Jesus (Mt 5.46; 9.9-13; 21.31-32). It would be more a Jewish tradition to expel than an expression of Jesus who loved and cared for the Gentile and tax collector. **18:** The authority given earlier to Peter (16.19) was now given to all the disciples or to the church. **19-20:** *Again, truly I tell you* indicated a lose transition between what was stated and what followed. These verses may have originally referred to prayer, but Matthew used them to teach what was permitted or prohibited (Jn 14.13-14). *In my name,* the *Mishnah Avot*, 3.2 reads, "If two sit together and there are no words of the Torah between them, this is the seat of the scornful, as it is written, 'or set in the seat of the scornful' (Ps 1.1); but if two sit together and there are words of the Torah between them, the Shekinah (the presence of God) rests between them, as it is written, 'Those who feared the Lord spoke with one another'" (Mal 3.16). An ancient teaching about the presence of God was reworked to refer to the presence of Christ.

Forgiveness, 18.21-35

21: Peter understood the need to forgive others (Mk 11.25; Lk 6.36; 11.4; 17.3), but he wanted to know *how often should I forgive?* Jewish tradition held that if the offender repented, apologized, and made right the wrong, it was the duty of the injured party to forgive him. Jesus reverses the law of vengeance (Gen 4.24) where the song of Lamech states, "If Cain is avenged sevenfold, truly Lamech seventy-sevenfold." That was the blood feud carried on without mercy and without limit. **22:** Jesus said, just as in the old days there was no limit to hatred and vengeance, so mercy and forgiveness should be beyond calculating.

23-35: The parable taught that only a forgiving spirit could receive forgiveness (25.19). **23:** *A king* was regarding an earthly king rather than the heavenly Father (18.35). **24:** *Ten thousand talents* was an enormous amount. A *talent* equivalent to six thousand denarii, was a lot considering that two denarii, was the daily wage for the common laborer. **25:** *To be sold* was permitted by the law of Moses (Lev 25.39; 2 Kings 4.1). **27:** The *debt* was literally a loan (18.24). **28:** *A hundred denarii* was a little over a month and a half's wages. **30:** The callous refusal resulted in throwing *him into prison.* **32-33:** The king was angry at his lack of mercy and in turn did not show him any mercy (Lk 7.41-43). **34:** *To be tortured* until the debt was paid, thus for a very long time.

Chapter 18 Study Guide

1. Describe how the example of the child related to the kingdom of heaven.
2. What do verses 5 and 6 mean to you?
3. What is your understanding of "angels in heaven"?
4. Does the suggested approach toward a fellow Christian appear to follow the teachings of Jesus or that of Judaism?
5. How many times should you forgive your fellow Christian?

Chapter 19
From Galilee to Jerusalem, 19.1-20.34
(Mk 10.1-52; Lk 18.15-19.27)
Marriage and divorce, 19.1-12
(Mk 10.1-12)

Matthew. When **(M)**(Jesus had finished saying these things,) he left Galilee and went to the region of Judea beyond the Jordan. [2]Large crowds followed him, and he cured them there.

[3]Some Pharisees came to him, and to test him they asked,

Pharisees. "Is it lawful for a man to divorce his wife **(M)**(for any cause?")

Matthew. He answered,

Jesus. [4]"Have you not read that the one who made them at the beginning

God. (P)('made them male and female,' [a])

Jesus. [5]and said,

Editor. (LJ)("'For this reason a man shall leave his father and mother and be joined to his wife, and the two shall become one flesh'? [6]So they are no longer two, but one flesh. Therefore what God has joined together, let no one separate." [b])

Matthew. [7]They said to him,

Pharisees. "Why then did Moses command us to give a certificate of dismissal and to divorce her?"

Matthew. [8]He said to them,

---

[a] Gen 1.27 (humankind)
[b] Gen 2.24

Jesus. "It was because you were so hard-hearted that Moses allowed you to divorce your wives, but from the beginning it was not so. [9]And I say to you, whoever divorces his wife, **(M)**(except for unchastity,) and marries another commits adultery."[c]

Matthew. (M) ([10]His disciples said to him,

Disciples. "If such is the case of a man with his wife, it is better not to marry."

Matthew. [11]But he said to them,

Jesus. "Not everyone can accept this teaching, but only those to whom it is given. [12]For there are eunuchs who have been so from birth, and there are eunuchs who have been made eunuchs by others, and there are eunuchs who have made themselves eunuchs for the sake of the kingdom of heaven. Let anyone accept this who can.")

Blessing the children, 19.13-15
(Mk 10.13-16; Lk 18.15-17)

Matthew. [13]Then little children were being brought to him in order that he might lay his hands on them and pray. The disciples spoke sternly to those who brought them; [14]but Jesus said,

Jesus. "Let the little children come to me, and do not stop them; for it is to such as these that the kingdom of heaven belongs."

Matthew. [15]And he laid his hands on them and went on his way.

---

[c] Other ancient authorities read *except on the ground of unchastity, causes her to commit adultery*; others add at the end of the verse *and he who marries a divorced woman commits adultery*

The rich young man, 19.16-30
(Mk 10.17-31; Lk 18.18-30)

Matthew. [16]Then someone came to him and said,

Rich young ruler. "Teacher, what good deed must I do to have eternal life?"

Matthew. [17]And he said to him,

Jesus. "Why do you ask me about what is good? There is only one who is good. **(M)**(If you wish to enter into life,) keep the commandments."

Matthew. (M) ([18]He said to him,

Rich young ruler. "Which ones?"

Matthew. And Jesus said,)

LORD. (J)("You shall not murder; You shall not commit adultery; You shall not steal; You shall not bear false witness; [19]Honor your father and mother; [d])

Jesus. (M)(also,

Moses. (P)(You shall love your neighbor as yourself."[e]))

Matthew. [20]The young man said to him,

Rich young ruler. "I have kept all these;[f] **(M)**(what do I still lack?")

Matthew. [21]Jesus said to him,

---

[d] Ex 20.12; Deut 5.16-20
[e] Lev 19.18
[f] Other ancient authorities add *from my youth*

Jesus. "If you wish to be perfect, go, sell your possessions, and give the money[g] to the poor, and you will have treasure in heaven; then come, follow me."

Matthew. [22]When the young man heard this word, he went away grieving, for he had many possessions.
[23]Then Jesus said to his disciples,

Jesus. (M)("Truly I tell you,) it will be hard for a rich person to enter the kingdom of heaven. [24]Again I tell you, it is easier for a camel to go through the eye of a needle than for someone who is rich to enter the kingdom of God."

Matthew. (M)([25]When the disciples heard this,) they were greatly astounded and said,

Disciples. "Then who can be saved?"

Matthew. [26]But Jesus looked at them and said,

Jesus. "For mortals it is impossible, but for God all things are possible."

Matthew. [27]Then Peter said in reply,

Peter. "Look, we have left everything and followed you. What then will we have?"

Matthew. [28]Jesus said to them,

Jesus. [Q₃]["Truly I tell you, at the renewal of all things, when the Son of Man is seated on the throne of his glory, you who have followed me will also sit on twelve thrones, judging the twelve tribes of Israel.] [29]And everyone who has left houses or brothers or sisters or father or mother or children or fields, for my name's sake, will

---

[g] Gk lacks *the money*

receive a hundredfold,[h] and will inherit eternal life. [30]But many who are first will be last, and the last will be first."

Chapter 19 Notes
From Galilee to Jerusalem, 19.1-20.34

Jesus took the Perean route from Galilee to Jerusalem, traveling on the eastern side of the Jordan, to avoid Samaria, whose hostile inhabitants sometimes attacked Jewish pilgrim bands.

Marriage and divorce, 19.1-12

1: *When Jesus had finished saying these things,* this (or a similar) formula marked the conclusion of each of the five main discourses in the gospel (see Introduction and 7.28; 11.1; 13.53; 26.1).

3: The question about divorce seemed to be presented from the Christian perspective, rather than the Jewish point of view, since divorce had always been possible in Judaism. What was debated among the Pharisees was not if a man could divorce his wife, but for what cause? The school of Shammai permitted divorce only if the wife was guilty of unchastity or gross immodesty, while the school of Hillel permitted a man to divorce his wife even if she spoiled his food. Jewish marriage was not a contract between equals because a woman did not marry, she was given in marriage. The Mosaic law (teaching) gave no answer to this question and the rabbis differed in their opinions. **4:** Matthew and Mark have Jesus quote from Genesis (Gen 1.27; 2.24) in his response to the Pharisees. **6:** Matthew and Mark added, *"Therefore, what God has joined together, let no one separate."* **7:** *A certificate of dismissal* was referred to as a "certificate of divorce" (see 5.31n). **8:** This commandment was written for you not because of your dull minds, and uncivilized emotions, but your hardness of heart. Jesus proclaimed that the Law was shaped to the character of those for whom it was written. **9:** Rather than being drawn

---

[h] Other ancient authorities read *manifold*

into the controversy between the two schools of Jewish thought, Jesus pointed out that divorce was contrary to divine intention in marriage in that the two shall become one flesh (Gen 1.27; 2.24). Jesus protested against the cruelty of men in divorcing their wives (Mal 2.13-16), and leaving the woman with no protection and with no choice but to be remarried (see 5.32n; Lk 16.18; 1 Cor 7.10-13).

11-12: Jesus recognized a place for voluntary celibacy in the service of God's kingdom (cf 1 Cor 7.1-9).

Blessing the children, 19.13-15

13: Placing a value on family life, Jewish parents would bring their children to have the rabbis bless them that included laying *his hands on them and* praying. **14:** The disciples *spoke sternly* to the parents, wanting to protect Jesus from what they considered trivial matters, as the crowds often made it difficult for him to function or even move. Both Matthew and Luke omit Mark's comment that Jesus was indignant, and that he embraced the children as he blessed them. *For it is to such as these that the kingdom of heaven belongs* meaning those who depend in trustful simplicity share in God's kingdom.

The rich young man, 19.16-30

16: The ruler usually has been identified as "the rich young ruler" resulting from the combined information from the Synoptics. Mark called him a rich man, and Matthew called him a *young man* (19.20), while Luke identified him as a ruler, a member of the governing body of a synagogue. *Gospel of the Nazaraeans* (in Origen, *Commentary on Matthew*, 15.14 in the Latin version), "The second of the rich people said to Jesus, 'Teacher, what good things can I do and live?' Jesus answered, 'Fulfill the law and the prophets.' The person answered, 'I have.' Jesus said, 'Go, sell all that you have and distribute to the poor; and come, follow me.' But the rich man began to scratch his head, for it did not please him. And the Lord said to him, 'How can you say, I have fulfilled the law and the prophets, when it is written in the law;

You shall love your neighbor as yourself; and look, many of your neighbors, children of Abraham and Sarah, are covered with filth, dying of hunger, and your house is full of good things, none of which is given to them? And Jesus turned and said to Simon, the disciple, who was sitting nearby, 'Simon, son of Jonah, it is easier for a camel to go through the eye of a needle than for a rich person to enter the kingdom of heaven.'" **17:** *Gospel of the Naassenes,* (in Hippolytus, *Refutation of All Heresies,* v.7.26) reads, "Why do you call me good? One there is who is good – my Father who is in heaven – who makes his sun to rise on the just and on the unjust, and sends rain on the pure and on sinners" (cf 5.45). Jesus replied that the good way of life was obedience to God's will (15.2-3, 6). The Greek tense of the phrase *keep the commandments* implied not a single action but a continued process. *Eternal life* meant to share in the life to come, the kingdom of God. **18-19:** The commandments in Matthew were taken from Mark (Mk 10.19; Ex 20.10-16) and Jesus added, *"You shall love your neighbor as yourself"* (Deut 5.16-20; Rom 13.9; Jas 2.11). **20:** *I have kept all these* represented an honest claim. Rabbinical teachers believed that it was possible for individuals to fulfill their obligations to the whole law. **21:** Jesus consistently turned people's attention from concern over their own religious standing, calling them to involve themselves in the basic, vital interests of others. Wealth, poverty, or formal piety was not as important as sharing in the working out of God's life-giving design for all people (5.23-24, 43-48; 6.33). **22:** While it was difficult, many rich men became disciples such as Matthew (9.9), Joseph of Arimathea (27.57), Zacchaeus (Lk 19.9) but this rich man felt that discipleship would cost him too much.

 23-24: Luke had Jesus address the rich man, while both Matthew and Mark have him make the comment to the disciples. The *camel* was the largest beast of burden known in Palestine. The *needle's eye* was the name of a small gate in the wall that surrounded Jerusalem, and it should not be explained away by the Greek use of the *eye of a needle* on a "rope" or "cable." **26:** What was impossible for man became the summation of all of the laws, *but for God all things are possible* (Gen 18.14; Jer 32.17).

27: Peter again fulfilled the role of spokesman for the disciples. *We have left everything* meaning the disciples were not like the rich man. **28:** *The renewal of all things* referred to the consummation of God's purpose (cf Rom 8.18-25). **29-30:** *Jesus* assured the disciples they would receive more in this age and in the life to come. So much for serving God with no reward, unless this was used to assure the early church that God noticed their sacrifices (Mt 20.16; Mk 10.31; Lk 13.30).

Chapter 19 Study Guide

1. What was your reaction to the discourse on marriage and divorce?
2. What role did children play in Jesus' ministry?
3. Why did the rich man find it difficult to become a disciple of Jesus?
4. Explain the use of Peter's response in verse 27 by the early church.
5. What does the statement, "many who are first will be last, and the last will be first" mean for you?

Chapter 20
Laborers in the vineyard, 20.1-16

Jesus. (M)("For the kingdom of heaven is like a landowner who went out early in the morning to hire laborers for his vineyard. ²After agreeing with the laborers for the usual daily wage,ª he sent them into his vineyard. ³When he went out about nine o'clock, he saw others standing idle in the marketplace; ⁴and he said to them,

Vineyard owner. 'You also go into the vineyard, and I will pay you whatever is right.'

ª Gk *a denarius*

Jesus. So they went. [5]When he went out again about noon and about three o'clock, he did the same. [6]And about five o'clock he went out and found others standing around; and he said to them,

Vineyard owner. 'Why are you standing here idle all day?'

Jesus. [7]They said to him,

Unemployed. 'Because no one has hired us.'

Jesus. He said to them,

Vineyard owner. 'You also go into the vineyard.'

Jesus. [8]When evening came, the owner of the vineyard said to his manager,

Vineyard owner. 'Call the laborers and give them their pay, beginning with the last and then going to the first.'

Jesus. [9]When those hired about five o'clock came, each of them received the usual daily wage.[b] [10]Now when the first came, they thought they would receive more; but each of them also received the usual daily wage.[c] [11]And when they received it, they grumbled against the landowner, [12]saying,

Workers. 'These last worked only one hour, and you have made them equal to us who have borne the burden of the day and the scorching heat.'

Jesus. [13]But he replied to one of them,

Vineyard owner. 'Friend, I am doing you no wrong; did you not agree with me for the usual daily wage?[d] [14]Take what belongs to you

---

[b] Gk *a denarius*
[c] Gk *a denarius*
[d] Gk *a denarius*

and go; I choose to give to this last the same as I give to you. ¹⁵Am I not allowed to do what I choose with what belongs to me? Or are you envious because I am generous?"ᵉ)

Jesus. [Q₂][¹⁶So the last will be first, and the first will be last."ᶠ**]**

The Passion foretold a third time, 20.17-19
(Mk 10.32-34; Lk 18.31-34)

Matthew. ¹⁷While Jesus was going up to Jerusalem, he took the twelve **(M)(disciples aside)** by themselves, and said to them on the way,

Jesus. ¹⁸"See, we are going up to Jerusalem, and the Son of Man will be handed over to the chief priests and scribes, and they will condemn him to death; ¹⁹then they will hand him over to the Gentiles to be mocked and flogged and crucified; and on the third day he will be raised."

James and John seek honor, 20.20-28
(Mk 10.35-45; Lk 22.24-27)

Matthew. ²⁰Then the mother of the sons of Zebedee came to him with her sons, and kneeling before him, she asked a favor of him. ²¹And he said to her,

Jesus. "What do you want?"

Matthew. She said to him,

Salome. "Declare that these two sons of mine will sit, one at your right hand and one at your left, in your kingdom."

Matthew. ²²But Jesus answered,

ᵉ Gk *is your eye evil because I am good?*
ᶠ Other ancient authorities add *for many are called but few are chosen*

163

Jesus. "You do not know what you are asking. Are you able to drink the cup that I am about to drink?"[g]

Matthew. They said to him,

James and John. "We are able."

Matthew. [23]He said to them,

Jesus. "You will indeed drink my cup, but to sit at my right hand and at my left, this is not mine to grant, but it is for those for whom it has been prepared by my Father."

Matthew. [24]When the ten heard it, they were angry with the two brothers. [25]But Jesus called them to him and said,

Jesus. "You know that the rulers of the Gentiles lord it over them, and their great ones are tyrants over them. [26]It will not be so among you; but whoever wishes to be great among you must be your servant, [27]and whoever wishes to be first among you must be your slave; [28]just as the Son of Man came not to be served but to serve, and to give his life a ransom for many."

Two blind men of Jericho, 20.29-34
(Mk 10.46-52; Lk 18.35-43)

Matthew. [29]As they were leaving Jericho, a large crowd followed him. [30]There were two blind men sitting by the roadside. When they heard that Jesus was passing by, they shouted,

Blind. "Lord,[h] have mercy on us, Son of David!"

Matthew. [31]The crowd sternly ordered them to be quiet; but they shouted even more loudly,

---

g Other ancient authorities add *or to be baptized with the baptism that I am baptized with?*
h Other ancient authorities lack *Lord*

Blind. (M)("Have mercy on us,) Lord, Son of David!"

Matthew. [32]Jesus stood still and called them, saying,

Jesus. "What do you want me to do for you?"

Matthew. [33]They said to him,

Blind. "Lord, let our eyes be opened."

Matthew. (M)([34]Moved with compassion,) Jesus touched their eyes. Immediately they regained their sight and followed him.

Chapter 20 Notes
Laborers in the vineyard, 20.1-16

Matthew continued with the parable about unexpected reversals after two difficult statements in the previous chapter. The first statement was made by Peter, "Look, we have left everything and followed you." Followed by the question, "What then will we have" (Mk 19.27)? Peter and the other disciples expected to be rewarded for their extended devotion to Jesus. What they received was a confusing statement by Jesus, "But many who are first will be last, and the last will be first" (Mk 19.30). Added to this statement was the reality that Jesus had an extensive ministry among the country people, those having limited contact with the religious leaders. John provided insight into the Pharisees' attitude toward these people, "But this crowd, which does not know the law – they are accursed" (Jn 7.49). As a result, the "people of the land" in return held the Pharisees in contempt. Therefore, Jesus presented this parable to make the point that rankings based upon length of service or prominence would be disregarded and God's grace would be given to all, an act that seemed unfair and unjust to some.

1: *Early* meant approximately six a.m. The term *vineyard* was often used as a symbol of Israel, the place of God's activity (Isa

5.1; Jer 12.10). **2:** *The usual daily wage* was literally in Greek "two denarius" for laborers. Smaller coins, the copper or penny, existed (Lk 12.59); therefore, payment could have been made on an hourly basis. **3-5:** *Others* were those hired at 9 a.m., noon and 3 p.m. and were promised to receive *whatever is right.* **6-7:** *About five o'clock* meant about an hour before the end of the workday. The story did not blame them for earlier idleness, *no one has hired us.* **8:** *When evening came* each of the workers were paid daily according to Jewish custom by the *manager* (Lev 19.13; Deut 24.14-15), but in this case by reverse order. **10-12:** The workers hired earlier in the day *thought they would receive more* because they had worked all *day and* in *the scorching heat.* Their attitude reflected that of the elder brother in Luke (Lk 15.29). **14:** *Take what belongs to you and go,* as each will be paid according to the contract. However, Jesus was not dealing with an economic theory, but the gift of divine grace and the motive for laboring in God's vineyard. The rabbis taught, *Mishnah Avot,* 1.3, "Do not be like slaves who serve the master for the sake of reward, but be like slaves who serve the master not for sake of reward, and let the fear of heaven be upon you." **15:** *Are you envious* in the Greek literally meant, "Is your eye evil because I am good?" The term "evil eye" was often used in place of "grudging, envy and jealousy" (Prov 22.9; 23.6; 28.22). God can do what he chooses *with what belongs to* him. **16:** Repeating the message of 19.30 in reverse added emphasis, but it may be an editorial addition.

The Passion foretold a third time, 20.17-19

17-19: The passion foretold for the third time indicated that Jesus was now on the way to Jerusalem for the final time (cf 16.21; 17.22). Matthew and Mark reported that *the Son of Man* would *be handed over to the chief priest and scribes* before being handed *over to the Gentiles.* Luke just had the Son of Man being handed directly over to the Gentiles. All three gospel writers implied that Jesus tried to explain the passion to the disciples, but Luke made it clear that "they understood nothing about these things" (Lk 18.34), and that their failure to understand was in accordance with God's purpose.

James and John seek honor, 20.20-28

20: While in Mark (Mk 10.35-45) James and John made the request for seats of honor, Matthew had their *mother*, Salome, making the request (*see* Salome, wife of Zebedee; see 27.56 and Mk 15.40-41). **22:** *Cup* was a frequent metaphor in the OT to describe suffering by the hand of God (Isa 51.17). *Gospel of the Naassenes,* (in Hippolutus, *Refutation of All Heresies,* v.8.11),"But" Jesus says, "even if you drink the cup which I drink, you will not be able to enter where I go." **23:** James was the first of the Twelve to suffer martyrdom under Herod Agrippa in 44 CE (Acts 12.2) while John was believed to have died in old age at Ephesus. Jesus declared that the *Father* would assign the chief places according to the divine plan.

24: *They were angry with the two brothers* referred to the ten who were afraid of losing something themselves. It also indicated that James and John either were a part of, or knew about their mother's request. Based upon Jesus' response (v 22) James and John were present when their mother made the request. **25:** *Rulers of the Gentiles* were probably in reference to the Romans. **26:** Greatness to the rulers meant power to dominate and dictate to others. Greatness to Jesus came in the ability to serve and help others (Mk 9.35). **28:** *To give his life a ransom for many* was an introduction of a new idea but did not indicate that a ransom was paid to someone, God or the devil (26.39; 1 Tim 2.5-6; Jn 13.15-16; Titus 2.14; 1 Peter 1.18). The thought seemed based on Isaiah (Isa 53.12) as the Suffering Servant. *Many* did not limit the number but that the benefit would be widely effective.

Two blind men of Jericho, 20.29-34

29: *Jericho* was a village in Judea near an important ford over the Jordan River, which travelers used when they went from Galilee to Jerusalem by way of Perea to avoid contact with the Samaritans. Matthew reworked Mark's account of the healing of Bartimaeus (Mk 10.46-52) where the emphasis was upon the man's persistence and where Jesus proclaimed, "Go, your faith has made you well." Matthew omitted these details and had Jesus touching the eyes of the two blind men, with no mention of faith. **30:** The messianic title, *Son of David* (9.27) was used by all three Synoptic Gospel writers, Jesus did not respond to it, but to the cries *"Have mercy"* (Mk 10.48; Lk 18.39). Mark and Luke both used this title and assumed in their writings that Jesus' true nature was now in the open and the reader was prepared for the triumphal entry into Jerusalem. He was told to be quiet *but shouted even more loudly.* **32-33:** Jesus asked, *"What do you want me to do for you?"* The two men asked to see. **34:** Matthew said that Jesus was *moved with compassion* so he *touched their eyes, Immediately they regained their sight* and they *followed him* as disciples.

Chapter 20 Study Guide

1. What purpose did Matthew have in placing the parable of the workers in the vineyard in his gospel?
2. Why was Jesus handed over to the Gentiles to be mocked, flogged and crucified?
3. Where were the disciples, James and John, when Jesus was discussing the last shall be first and the first shall be last?
4. Explain the account of the two blind men or Bartimaeus.
5. Why does Matthew have Jesus touching the eyes to heal them when in Mark and Luke he just gave a command?

Chapter 21
The last week, 21.1-27.66
(Mk 11.1-15.47; Lk 19.28-23.56)
Palm Sunday, 21.1-11
(Mk 11.1-10; Lk 19.28-38; Jn 12.12-18)

Matthew. When they had come near Jerusalem and had reached Bethphage, at the Mount of Olives, Jesus sent two disciples, ²saying to them,

Jesus. "Go into the village ahead of you, and immediately you will find **(M)**(a donkey tied, and) a colt with her; untie them and bring them to me. ³If anyone says anything to you, just say this,

Disciples. 'The Lord needs them.'

Jesus. And he will send them immediately.ᵃ"

Matthew. (M)(⁴This took place to fulfill what had been spoken through the prophet, saying,

Lord. (T-I)(⁵"Tell the daughter of Zion ᵇ)

Zechariah. Look, your king is coming to you, humble, and mounted on a donkey, and on a colt, the foal of a donkey."ᶜ

Matthew. ⁶The disciples went and did as Jesus had directed them; ⁷they brought **(M)**(the donkey and) the colt, and put their cloaks on them, and he sat on them. ⁸A very large crowdᵈ spread their cloaks on the road, and others cut branches from the trees and spread them on the road. ⁹The crowds that went ahead of him and that followed were shouting,

---

ᵃ Or *'The Lord needs them and will send them back immediately.'*
ᵇ Isa 62.11
ᶜ Zech 9.9
ᵈ Or *Most of the crowd*

Crowd. "Hosanna **(M)**(to the Son of David!) Blessed is the one who comes in the name of the Lord! Hosanna in the highest heaven!"[e]

Matthew. [10]When he entered Jerusalem, **(M)**(the whole city was in turmoil, asking,

Citizens. [11]"Who is this?"

Matthew. The crowds were saying,

Crowds. "This is the prophet Jesus from Nazareth in Galilee.")

Cleansing the temple, 21.12-17
(Mk 11.11, 15-19; Lk 19.45-48; Jn 2.13-17)

Matthew. [12]Then Jesus entered the temple[f] and drove out all who were selling and buying in the temple, and he overturned the tables of the money changers and the seats of those who sold doves. [13]He said to them,

Jesus. "It is written,

Lord. (T-I)('My house shall be called a house of prayer'; [g]) **(B)**(but you are making it a den of robbers." [h])

Matthew. [14]The blind and the lame came to him in the temple, and he cured them. [15]But when the chief priests and the scribes saw the amazing things that he did, and heard [i] the children crying out in the temple,

Children. "Hosanna to the Son of David,"

---

[e] Ps 118.26
[f] Other ancient authorities add *of God*
[g] Isa 56.7
[h] Jer 7.11
[i] Gk lacks *heard*

Matthew. they became angry [16] and said to him,

Chief priests and Scribes. "Do you hear what these are saying?"

Matthew. Jesus said to them,

Jesus. "Yes; have you never read,

Temple singer. 'Out of the mouths of infants and nursing babies you have prepared praise for yourself'?" [j]

Matthew. [17]He left them, went out of the city to Bethany, and spent the night there.

Fig tree cursed, 21.18-22
(Mk 11.12-14, 20-25)

Matthew. [18]In the morning, when he returned to the city, he was hungry. [19]And seeing a fig tree by the side of the road, he went to it and found nothing at all on it but leaves. Then he said to it,

Jesus. "May no fruit ever come from you again!"

Matthew. And the fig tree withered at once. [20]When the disciples saw it, they were amazed, saying,

Disciples. "How did the fig tree wither at once?"

Matthew. [21]Jesus answered them

Jesus. "Truly I tell you, if you have faith and do not doubt, **(M)**(not only will you do what has been done to the fig tree, but even) if you say to this mountain,

Disciples. 'Be lifted up and thrown into the sea,'

---

[j] Ps 8,2

Jesus. it will be done. [22]Whatever you ask for in prayer with faith, you will receive."

Jesus' authority, 21.23-32
(Mk 11.27-33; Lk 20.1-8)

Matthew. [23]When he entered the temple, the chief priests and the elders **(M)**(of the people came to him as he was teaching,) and said,

Chief priests and Elders. "By what authority are you doing these things, and who gave you this authority?"

Matthew. [24]Jesus said to them,

Jesus. "I will also ask you one question; if you tell me the answer, then I will also tell you by what authority I do these things. [25]Did the baptism of John come from heaven, or was it of human origin?"

Matthew. And they argued with one another,

Chief priests and Elders. "If we say, 'From heaven,' he will say to us,

Jesus. 'Why then did you not believe him?'

Another Argument. [26]But if we say, 'Of human origin,' we are afraid of the crowd; for all regard John as a prophet."

Matthew. [27]So they answered Jesus,

Chief priests and Elders. "We do not know."

Matthew. And he said to them,

Jesus. "Neither will I tell you by what authority I am doing these things."
    (M)([28]"What do you think? A man had two sons; he went to the first and said,

Father. 'Son, go and work in the vineyard today.'

Jesus. ²⁹He answered,

Son. (first) 'I will not';

Jesus. but later he changed his mind and went. ³⁰The father[k] went to the second and said the same; and he answered,

Son. (second) 'I go, sir';

Jesus. but he did not go. ³¹Which of the two did the will of his father?"

Matthew. They said,

Chief priests and Elders. "The first."

Matthew. Jesus said to them,

Jesus. "Truly I tell you, the tax collectors and the prostitutes are going into the kingdom of God ahead of you.) [Q₂][³²For John came to you in the way of righteousness and you did not believe him, but the tax collectors and the prostitutes believed him; and even after you saw it, you did not change your minds and believe him."]

Parable of the vineyard, 21.33-46
(Mk 12.1-12; Lk 20.9-19)

Jesus. ³³"Listen to another parable. There was a landowner who planted a vineyard, put a fence around it, dug a wine press in it, and built a watchtower. Then he leased it to tenants and went to another country. ³⁴When the harvest time had come, he sent his slaves to the tenants to collect his produce. ³⁵But the tenants seized **(M)(his slaves)** and beat one, **(M)** (killed another, and stoned another.) ³⁶Again he

---

ᵏ Gk *He*

173

sent other slaves, more than the first; and they treated them in the same way. [37]Finally he sent his son to them, saying,

Vineyard owner. 'They will respect my son.'

Jesus. [38]But when the tenants saw the son, they said to themselves,

Tenants. 'This is the heir; come, let us kill him and get his inheritance.'

Jesus. [39]So they seized him, threw him out of the vineyard, and killed him. [40]Now when the owner of the vineyard comes, what will he do to those tenants?"

Matthew. [41]They said to him,

Chief priests and Elders. "He will put those wretches to a miserable death, and lease the vineyard to other tenants who will give him the produce at the harvest time."

Matthew. [42]Jesus said to them,

Jesus. "Have you never read in the scriptures:

Temple singer. 'The stone that the builders rejected has become the cornerstone;[l] this was the Lord's doing, and it is amazing in our eyes'? [m]

Jesus. (M)([43]Therefore I tell you, the kingdom of God will be taken away from you and given to a people that produces the fruits of the kingdom.[n]**)** [44]The one who falls on this stone will be broken to pieces; and it will crush anyone on whom it falls."[o]

---

[l] Or *keystone*
[m] Ps 118.22-23
[n] Gk *the fruits of it*
[o] Other ancient authorities lack verse 44

Matthew. ⁴⁵When the chief priests and the Pharisees heard his parables, they realized that he was speaking about them. ⁴⁶They wanted to arrest him, but they feared the crowds, **(M)**(because they regarded him as a prophet.)

Chapter 21 Notes
The last week, 21.1-27.66

The next few chapters (21.1-27.66) were devoted to Jesus' ministry, arrest, trial, death, burial, and resurrection. Church tradition held that all of these events took place within a single week, just a few days before the Passover Festival. The Synoptic Gospels presented that this was Jesus' first visit to Jerusalem during his ministry, yet he had friends in the city (Mt 21.2-3; Mk 11.2-3; Lk 19.30-31), and he seemed known by Simon the Leper (Mt 26.6; Mk 14.3). The statement about Jerusalem by Jesus could be interpreted that Jesus had visited the Holy City (Mt 23.37-39; Lk 13.34-45). John the Evangelist, in his gospel, had Jesus making several trips to Jerusalem with his disciples, most of them for festivals.

The length of stay in Jerusalem presents other issues. The triumphal entry is conventionally placed on Palm Sunday with Jesus spending the previous sabbath just east of Jericho. This would have him arrive in Jerusalem on Sunday evening, which agreed with Mark where he went to the temple, but "it was already late" so "he went out to Bethany with the Twelve" (Mk 11.11). This would make the cursing of the fig tree and the cleansing of the temple taking place on Monday (Mk 11.12-19). The story of the disciples calling attention to the withered fig tree then took place on Tuesday with nothing said about the end of the day (Mk 11.20-26). One may assume that "again they came to Jerusalem" (Mk 11.27) happened on Wednesday, with the preparation for the Passover Seder or searching for the leaven, with the Seder or the Last Supper being held on Thursday evening.

Then there was the cursing of the fig tree because of its lack of fruit, "When it was not the season." In Jerusalem, figs rarely ripened until summer time and the fig trees would continue to bear fruit for ten months. Therefore, figs would be available during the fall Tabernacle Festival, but not during the spring Passover Festival. Using cut branches or foliage from trees and shouts of *"Hosanna"* and *"Blessed is the one who comes in the name of the Lord!"* suggest the temple ritual during the Tabernacle Festival rather than the Passover Festival. Therefore, it could be suggested that the Triumphal Entry was part of the Tabernacle Festival while at least the Seder service was part of the Passover service. Therefore, Jesus and the disciples were in Jerusalem for an extended period, or upon several occasions, where Jesus aroused the anger of the religious establishment.

At the beginning of the Christian era, a majority of the Jewish people believed in the coming of a mighty, warrior-Messiah of David's line. The Qumran Community looked forward to the time when such a Messiah would lead them in the great, final battle between "the sons of darkness" and the "sons of light." The Zealots were also ready at any moment to flock to the Messiah's standard and to fight by his side with naked sword. When the Messiah would come, the people would "Rejoice greatly, O daughter of Zion! Shout aloud, O daughter of Jerusalem! Lo, your king comes to you; triumphant and victorious is he, humble and riding on a donkey, on a colt, the foal of a donkey" (Zech 9.9).

Each year Jewish people from all around would make pilgrimages to Jerusalem to celebrate three major festivals; the Passover, Weeks and Booths. During these three festivals, messianic expectations would run high among the people. Jesus was a popular figure and no stranger to many of these visitors, including the leaders of Jerusalem. When he entered the city on a donkey, the messianic expectations took on an air of excitement.

Palm Sunday, 21.1-11

1: Jesus, while putting an emphasis on humility, offered himself as the Messiah. Like a parable, his action had to be understood and accepted (Jn 6.14; 7.40; Acts 3.22; Mk 6.15; Lk 13.33). Jesus, his disciples and the crowd (20.29) traveled up the steep road from Jericho to *Jerusalem. Bethphage* was not mentioned before in the gospels, but it was near Bethany, less than two miles southeast of Jerusalem. **2:** Matthew had Jesus telling the *two disciples* to *untie* and bring both the *donkey* and *a colt with her* while Mark and Luke only mention a colt. **3:** *And he will send them immediately* suggested the owner was a secret disciple of Jesus. **5:** *Tell the daughter of Zion* was from Isaiah (Isa 62.11). The rest of the quotation was from Zechariah (Zech 9.9). The Hebrew text referred not to two animals, but to one. The reference to the two in vv 5 and 7 may have arisen through misunderstanding the form of Hebrew poetic expression in Zechariah (Zech 9.9), and Mark had to correct, "sat on it," as *he sat on them* did not work well. **8:** Mark had those shouting as "many people" (Mk 10.8) and Matthew expanded the group to a *very large crowd* that treated Jesus as a kingly leader coming to take his throne. Luke identified the group as a "multitude of the disciples" meaning more than the Twelve. **9:** *Cloaks* and *cut branches from the trees* were tokens of honor (2 Kings 9.13). *Hosanna,* originally a Hebrew invocation addressed to God, meaning "Save now" which was later used as a cry of joyous acclamation. *Blessed is the one who comes in the name of the Lord* (Ps 118.26) was a greeting to pilgrims approaching the temple. *Hosanna in the highest heaven* meant either "raise the cry of hosanna to the heavens" or "God in heaven save." Jesus did not encourage the use of *Son of David* and asked his disciples to not call him the Messiah as it encouraged ideas of a political and military deliverer. **10-11:** Those traveling with Jesus from Galilee praised Jesus, while the people in Jerusalem asked, *"Who is this?"* Jesus was not called *"Son of David"* but *the prophet Jesus from Nazareth in Galilee* as Matthew drew attention away from the political messiahship to the prophetic message of Jesus.

Cleansing the temple, 21.12-17

According to Mark, the cleansing of the temple did not take place until the next day, "as it was already late" (Mk 11.11). **12:** The animals for sale were acceptable for sacrifice; the moneychangers converted Gentile coins into Jewish money that could properly be presented in the temple (Ex 30.13; Lev 1.14). *Entered the temple,* or the large outer court called the Court of the Gentiles, the only place Gentiles were permitted. **13:** Matthew and Luke compress Mark's account of cleaning the temple by omitting a house of prayer "for all nations" (Mk 11.17; Lk 19.46). Jesus protested the commercialization even in this one area where Gentiles could enter. Only in John's gospel are we told that Jesus made a whip of cords and used strong violence to achieve his end (Jn 2.13-17). In their desire to make a profit, the sellers reduced the *house of prayer* into *a den of robbers.*

14: Matthew did not have Jesus do any teaching on the first day, but he *cured* the *blind and the lame* revealing the power of God in his temple, to the amazement of the *chief priests and the scribes.* **15:** *The children* now echoed the words of the crowd causing the religious leaders to *become angry.* **16:** God had prepared praise for himself *out of the mouths of infants and nursing babies* (Ps 8.2). **17:** The lines of conflict were established as Jesus exercised authority over the temple by cleaning it, by healing those in need, and accepting the praise of pilgrims and children. On the other side of the conflict, were the temple and city religious leaders as Jesus *went* to *Bethany,* and *spent the night there.*

Fig tree cursed, 21.18-22

18-20: Mark said, "It was not the season for figs" (Mk 11.13), then why would Jesus curse the fig tree, as it seemed against his nature? Some hold the leaves showed the possibility of green fruit and in disappointment Jesus cursed the tree. However, what should be done with the fact that the leaves of the fig tree normally appear after the fruit. Probably the early church used this parable to condemn Israel for failing to produce the fruit of faith and obedience. **21-22:** These verses reflected some independent sayings used by Mark and later Matthew to express the importance and power *in prayer with* *faith.* Faith was concerned with doing God's will, not with moving mountains (17.20; Mk 11.22-23; Lk 17.6; I Cor 13.2; Jas 1.6).

Jesus' authority, 21.23-32

23-32: The Sanhedrin (*see* Sanhedrin) heard of Jesus' activities in Galilee, and they were watching him with suspicion. However, as long as he remained in the northern providence he was under the rule of Herod Antipas, and they were restricted from taking any direct action against him. However, when he entered Judea he came under their authority, and as someone who might cause a political uprising or ignite the messianic hopes, he became a matter of their concern. **23:** So they sent a delegation of *chief priests,* and *elders* to trap Jesus into admitting something that they could use against him before the Roman procurator. Mark and Luke added "scribes" to this delegation. Mark had this incident happening on the day following the cleansing of the temple, an act challenged by the Sanhedrin. Matthew and Luke have Jesus *teaching* the people in the temple, telling the good news, as the basis for the challenge of his *authority,* since he had not been trained and ordained as a rabbi. The issue here was they wanted to obtain from Jesus a messianic claim. **24-25:** Jesus wanted to establish there was a connection between his ministry and that of John's and that his authority came *from heaven.* Their refusal to answer his question freed Jesus from having to reply to their challenges. While Mark and Matthew make their hesitation to answer because *"we are afraid of the crowd,"* Luke made the consequences more violent, "all the people will stone us."

28-30: The message of the parable of the two sons was that God wants obedience and not just lip service. Even those who did not know that they were working for God would be rewarded (7.21; 25.31-46). **31-32:** The second half of verse 31 is difficult to understand, but the idea is found in Luke (Lk 18.10-14). Those who do not profess to be religious could be awaken to a realization of a spiritual need, while the righteous ones could be closed to the teachings of Jesus and the will of God in their lives (Lk 7.29-30).

Parable of the vineyard, 21.33-46

While it may be possible that the parable was part of one of Jesus' parables, it appeared to reflect the beliefs of the early church. God was the owner of the vineyard and the vineyard was Israel. The tenants were the leaders of Judaism and the slaves (servants) are the OT prophets. The beloved son was Jesus and the murder of the heir was the crucifixion of the Jesus. The destruction of the wicked was the destruction of the temple and the new tenants were to be understood as the apostles and the early church.

33: Matthew and Mark (Mk 12.1) had this parable presented to the Sanhedrin delegation while Luke had it addressed to the people (Lk 20.9). The parable in Mark, and later Matthew, was closely modeled from the ancient parable in Isaiah (Isa 5.1-7). *Fence around it* missed the point where the "wall that was made from stones gathered from the field" was built to keep the wild beasts out of the *vineyard.* A *wine press* was usually hollowed out of rock, with the grapes being crushed in the upper part while the lower part collected the grape-juice. The new wine was stored in an enclosed structure called a *watchtower.* A watchman used the flat roof to guard the vineyard and wine against beasts and thieves. Luke adapted his version and added the owner going to another country for a long time, emphasizing the time since the covenant God made with Moses (Lk 20.10). This may have reflected conditions regarding absentee ownership in Israel, or that God was not present to help the people. **34:** The vineyard owner sent several slaves to *collect* from the tenants the master's share of the *produce,* usually a quarter or a half of the amount, paid annually. **35-36:** The tenants *beat one, killed another, and stoned another* with the same results when an even larger group of slaves was sent. **37-39:** The introduction of his *son,* as the "beloved son" in Mark and Luke, took what might have been a real situation and made it an allegory. Mark and Luke said, "Perhaps they will respect him" while Matthew was more positive, *"they will respect my son."* The foolish tenants thought if *they* would *kill* the heir, then the landowner would abandon the vineyard allowing them to seize possession . Matthew and Luke had the son thrown *"out of the vineyard"* implying rejection and *"killed him"* (Lk 20.15), while Mark reverses the order (Mk 12.8). This may correspond to the Christian tradition that Jesus was crucified "outside the gate." **41:** In real life, Roman law permitted no Jewish master to take matters into his own hands and kill the tenants, but the prophets had repeatedly predicted the destruction of the sinful nation. Matthew and Luke's readers may have thought of the destruction of Jerusalem in 70 CE.

42: Both the Jews and the early Christians interpreted this quote from Psalms (Ps 118.22-23) *this was the* LORD's *doing (see* LORD) to be messianic (Acts 4.11; 1 Peter 2.4-7). **43:** Matthew was the only one that implied that the vineyard *will be taken away* from Israel and given *to a people that produces the fruits of the kingdom,* probably meaning the apostles and the church were now the true Israel. Luke added the protest, "Heaven forbid" by Jesus' listeners (Lk 20.16). **45-46:** *They wanted to arrest him* was an editorial note, but Matthew added the reason why, the chief priests and Pharisees *feared the crowd* was because the crowd *regarded him as a prophet.*

Chapter 21 Study Guide

1. Why did Jesus go to Jerusalem?
2. Examine some of the messianic expectations present at the triumphal entry.
3. What impact did the very large crowd have upon Jesus cleansing the temple?
4. Why was the fig tree cursed? What symbol did this represent in the gospels?
5. Why did Jesus tell the parables of the two sons and the vineyard owner?

Chapter 22
The marriage feast, 22.1-14
(Lk 14.16-24)

Matthew. Once more Jesus spoke to them in parables, saying:

Jesus. [Q₁][²"The kingdom of heaven may be compared to a king who gave a wedding banquet for his son. ³He sent his slaves to call those who had been invited to the wedding banquet, but they would not come. ⁴Again he sent other slaves, saying,

King. 'Tell those who have been invited:

Slaves. Look, I have prepared my dinner, my oxen and my fat calves have been slaughtered, and everything is ready; come to the wedding banquet.'

Jesus. ⁵But they made light of it and went away, one to his farm, another to his business, ⁶while the rest seized his slaves, mistreated them, and killed them. ⁷The king was enraged. He sent his troops, destroyed those murderers, and burned their city. ⁸Then he said to his slaves,

King. 'The wedding is ready, but those invited were not worthy. ⁹Go therefore into the main streets, and invite everyone you find to the wedding banquet.'

Jesus. ¹⁰Those slaves went out into the streets and gathered all whom they found, both good and bad; so the wedding hall was filled with guests."]
    (M)(¹¹"But when the king came in to see the guests, he noticed a man there who was not wearing a wedding robe, ¹²and he said to him,

King. 'Friend, how did you get in here without a wedding robe?'

Jesus. And he was speechless. ¹³Then the king said to the attendants,

King. 'Bind him hand and foot, and throw him into the outer darkness,) where there will be weeping and gnashing of teeth.'

Jesus. (M)([14]For many are called, but few are chosen.")

Paying taxes to Caesar, 22.15-22
(Mk 12.13-17; Lk 20.20-26)

Matthew. [15]Then the Pharisees went and plotted to entrap him in what he said. **(M)(**[16]So they sent their disciples to him, along with the Herodians,) saying,

Disciples (Pharisee's) and Herodians. "Teacher, we know that you are sincere, and teach the way of God in accordance with truth, and show deference to no one; for you do not regard people with partiality. **(M)(**[17]Tell us, then, what you think.) Is it lawful to pay taxes to the emperor, or not?"

Matthew. [18]But Jesus, aware of their malice, said,

Jesus. "Why are you putting me to the test, **(M)(**you hypocrites?) [19]Show me the coin used for the tax."

Matthew. And they brought him a denarius. [20]Then he said to them,

Jesus. "Whose head is this, and whose title?"

Matthew. [21]They answered,

Disciples (Pharisee's) and Herodians. "The emperor's."

Matthew. Then he said to them,

Jesus. "Give therefore to the emperor the things that are the emperor's, and to God the things that are God's."

Matthew. ²²When they heard this, they were amazed; and they left him and went away.

Question about the resurrection, 22.23-33
(Mk 12.18-27; Lk 20.27-40)

Matthew. (M)(²³The same day some**)** Sadducees came to him, saying there is no resurrection;ᵃ and they asked him a question, saying,

Sadducees. ²⁴"Teacher, Moses said,

Moses. (D)('If a man dies childless, his brother shall marry the widow, and raise up children for his brother.' ᵇ**)**

Sadducees. ²⁵Now there were seven brothers among us; the first married, and died childless, leaving the widow to his brother. ²⁶The second did the same, so also the third, down to the seventh. ²⁷Last of all, the woman herself died. ²⁸In the resurrection, then, whose wife of the seven will she be? For all of them had married her."

Matthew. ²⁹Jesus answered them,

Jesus. "You are wrong, because you know neither the scriptures nor the power of God. ³⁰For in the resurrection they neither marry nor are given in marriage, but are like angelsᶜ in heaven. ³¹And as for the resurrection of the dead, have you not read what was said to you by God,

God. (E)(³²'I am the God of Abraham, the God of Isaac, and the God of Jacob'? ᵈ**)**

Jesus. He is God not of the dead, but of the living."

ᵃ Other ancient authorities read *who say that there is no resurrection*
ᵇ Deut 25.5
ᶜ Other ancient authorities add *of God*
ᵈ Ex 3.6, 16

Matthew. ³³And when the crowd heard it, they were astounded at his teaching.

The great commandment, 22.34-40
(Mk 12.28-34; Lk 10.25-28)

Matthew. ³⁴When the Pharisees heard that he had silenced the Sadducees, they **(M)**(gathered together, ³⁵and one of them, a lawyer,) asked him a question to test him.

Lawyer. ³⁶"Teacher, which commandment in the law is the greatest?"

Matthew. ³⁷He said to them,

Moses. (D)("'You shall love the Lord your God with all your heart, and with all your soul, and with all your mind' ᵉ)

Jesus. (M)(³⁸This is the greatest and first commandment.) ³⁹And a second is like it:

Moses. (P)('You shall love your neighbor as yourself.'ᶠ)

Jesus. ⁴⁰On these two commandments hang all the law and the prophets."

David's son, 22.41-46
(Mk 12.35-37; Lk 20.41-44)

Matthew. ⁴¹Now while the Pharisees were gathered together, Jesus asked them this question:

Jesus. ⁴²"What do you think of the Messiah?ᵍ Whose son is he?"

Matthew. They said to him,

ᵉ Deut 6.5
ᶠ Lev 19.18
ᵍ Or *Christ*

Pharisees. "The son of David."

Matthew. [43]He said to them,

Jesus. "How is it then that David by the Spirit[h] calls him Lord, saying,

David. [44]'The Lord said to my Lord,

LORD. "Sit at my right hand, until I put your enemies under your feet"'? [i]

Jesus. [45]If David thus calls him Lord, how can he be his son?"

Matthew. [46]No one was able to give him an answer, nor from that day did anyone dare to ask him any more questions.

Chapter 22 Notes
The marriage feast, 22.1-14

1-14: Matthew's source for this parable may have differed from Luke's as it identified the "great dinner" as a *wedding banquet* given by a king *for his son* (Lk 14.16-24). This parable may have been a continuation of the two parables in the previous chapter and reflected the attitude of the early church, where not only the religious leaders, but also the people mistreated and refused the messenger. Therefore, the invitation was given to others who were outcasts, the tax collectors, sinners and Gentiles, who did accept (cf Jn 1.11-12).

4-5: *Everything is ready* and those who have been invited are called to come *to the wedding banquet,* but *they made light of it* continuing with their own matters and ignoring the King's invitation. **6-7:** These two verses may be a later addition as they reference the persecution of the Christians, such as the apostles and Stephen (Acts 7.57-8.1), and the destruction of Jerusalem in 70 CE

---

[h] Gk *in spirit*
[i] Ps 110.1

9-10: *Go therefore into the main streets,* since those who were regular guests rejected the summons, the invitation was extended to those considered both *good and bad* (13.47). Luke expanded the parable by adding another invitation to the Gentiles after all the poor, crippled, blind and lame had been received.

11-14: These verses were only in Matthew and may have been part of a different parable. Those attending the banquet were expected to be clean and wear proper clothing. The point seemed to be that the king would judge all who came to the banquet without doing what the king expected. **13:** *Throw him into the outer darkness, where there will be weeping and gnashing of teeth* was a common expression of disappointment and pain (see 8.12n). While the other gospel writers included an aspect of judgment, it became more evident in Matthew. **14:** This verse appeared to be an independent saying that Matthew used as a climax to the parable. Many were invited, but only a few accepted the invitation. Those *few* were the *chosen* or the remnant spoken of by Isaiah (Isa 10.21-22) that would reverse the present attitude of the nation. (*Gospel of Thomas*, Logion 23), "Jesus said, 'I will choose you, one out of a thousand, and two out of ten thousand, and they will stand as a single one.'"

Paying taxes to Caesar, 22.15-22

15: (*Egerton Papyrus 2*), "And coming to Jesus to test him, they said, 'Teacher Jesus, we know that you are from God, for what you do testifies to you beyond all the prophets. Tell us, then, is it lawful to give to kings what pertains to their rule? Shall we pay them or not?' And Jesus, knowing their thoughts and being moved with indignation, said to them, 'Why do you call me teacher with your mouth and do not hear what I say? Well did Isaiah prophecy of you, when he said: 'This people honors me with their lips, but their heart is far from me; in vain do they worship me, teaching as doctrines the precepts of human beings.'" **16:** *Herodians* were apparently a group supporting the royal family. Nothing definite was known about them, but probably their interests were secular. The Pharisees sought allies wherever they might be found (Mk 3.6; 8.15; 12.13). In asking Jesus for a pronouncement affecting all Judeans, his enemies thought to bring him into conflict with sectarian views. **17:** The Romans collected an unpopular annual poll *tax* from every adult male in Judea over the age of fourteen and all females over twelve, up to the age of sixty-five. This tax was interpreted as a mark of Jewish subjection to a foreign power. The question from the Pharisees and Herodians was carefully presented. If Jesus approved paying taxes, he would offend the nationalistic parties, but if he disapproved payment, he could be reported as disloyal to the empire (Acts 5.37). **18:** The term, *hypocrites* did not appear in Mark or Luke but the crafty and malicious intent was obvious. **19-20:** *The coin* minted by the Romans with the likeness of the *emperor* was worth about twenty cents. Jewish coins had emblems of olive branches and palms as the Jewish law prohibited the use of images. **21-23:** If coins bearing Caesar's image were circulated, they belonged to the emperor Tiberius, even if the image was his or his predecessor, Augustus and he had a right to demand them. At the same time, there were duties and debts that are owed to God (Rom 13.7; 1 Pet 2.17). (*Gospel of Thomas,* Logion 100), "They showed Jesus a gold (coin) and said to him, 'Caesar's officers demand taxes from us.' Jesus said to them, 'Give to Caesar what belongs to Caesar, give to God what belongs to God and give to me what is mine.'"

Question about the resurrection, 22.23-33

The Sadducees failed to see God's purpose and did not trust his power. Those who were related to God in faith have life even though physically dead; Resurrection was the divine act by which they would achieve the fullness of life intended in creation and lost through sin and death.

23: *The Sadducees* accepted only the written tradition as authorative. Because the belief in a life to come, based on a physical resurrection, emerged after the Pentateuch (first five books of the OT) was compiled and was not evident in it, they declared *there is no* *resurrection* (Ex 3.5; Acts 4.1-2; 23.6-10). **24-26:** This was an effort to show that Moses could not have contemplated any resurrection. The reference to the "levirate" marriage law in Deuteronomy (Deut 25.5-6) and Genesis (Gen 38.8) was an ancient Hebrew idea associated with ancestor worship. It was the duty of the brother to have a male descendant for his deceased brother and perpetuate his name and inheritance. By the time of Jesus, this law was in question and was probably obsolete. The case presented by the Sadducees was more about the controversy over the resurrection.

30-31: All three of the evangelists make the same point, but in somewhat different language; human relationships in the home did not exist in the same way beyond death. Jesus distinguished two ages and kinds of existence. Mortals were part of this age by the fact of physical birth, and of the age to come by resurrection. Marriage was necessary to continue the race, but this disappeared when men and women became *like angels in heaven* and "cannot die anymore" (Lk 20.36). **32-33:** Mark and Luke said, "In the story about the bush" (Ex 3.2-6), it would have been nonsense for Moses to speak of the LORD (*see* LORD) as the God of the patriarchs, if they had only lived and died long ago. To him all of them were alive (Mk 12.26-27; Lk 20.37-40). Interesting parallels are in Fourth Maccabees (4 Macc 7.19; 16.25), written during the same period as Matthew and Luke.

The great commandment, 22.34-40

35-40: Matthew and Luke used the term *lawyer* in place of Mark's "scribe" to identify someone educated in the religious law. In Matthew and Mark, the scribe asked about the greatest commandment, and Luke substituted it with one that would have more appeal to the Gentiles, "what must I do to inherit eternal life?" In Luke, the lawyer combined the Shema in Deuteronomy (Deut 6.4-5) and Leviticus (Lev 19.18), while in Matthew and Mark Jesus made the connection between these OT texts. Jesus stressed that acts of love are the final requirement of the law. Paul quoted this passage in Galatians (Gal

3.12). (*Gospel of Thomas,* Logion 25), "Jesus said, 'Love your brother or sister as your soul, and guard them as the apple of your eye.'"

David's son, 22.41-46

These verses rejected that the Messiah must be "David's Son" and suggested that he should be described as LORD. **41:** All three Synoptic Gospel writers had Jesus ask *them,* meaning the *Pharisees,* if the Messiah was David's son. Jesus quoted the first verse of Psalm 110 (Ps 110.1), regarded as a royal Psalm. **44:** A lot was lost from the various translations, because in the OT when the word *"LORD"* was used regarding God it was capitalized as *"LORD"* rather than *"Lord"* that was regarding a king or the Messiah. Therefore, the first LORD referred to God, the second *Lord* was taken to refer to the Messiah. This quote from Psalms (Ps 110.1), ascribed to David long before the NT, proclaimed the words that the king *(my lord)* was invited by Israel's God *(the LORD)* to ascend the throne. The early church interpreted this as prophetic of the ascension in Acts 2.34-35 and Christ's work as high priest in Hebrews (Heb 1.13; 10.12-13; *see* Jesus as high Priest). Jesus used the opening words of the Psalm to question how the Messiah could be David's descendant, if David calls him *Lord.* This does not deny that Jesus was a descendant of David, only that for Jesus the title "son of David," with its political overtones did not do justice to his mission.

Chapter 22 Study Guide

1. Who are those who were brought into the wedding banquet from the streets?
2. What is a Christian's position on paying taxes?
3. What did Jesus teach about family relationships in heaven?
4. What does the great commandment mean to you?
5. What do you think of the Messiah?

Chapter 23
Woe to scribes and Pharisees, 23.1-36

Matthew. Then Jesus said to the crowds and to his disciples,

Jesus. (M)(²"The scribes and the Pharisees sit on Moses' seat; ³therefore, do whatever they teach you and follow it; but do not do as they do, for they do not practice what they teach.) [Q₂][⁴They tie up heavy burdens, hard to bear,ᵃ and lay them on the shoulders of others; but they themselves are unwilling to lift a finger to move them.] (M) (⁵They do all their deeds to be seen by others; for they make their phylacteries broad and their fringes long.) [Q₂][⁶They love to have the place of honor at banquets and the best seats in the synagogues, ⁷and to be greeted with respect in the marketplaces, and to have people call them rabbi.] (M)(⁸But you are not to be called rabbi, for you have one teacher, and you are all students.ᵇ ⁹And call no one your father on earth, for you have one Father—the one in heaven. ¹⁰Nor are you to be called instructors, for you have one instructor, the Messiah.ᶜ) ¹¹The greatest among you will be your servant. [Q₁] [¹²All who exalt themselves will be humbled, and all who humble themselves will be exalted.]

[Q₂][¹³"But woe to you, scribes and Pharisees, hypocrites! For you lock people out of the kingdom of heaven.] For you do not go in yourselves, and when others are going in, you stop them.ᵈ (M)(¹⁵Woe to you, scribes and Pharisees, hypocrites! For you cross sea and land to make a single convert, and you make the new convert twice as much a child of hellᵉ as yourselves.

ᵃ Other ancient authorities lack *hard to bear*
ᵇ Gk *brothers*
ᶜ Or *the Christ*
ᵈ Other authorities add here (or after verse 12) verse 14, *Woe to you, scribes and Pharisees, hypocrites! For you devour widows' houses and for the sake of appearance you make long prayers; therefore you will receive the greater condemnation*
ᵉ Gk *Gehenna*

[16]"Woe to you, blind guides, who say,

Pharisees and Scribes. 'Whoever swears by the sanctuary is bound by nothing, but whoever swears by the gold of the sanctuary is bound by the oath.'

Jesus. [17]You blind fools! For which is greater, the gold or the sanctuary that has made the gold sacred? [18]And you say,

Pharisees and Scribes. 'Whoever swears by the altar is bound by nothing, but whoever swears by the gift that is on the altar is bound by the oath.'

Jesus. [19]How blind you are! For which is greater, the gift or the altar that makes the gift sacred? [20]So whoever swears by the altar, swears by it and by everything on it; [21]and whoever swears by the sanctuary, swears by it and by the one who dwells in it; [22]and whoever swears by heaven, swears by the throne of God and by the one who is seated upon it.")

[Q₂][[23] "Woe to you, scribes and Pharisees, hypocrites! For you tithe mint, dill, and cummin, and have neglected the weightier matters of the law: justice and mercy and faith. It is these you ought to have practiced without neglecting the others.] (M)([24]You blind guides! You strain out a gnat but swallow a camel!)

[Q₂][[25]"Woe to you, scribes and Pharisees, hypocrites! For you clean the outside of the cup and of the plate, but inside they are full of greed and self-indulgence.] [26]You blind Pharisee! First clean the inside of the cup,[f] [Q₂][so that the outside also may become clean."

[27]"Woe to you, (M)(scribes and Pharisees, hypocrites!) For you are like whitewashed tombs, which on the outside look beautiful, but inside they are full of the bones of the dead and of all kinds of filth.] (M)([28]So you also on the outside look righteous to others, but inside you are full of hypocrisy and lawlessness.)

---

[f]   Other ancient authorities add *and of the plate*

[**Q₂**][²⁹"Woe to you, **(M)**(scribes and Pharisees, hypocrites!) For you build the tombs of the prophets and decorate the graves of the righteous,] **(M)**(³⁰ and you say,

Pharisees and Scribes. 'If we had lived in the days of our ancestors, we would not have taken part with them in shedding the blood of the prophets.')

Jesus. ³¹Thus you testify against yourselves that you are descendants of those who murdered the prophets. **(M)**(³²Fill up, then, the measure of your ancestors.) ³³You snakes, you brood of vipers! How can you escape being sentenced to hell?ᵍ [**Q₂**][³⁴ Therefore I send you prophets, sages, and scribes, some of whom you will kill **(M)**(and crucify, and some you will flog in your synagogues) and pursue from town to town, ³⁵so that upon you may come all the righteous blood shed on earth, from the blood of **(M)**(righteous) Abel to the blood of Zechariah **(M)**(son of Barachiah,) whom you murdered between the sanctuary and the altar. ³⁶Truly I tell you, all this will come upon this generation."]

Lament over Jerusalem, 23.37-39
(Lk 13.34-35)

Jesus. [**Q₃**][³⁷"Jerusalem, Jerusalem, the city that kills the prophets and stones those who are sent to it! How often have I desired to gather your children together as a hen gathers her brood under her wings, and you were not willing! ³⁸See, your house is left to you, desolate.ʰ ³⁹For I tell you, you will not see me again until you say,

Aaronic priesthood. 'Blessed is the one who comes in the name of the Lord.'" ⁱ]

ᵍ Gk *Gehenna*
ʰ Other ancient authorities lack *desolate*
ⁱ Ps 118.26

Chapter 23 Notes
Woe to scribes and Pharisees, 23.1-36

1: Jesus directed his teaching about the scribes and Pharisees *to the crowds and to his disciples.* While Jesus clashed with the scribes and Pharisees sometimes, he was in agreement with them (22.15-33). After the destruction of the temple in 70 CE, they were the only important influence in Judaism and were in bitter conflict with the early church. **2:** *Moses' seat* was a seat in the synagogue that symbolized the origin and authority of the law and was reserved for the *scribes and the Pharisees.* These two groups were pledged to obey and teach both the written law and the oral tradition that went back to Moses. **3:** *They do not practice what they teach* as a result they were called "hypocrites" (cf Rom 2.21). **4:** *Heavy burdens* or minute and perplexing interpretations of the law were laid upon *the shoulders of others* with no desire to help them (Lk 11.46; Mt 11.28-30; Acts 15.10). **5:** *Phylacteries,* meaning "amulets" or "charms", were little leather boxes worn on the left arm and forehead, containing strips of parchment bearing the text of Exodus (Ex 13.9, 16) and Deuteronomy (Deut 6.4-9; 11.18-20). *Fringes* were the blue twisted threads at the four corners of male garments, as a reminder to obey God's commandments. Since no maximum length was established, those wishing to display their piety made them as *long* as desired. **6-8:** *Rabbi* was a title of respect used by disciples in addressing their elders. This title was commonly used after the destruction of the temple in 70 CE (Mk 12.38-39; Lk 11.43; 14.7-11; 20.46; Jas 3.1). **10:** The Greek word "kathegetes" was translated "instructor" and only occurred here in the NT. In Modern Greek, it means "professor" or "an interpreter of the law." **11-12:** These verses have several parallels in the NT on humility (Lk 14.11; 18.14; Mt 18.4; 1 Pet 5.6).

13: The seven "woes," known as the denunciations were an indictment of some, but not all, Pharisees (Lk 11.52). (*Gospel of Thomas,* Logion 39), "Jesus said, 'The Pharisees and the scribes have received the keys of knowledge and have hidden them. They themselves did not enter, and they did not allow to enter those who wished to. But you, become as wise as serpents and as innocent as doves.'" **15:** The synagogues of the Dispersion (scattered to other cities and lands) were centers for Jewish beliefs and propaganda. Gentile converts or "God fearers" could worship the God of the Jews, but they did not become part of the Jewish community until they had been properly instructed in the Torah (the Law), males must be circumcised, submit to a proselyte bath, and offer a sacrifice in the temple (Acts 2.10; 6.5; 13.43). *Twice as much a child of hell* meant literally "double a son of Gehenna."

16-17: Because it was a common practice among the people to make *oaths* or vows, the rabbis were forced to divide oaths into two categories, those that must be followed or face punishment and others that were not expected to be kept, therefore, no penalty was received (5.33-37; 15.14; Ex 30.29). **19:** That which made the *gold sacred* was more important than the gold. **21:** These verses were directed against the careless use of an oath, which called upon God (1 Kings 8.13; Ps 26.8). **23-24:** *Dill and cumin* were both aromatic plants. The tithing of *mint, dill and cumin* was demanded by the law. However, Jesus said that *justice and mercy and faith* were more important (Lev 27.30; Mic 6.8). Luke used "rue" a similar aromatic plant instead of *dill* (Lk 11.42). The identification of these herbs indicated the excessive nature of the Pharisees in tithing, but they should not be at the expense of doing *justice and mercy and faith. Strain out a gnat,* which had fallen into the wine before drinking it, *but swallow a camel.* Only Matthew made the comparison between the small and large. Why make a fuss over the little things while neglecting matters that were more important?

25-26: *First clean the inside* was making the point that effective cleansing must start within (Lk 11.39-41; Mk 7.4). **27-28:** Tombs were *whitewashed* before Passover so Jewish travelers, especially the priests, would not accidentally touch them and become ceremonially unclean. The whitewash covered up all the tombs ugliness making them beautiful on the outside. This same application applied to *the scribes and Pharisees* (Lk 11.44; Acts 23.3; Ps 5.9). *Gospel of the Naassenes,* (in Hippolytus, *Refutation of all Heresies,* v.8.23), "You are whitewashed tombs with the bones of the dead, that is, no life is within you."

29-32: *Tombs of the prophets* and *graves of the righteous* were decorated, but it was not in a manner that honored their *ancestors* (Lk 11.47-48; Acts 7.51-53). **30:** Even though only one prophet's murder was mentioned in the Hebrew Scriptures (2 Chr 24.20-22), Jewish legend had added others to the list of national martyrs, thus *blood of the prophets*. **31:** The scribes and Pharisees would admit to being *descendants of those who murdered the prophets;* Jesus insisted that their attitudes were also similar (v 28). **32:** *Fill up, then the measure of your ancestors* could be translated, "come up to you ancestors standard." **33:** The scribes and Pharisees were compared to a *brood of vipers,* those low and poisonous creatures that fled in haste before the onrushing fire that swept across the wilderness (3.7; Lk 3.7). **34-36:** *Prophets, sages and scribes* were terms of Jewish origin applied here to Christian missionaries. *Kill and crucify* seemed to refer to the death of Jesus, but the flogging and pursuing seemed to mean the treatment of the Christians (Lk 11.49-51). *Abel* was the first martyr (Gen 4.8) and *Zechariah* was the last martyr to be mentioned in the Hebrew Bible (2 Chr 24.20-22). Matthew may have been confused between Zechariah the priest, the son of Jehoiada, and Zechariah the prophet, the son of Berechiah (Zech 1.1). *Gospel of the Nazaraeans,* (in Jerome, *Commentary on Matthew,* 23.35), "In the gospel which the Nazarenes use, for "son of Barachiah" we find written, "son of Johoiada." Peter of Laodicea, (*Commentary on Matthew,* 23.35, ed. Heinrici, V.267), "And Zechariah the son of Johoiada said, "For he was of two names."

Lament over Jerusalem, 23.37-39

37: Any association with the previous saying can only be made because of the reference to "Jerusalem as the place where prophets are killed." If these verses were to be understood as the sayings of Jesus, they must be a Christian addition that not only reflected upon

Jesus' death, but on the destruction of Jerusalem and the temple. The words *how often* suggest repeated efforts, made perhaps during an earlier Judean ministry (Lk 4.44). **38:** *Your house* meant the city itself, but included the temple (1 Kings 9.7; Jer 12.7; 22.5). **39:** This quote was shouted by the crowd at the triumphal entry into Jerusalem (21.9; Ps 118.26) and was used again by Matthew to express the return of the heavenly Messiah. *In the name of the Lord,* should have read "LORD" (*see* LORD).

Chapter 23 Study Guide

1. If the Messiah was the only instructor (23.10), what was the role of the Holy Spirit?
2. What was more sacred, a sacred gift or that which made the gift sacred? What then deserves your worship?
3. Why make a fuss over the little things while neglecting matters that are more important?
4. Why did Jesus call the scribes and Pharisees a "brood of vipers"?
5. How much influence did the persecution of the early Christians have upon the words of judgment expressed in this chapter?

Chapter 24
Destruction of the temple foretold, 24.1-3
(Mk 13.1-2; Lk 21.5-7)

Matthew. As Jesus came out of the temple and was going away, his disciples came to point out to him the buildings of the temple. ²Then he asked them,

Jesus. "You see all these, do you not? **(M)**(Truly I tell you,) not one stone will be left here upon another; all will be thrown down."

Matthew. ³When he was sitting on the Mount of Olives, the disciples came to him privately, saying,

Disciples. "Tell us, when will this be, and what will be the sign of your coming and of the end of the age?"

On the end of the age, 24.4-51
(Mk 13.3-37; Lk 21.8-36)

Matthew. ⁴Jesus answered them,

Jesus. "Beware that no one leads you astray. ⁵For many will come in my name, saying,

Messiah. (false) 'I am the Messiah!'ᵃ

Jesus. and they will lead many astray. ⁶And you will hear of wars and rumors of wars; see that you are not alarmed; for this must take place, but the end is not yet. ⁷For nation will rise against nation, and kingdom against kingdom, and there will be faminesᵇ and earthquakes in various places: ⁸all this is but the beginning of the birth pangs.

⁹"Then they will hand you over to be tortured and will put you to death, and you will be hated by all **(M)(nations)** because of my name. **(M)(**¹⁰Then many will fall away,ᶜ and they will betray one another and hate one another. ¹¹And many false prophets will arise and lead many astray. ¹²And because of the increase of lawlessness, the love of many will grow cold.**)** ¹³But the one who endures to the end will be saved. **(M)(**¹⁴And this good newsᵈ of the kingdom will be proclaimed throughout the world, as a testimony to all the nations; and then the end will come.**)**

¹⁵"So when you see the desolating sacrilege standing in the holy place, **(M)(**as was spoken of by the prophet Daniel**)**

ᵃ Or *the Christ*
ᵇ Other ancient authorities add *and pestilences*
ᶜ Or *stumble*
ᵈ Or *gospel*

Matthew. (let the reader understand),

Jesus. [16]then those in Judea must flee to the mountains; [17]the one on the housetop must not go down to take what is in the house; [18]the one in the field must not turn back to get a coat. [19]Woe to those who are pregnant and to those who are nursing infants in those days! [20]Pray that your flight may not be in winter or on a sabbath. [21]For at that time there will be great suffering, such as has not been from the beginning of the world until now, no, and never will be. [22]And if those days had not been cut short, no one would be saved; but for the sake of the elect those days will be cut short. [Q₂][[23]Then if anyone says to you,

Scoffers. 'Look! Here is the Messiah!'[e]

Jesus. or

Scoffers. 'There he is!'

Jesus. —do not believe it.] [24]For false messiahs[f] and false prophets will appear and produce great signs and omens, to lead astray, if possible, even the elect. [25]Take note, I have told you beforehand. [Q₂] [[26]So, if they say to you,

Scoffers. 'Look! He is in the wilderness,'

Jesus. do not go out. (M)(If they say,

Scoffers. 'Look! He is in the inner rooms,'

Jesus. do not believe it.) [27]For as the lightning comes from the east and flashes as far as the west, so will be the coming of the Son of Man. [28]Wherever the corpse is, there the vultures will gather."]

---

[e] Or *the Christ*
[f] Or *christs*

²⁹"Immediately after the suffering of those days the sun will be darkened, and the moon will not give its light; the stars will fall from heaven, and the powers of heaven will be shaken.

(M)(³⁰Then the sign of the Son of Man will appear in heaven, and then all the tribes of the earth will mourn,) and they will see

Daniel. (A)('the Son of Man coming on the clouds of heaven' ᵍ)

Jesus. with power and great glory. ³¹And he will send out his angels with a loud trumpet call, and they will gather his elect from the four winds, from one end of heaven to the other.

³²"From the fig tree learn its lesson: as soon as its branch becomes tender and puts forth its leaves, you know that summer is near. ³³So also, when you see all these things, you know that heʰ is near, at the very gates. ³⁴Truly I tell you, this generation will not pass away until all these things have taken place. ³⁵Heaven and earth will pass away, but my words will not pass away."

³⁶"But about that day and hour no one knows, neither the angels of heaven, nor the Son,ⁱ but only the Father. **[Q₂][**³⁷For as the days of Noah were, so will be the coming of the Son of Man. **(M)**(³⁸For as in those days before the flood) they were eating and drinking, marrying and giving in marriage, until the day Noah entered the ark, ³⁹and **(M)** (they knew nothing) until the flood came and swept them all away, **(M)**(so too will be the coming of the Son of Man.) ⁴⁰Then two will be in the field; one will be taken and one will be left. ⁴¹Two women will be grinding meal together; one will be taken and one will be left.] ⁴²Keep awake therefore, for you do not know on what dayʲ your Lord is coming. **[Q₂][**⁴³But understand this: if the owner of the house had known in what part of the night the thief was coming, he would have stayed awake and would not have let his house be broken into. ⁴⁴Therefore you also must be ready, for the Son of Man is coming at an unexpected hour."]

ᵍ Dan 7.13
ʰ Or *it*
ⁱ Other ancient authorities lack *nor the Son*
ʲ Other ancient authorities read *at what hour*

[Q₂][⁴⁵"Who then is the faithful and wise slave, whom his master has put in charge of his household, to give the other slavesᵏ their allowance of food at the proper time? ⁴⁶Blessed is that slave whom his master will find at work when he arrives. ⁴⁷Truly I tell you, he will put that one in charge of all his possessions. ⁴⁸But if that wicked slave says to himself,

Slave. 'My master is delayed,'

Jesus. ⁴⁹and he begins to beat his fellow slaves, and eats and drinks with drunkards, ⁵⁰the master of that slave will come on a day when he does not expect him and at an hour that he does not know. ⁵¹He will cut him in piecesˡ and put him with the hypocrites,**] (M)**(where there will be weeping and gnashing of teeth.")

Chapter 24 Notes
Destruction of the temple foretold, 24.1-3

Matthew presented the last of his five great discourses (5.1-7.27; 10.1-11.1; 13.1-52; 18.1-35), and this one dealt with the end of the age. He wanted to clarify it to his readers that Jesus would come again in glory, even if that coming had been delayed. Christians should do more than just read the times and seasons, because no one could tell exactly when the Lord would come. Jesus' followers should be ready at every moment and Matthew presented Jesus' teaching that each Christian would be judged on the time given to him, meaning how he had helped those in need.

Mark's little Apocalypse (Mk 13.1-37) was originally a Jewish document taken over by early Christian preachers to address the circumstances of the early church. It may have included some genuine sayings of Jesus, but they can no longer be isolated. Some of

---

ᵏ Gk *to give them*
ˡ Or *cut him off*

Matthew's and Luke's versions differ from Mark's, because they were written later and the beliefs of the early church were more developed.

1: These teachings set down by Matthew are placed within the historical events that took place between 30 and 70 CE and predicted what might happen at the end of human history. It remains unclear if Jesus predicted the fate of the temple before its destruction or if it was an after the fact statement by the early church. **2:** *Truly I tell you,* was a phrase only used by Matthew. The actual destruction of the temple was by fire.

3: Jesus' public ministry ended as he spoke *privately* with his disciples, who asked for a sign when the end would come. Jesus warned them not to expect the end to happen immediately (Lk 17.20-21: Mt 13.39, 40, 49; 16.27).

On the end of the age, 24.4-51

4: *Leads you astray* stressed the importance of not being misled by false prophets such as Simon Magus (Acts 8.9-11). **5:** Josephus, *(The History of the Jewish War)* reported in 66-70 CE there were many who claimed to be a Messiah (1 Jn 2.18). Luke agreed and added to the warning about false messiahs a sense of urgency with the warning, "the time is near" (Lk 21.8). **6-7:** *Wars, famines and earthquakes,* with other kinds of cosmic disorders were part of the rhetoric and predictions about the end of the age (2 Esd 9.3; 13.30-32; Rev 6.1-8), and any attempt to link them to specific events of the period of the early church becomes a waste of time. If they happened, it did not mean the end of time, only that people believed it to be the coming end. It was expected by some that the Jewish war would usher in the end of the age, but it did not happen (Rev 6.3-8, 12, 17). **8:** *The beginning of the birth pangs* signaled the imminence of the new age, which was announced at the beginning of Jesus' public ministry has come near (4.17), but it was to be realized only after a period of witnesses to Jesus' message (v 14). While this message was to the Twelve disciples, verses 5-14 seemed to include a larger community of followers.

9: Persecution, false prophets and apostasy (falling away) were predicted before the end. Matthew added *"nations"* to Mark and Luke's comments "you will be hated by all because of my name" (10.17-18, 22; Jn 15.18; 16.2). **10-12:** These verses were only in Matthew where he showed that before Christ's return *many will fall away* from the Christian cause. This position may have reflected the actual experiences of individuals like Stephen, Peter and Paul. For Luke the purpose for all of the persecutions was so it "will give you an opportunity to testify, and the disciples are called upon to make up their minds in advance what they will do" (Lk 21.13-14). *Hate one another* seemed directed to the divisions within the early church (Eph 4.14; 1 Jn 2.18-22). **12:** *The love of* Christians for one another would grow cold (10.22; Rev 2.7). **13:** Those *who* endure *to the end* during this trying period *will be saved.* **14:** *The good news of the kingdom will be proclaimed throughout the world* before *the end will come* were understood to be prophetic by believers today with a different understanding of our inhabited earth. Because the Roman Empire included several nations, it was commonly referred to as *"all the nations."* Therefore, this verse could be interpreted to mean that when the *good news of the kingdom* was *proclaimed* to all the inhabited earth, then the entire world would be *a testimony* to Rome, *and then the end will come* (28.19; Rom 10.18). Jesus' followers were to proclaim the good news of the kingdom throughout the world, and it became difficult to explain why most of the disciples remained in Jerusalem after the resurrection, leaving the mission to the Gentiles mostly to Paul.

15: *Desolating sacrilege standing in the holy place* referred to the establishment of a pagan alter in the temple (Dan 9.27; 11.31; 12.11). The prophecy from Daniel was reinterpreted and applied to the Roman Emperor Caligula (37-41 CE) who wanted to set up his image in the temple. Or it may be regarding the erection of Titus' statue on the site of the destroyed temple in 70 CE (Mk 13.14). Luke interpreted the expression to mean "When you see Jerusalem surrounded by armies, then you will know that its desolation has come near" (Lk 21.20), revealing some knowledge of the events in Jerusalem just before the siege. The Christian community in Jerusalem withdrew to Pella in Perea in response to the pending disaster. However, the Jewish people came to the city, because they did not believe the temple and the Holy City would be destroyed. According to Roman figures, ninety-seven thousand were taken prisoner and one million Jewish people were slain during this war. **16-18:** The people were to *flee to the mountains,* because the hill country in Judea had many caves and hiding places. *On the housetop* was regarding the flat roofs where people sat and rested. They were warned to not re-enter *the house* for any possessions but flee quickly. Nor should a field laborer attempt to retrieve any property. **19:** *Pregnant* women and mothers with *nursing infants* could not leave fast enough to escape danger. **20:** The mention of *winter,* a time of cold weather, *or on a sabbath* was unique for Matthew who provided this Jewish touch, and it indicated that Christians in Matthew's day might have still been observing the sabbath. **21:** Conflicts between family traditions and the Christian faith were real for the early Jewish and Gentile Christians. It was important for this issue to be addressed, as in 1 Peter, "Yet if any of you suffers as a Christian, do not consider it a disgrace, but glorify God because you bear this name" (1 Pet 4.16). **23:** (*Gospel of Thomas,* Logion 113), "Jesus' disciples asked him, 'When will the kingdom come? Jesus said, 'It will not come by waiting for it. People will not say, 'Here it is,' or 'There it is,' but the kingdom of the Father is spread upon the earth and people do not see it.'" **24:** The *great signs and omens* were regarding the acts of false prophets (Deut 13.1-5). **26-28:** In the wilderness, Moses saw God and both Christians and Jews looked back to those days. Josephus told of rebels who led the people into the wilderness promising them deliverance *(Jewish Antiquities,* XX.8.6, *10; The History of the Jewish War,* II.13.5; Acts 21.37-38). *In the inner rooms* suggested the Oriental doctrine of the hidden Messiah or redeemer (Jn 7.27). *The coming of the Son of Man* would be as sudden *as lightening* and visible for all to see.

29-31: The language here was drawn from the OT; God's victory over sin was to be established by the Son of Man whom he sent. *The sun will be darkened* reflected a feature in several Jewish descriptions of the end, "For the stars of the heavens and their constellations will not give their light; the sun will be dark at its rising, and the moon will not shed its light" (Isa 13.10; 34.4; Ezek 32.7; Joel 2.10-11; Zeph 1.15; Rev 8.12). **30:** *The sign of the Son of Man* may be regarding Isa 11.12, "He will raise a signal for the nations" (16.27; Dan 7.13; Rev 1.7). *All the tribes on earth will mourn* appeared to refer to Zechariah (Zech 12.10) and then expanded to a universal meaning. **31:** *With a loud trumpet call* was another feature in Jewish apocalyptic writings as the day of judgment was announced by a trumpet call (1 Cor 15.32; 1 Thess 4.16; Isa 27.13; Zech 2.10; 9.14). **34:** The normal meaning of *this generation* would be "people of our time," and the words would refer to a period of twenty to thirty years (10.23; 16.28). What Jesus meant, however, remains uncertain. **35:** *My words will not pass away* that was they were true and eternal (5.18; Lk 16.17).

36: No one knew *about the day and hour,* not even *the Son, but only the Father,* so every disciple must remain alert (Acts 1.6-7). **37-39:** Those in Noah's day were unprepared for the flood and so shall it be with be when the Son of Man comes (Lk 17.26-27; Gen 6.5-8; 7.6-24). There was nothing wrong with their *eating and drinking, marrying and giving in marriage.* However, it was wrong to continue with business as usual while neglecting what was happening around them, in spite of all the warnings. The conduct of the people would be like those who lived before the flood. **40-41:** *One will be taken,* the one who was alert and ready to respond, and *one will be left* because they are unprepared. *Grinding meal* was the work of a slave girl (Ex 11.5; Lk 17.34-35). **42:** *Keep awake* was to be continually prepared and ready (Mk 13.35; Lk 12.40; 21. 34-36; Mt 25.13). **43-45:** *The thief* could dig through the house wall and surprise the owner because he was not alert (Lk 12.39-46; 1 Thess 5.2; Rev 3.3.). (Epiphanius, *Ancoratus,* 21.2), "For he (the Son) said, 'That day will come like a thief in the night.'"

46-47: Matthew closed with another parable that emphasized the Lord would return suddenly. The point of this parable was that the disciples were to do more than just watch, they were to be *at work,* they were to be faithful in carrying out their duties. The reward for faithful service was greater opportunities and responsibilities, not an endless rest. **48-50:** But for the unfaithful one, who mistreated his fellow servants and thought the delay meant it would not happen, he would not be ready when the master returned. **51:** He would not receive greater opportunities and responsibilities, but *will* be *cut in pieces,* an ancient expression sometimes used to represent a brutal form of punishment. *Where there will be weeping and gnashing of teeth* was a common expression of disappointment and pain (see 8.12n). While the other gospel writers included an aspect of judgment, it became more evident in Matthew.

Chapter 24 Study Guide

1. Why did the disciples remain in Jerusalem after the resurrection, if Jesus told them that the good news must be proclaimed to the entire world?
2. What are you to look for concerning the end of time?
3. Do you believe that Jesus will come again?
4. React to the statement that the church has combined the second coming of Jesus with the end of time.
5. Why are people so concerned with the end of time and what will happen when it comes?

Chapter 25
Teaching on the coming of the kingdom, 25.1-46
The parable of the wise and foolish bridesmaids, 25.1-13

Jesus. (M)("Then the kingdom of heaven will be like this. Ten bridesmaids[a] took their lamps and went to meet the bridegroom.[b] [2]Five of them were foolish, and five were wise. [3]When the foolish took their lamps, they took no oil with them; [4]but the wise took flasks of oil with their lamps. [5]As the bridegroom was delayed, all of them became drowsy and slept. [6]But at midnight there was a shout,

[a] Gk *virgins*
[b] Other ancient authorities add *and the bride*

Messenger. 'Look! Here is the bridegroom! Come out to meet him.'

Jesus. ⁷Then all those bridesmaids[c] got up and trimmed their lamps. ⁸The foolish said to the wise,

Bridesmaids. (foolish) 'Give us some of your oil, for our lamps are going out.'

Jesus. ⁹But the wise replied,

Bridesmaids. (wise) 'No! there will not be enough for you and for us; you had better go to the dealers and buy some for yourselves.'

Jesus. [Q₂][¹⁰And while they went to buy it, the bridegroom came, and those who were ready went with him into the wedding banquet; and the door was shut. ¹¹Later the other bridesmaids[d] came also, saying,)

Bridesmaids. (foolish). 'Lord, lord, open to us.'

Jesus. ¹²But he replied,

Bridegroom. 'Truly I tell you, I do not know you.']

Jesus. (M)(¹³Keep awake therefore, for you know neither the day nor the hour.[e])

Parable of the talents, 25.14-30
(Lk 19.12-27)

Jesus. [Q₂][¹⁴ "For it is as if a man, going on a journey, summoned his slaves and entrusted his property to them; ¹⁵to one he gave five talents,[f] to another two, to another one, to each according to his

---

[c] Gk *virgins*
[d] Gk *virgins*
[e] Other ancient authorities add *in which the Son of Man is coming*
[f] A talent was worth more than fifteen years' wages of a laborer

ability. Then he went away.] **(M)**(¹⁶The one who had received the five talents went off at once and traded with them, and made five more talents. ¹⁷In the same way, the one who had the two talents made two more talents. ¹⁸But the one who had received the one talent went off and dug a hole in the ground and hid his master's money.¹⁹After a long time the master of those slaves came and settled accounts with them. ²⁰Then the one who had received the five talents came forward, bringing five more talents, saying,

Slave. (five talents) 'Master, you handed over to me five talents; see, I have made five more talents.')

Jesus. ²¹His master said to him,

Nobleman. 'Well done, good and trustworthy slave; you have been trustworthy in a few things, I will put you in charge of many things; enter into the joy of your master.'

Jesus. ²²And the one with the two talents also came forward, saying,

Slave. (two talents) 'Master, you handed over to me two talents; see, I have made two more talents.'

Jesus. (M) (²³His master said to him,)

Nobleman. 'Well done, good and trustworthy slave; you have been trustworthy in a few things, I will put you in charge of many things; enter into the joy of your master.'

Jesus. ²⁴Then the one who had received the one talent also came forward, saying,

Slave. (one talent) 'Master, I knew that you were a harsh man, reaping where you did not sow, **(M)**(and gathering where you did not scatter seed; ²⁵so I was afraid, and I went and hid your talent in the ground. Here you have what is yours.')

Jesus. [26]But his master replied,

Nobleman. 'You wicked and lazy slave! You knew, did you, that I reap where I did not sow, **(M)**(and gather where I did not scatter?) [27]Then you ought to have invested my money with the bankers, and on my return I would have received what was my own with interest. [28]So take the talent from him, and give it to the one with the ten talents. [29]For to all those who have, more will be given, and they will have an abundance; but from those who have nothing, even what they have will be taken away. **(M)**([30]As for this worthless slave, throw him into the outer darkness, where) there will be weeping and gnashing of teeth.'

The great judgment, 25.31-46

Jesus. (M)([31]"When the Son of Man comes in his glory, and all the angels with him, then he will sit on the throne of his glory. [32]All the nations will be gathered before him, and he will separate people one from another as a shepherd separates the sheep from the goats, [33]and he will put the sheep at his right hand and the goats at the left. [34]Then the king will say to those at his right hand,

King. 'Come, you that are blessed by my Father, inherit the kingdom prepared for you from the foundation of the world; [35]for I was hungry and you gave me food, I was thirsty and you gave me something to drink, I was a stranger and you welcomed me, [36]I was naked and you gave me clothing, I was sick and you took care of me, I was in prison and you visited me.'

Jesus. [37]Then the righteous will answer him,

Righteous followers. 'Lord, when was it that we saw you hungry and gave you food, or thirsty and gave you something to drink? [38]And when was it that we saw you a stranger and welcomed you, or naked and gave you clothing? [39]And when was it that we saw you sick or in prison and visited you?'

Jesus. [40]And the king will answer them,

King. 'Truly I tell you, just as you did it to one of the least of these who are members of my family,[g] you did it to me.'

Jesus. [41]Then he will say to those at his left hand,

King. 'You that are accursed, depart from me into the eternal fire prepared for the devil and his angels; [42]for I was hungry and you gave me no food, I was thirsty and you gave me nothing to drink, [43]I was a stranger and you did not welcome me, naked and you did not give me clothing, sick and in prison and you did not visit me.'

Jesus. [44]Then they also will answer,

Those at the left hand. 'Lord, when was it that we saw you hungry or thirsty or a stranger or naked or sick or in prison, and did not take care of you?'

Jesus. [45]Then he will answer them,

King. 'Truly I tell you, just as you did not do it to one of the least of these, you did not do it to me.'

Jesus. [46]And these will go away into eternal punishment, but the righteous into eternal life.")

Chapter 25 Notes
Teachings on the coming of the kingdom, 25.1-46
The parable of the wise and foolish bridesmaids, 25.1-13

The parable of the wise and foolish bridesmaids was based on the Palestinian custom that the groom moved his bride from her parents' home to his own. Weddings in Palestine were joyful events

---

[g] Gk *these my brothers*

even surpassing many of the festivals. Weddings even took greater importance than studying the Torah.

1: Matthew, like Luke, made the same point, that since no one knew the time of the end, all must be ready to meet the Son of Man (Lk 12.35-38; Mk 13.34). *Then* was regarding the end of the age, when the Lord was expected. The bride, who was not mentioned, waited at her home for the bridegroom. The *ten bridesmaids,* friends of the bride, would eagerly assemble to meet the groom as he came to the bride's home. **2:** The division of the bridesmaids into two groups reflected the twofold division characteristic of Matthew (7.24-27) and may have represented the divisions between Christians and Jewish or maybe between members within a church. **3-5:** All the bridesmaids had lamps with oil. The wise ones were prepared and *took flasks* containing extra *oil,* while the *foolish* ones had no reserve and were not prepared for the groom's delay. The party must have been boring, because they *became drowsy and slept.* **6-7:** *At midnight* when the announcement of the groom came, five bridesmaids were unprepared. **8-10:** The lamps had been burning and needed more oil, but there was not enough in the extra flasks for all ten of them. The foolish ones had to *go to the dealers and buy some.* It would be unusual for any *dealers* to be open at midnight. While they were gone to obtain more oil the groom came, *and those* who were *ready went into the wedding banquet; and the door was shut* (Rev 19.9). The parable may have originally ended here, as there was no reason to believe that the groom kept *the door shut.* **11-12:** Some believe that verses 11 and 12 were added later by the church to stress the need to be prepared, because someday it might be too late to share in the *wedding banquet* (Lk 13.25; Mt 7.21-23). **13:** The command to watch linked this parable with the previous one (24.42; Mk 13.35; Lk 12.40).

The parable of the talents, 25.14-30

This parable differed greatly from Luke's parable of the pounds (Lk 19.11-27) but it might be assumed that Matthew changed "pounds" to *"talents"* to stress those who wished to share in the future blessings must use their talents and time wisely in serving God. On the other hand, Luke had "the spokesman" give the same endowment of "ten pounds" to each of the ten slaves. **15-18:** On the value of this *talent,* see note f, where it was worth over fifteen years of a laborer's wages. Talents today are usually thought of as skills or gifts given and developed. The point of the parable was that gifts, hidden or unused, in serving God would be lost. **21:** *Enter into* meant to share in *the joy of your master* (Lk 16.10). **24-25:** The comment, *"you were a harsh man"* made it difficult for this parable to represent God or Christ. However, the servant *knew* the master to be *a harsh man.* **26-27:** *Ought to have invested my money with the bankers* where it would have at least earned some interest. In ancient times, the rates of interest were high. **29:** The statement, *from those who have nothing, even what they have will be taken away,* illustrated Jesus' way of speaking in two settings at once. The master's servant had his original talent, yet had earned nothing by it, so individuals can have their earthly existence and all that derives from it, yet lack merit in the final judgment (v 30). Talents are given to be used. (*Gospel of Thomas,* Logion 41*),* "Jesus said, 'All who have in their hands, to them will be given; and all who do not have, from them will be taken away, even the little they have.'" **30:** *Worthless* was to be without value to his master. *Where there will be weeping and gnashing of teeth* was a common expression of disappointment and pain (see 8.12n). While the other gospel writers include an aspect of judgment, it becomes more evident in Matthew (22.13; 24.51).

The great judgment, 25.31-46

Nowhere did Matthew express the ethical spirit of the OT and Judaism as he did in this picture of the end of the age. Yet it differed from most Jewish apocalyptic literature because the judge was the returning Son of Man rather than God. Note the favorite twofold division of Matthew, the sheep and the goats. An unusual note on this parable was that on the day of judgment some would discover that they have been on God's side all along (vs 37-39).

31: Since the *Son of Man* only occurred here in this parable and the "king" was used everywhere else, maybe the original parable referred to the king as the Messiah (16.27; 19.28). **32:** The sheep in Palestine were usually white and the goats were usually black, and a shepherd could easily separate them (Ezek 34.17). *All the nations,* a term usually used regarding Rome, only appeared here and in 24.14 by the Jewish Christians who compiled the M source (cf Rom 2.13-16). **34:** Reward in the age to come was described more than once as an inheritance (5.5; 19.29; Gal 4.1-7; 21-31; Lk 12.32; Mt 5.3; Rev 13.8; 17.8). To *inherit the kingdom* was to be recognized as a child of God. **35-37:** The surprise of the *righteous* was one of the most powerful aspects of this parable (Isa 58.7; Jas 1.27; 2.15-16; Heb 13.2; 2 Tim 1.16). **40:** The Messiah identified himself with the interests and needs of the *least of these who are members of my family* (10.42; Mk 9.41; Heb 6.10; Prov 19.17). **41:** *Eternal fire* (Gahanna) *prepared for the devil and his angels,* was for those who were indifferent to the needs of the least of God's family (Enoch 10.13; Mk 9.48; Rev 20.10). **46:** Dan 12.2; Jn 5.29. *Go away... into eternal life* expressed the same idea as *inherit the kingdom* (v 34).

Chapter 25 Study Guide

1. Were the five wise bridesmaids selfish in refusing to share their resources with the other five?
2. What was the point of the parable of the five wise and five foolish bridesmaids?
3. What does the parable of the talents mean to you? What talents has God given to you? How do you use them?
4. What does it mean to be blessed by God?
5. What does it mean to you to minister to one of the least of God's children?

Chapter 26
Jesus' death, 26.1-27.66
(Mk 14.1-15.47; Lk 22.1-23.56; Jn 13.1-19.42)

Matthew. (M)(When Jesus had finished saying all these things, he said to his disciples,)

Jesus. [2]"You know that after two days the Passover is coming, **(M)** (and the Son of Man will be handed over to be crucified.")

Matthew. [3]Then the chief priests and the elders **(M)**(of the people gathered in the palace of the high priest, who was called Caiaphas,) [4]and they conspired to arrest Jesus by stealth and kill him. [5]But they said,

Chief priests and Elders. "Not during the festival, or there may be a riot among the people."

Matthew. [6]Now while Jesus was at Bethany in the house of Simon the leper,[a] [7]a woman came to him with an alabaster jar of very costly ointment, and she poured it on his head **(M)**(as he sat at the table.) [8]But when the disciples saw it, they were angry and said,

Disciples. "Why this waste? [9]For this ointment could have been sold for a large sum, and the money given to the poor."

Matthew. [10]But Jesus, aware of this, said to them,

Jesus. "Why do you trouble the woman? She has performed a good service for me. [11]For you always have the poor with you, but you will not always have me. [12]By pouring this ointment on my body she has prepared me for burial. [13]Truly I tell you, wherever this good news[b] is proclaimed in the whole world, what she has done will be told in remembrance of her."

---

[a] The terms *leper* and *leprosy* can refer to several diseases
[b] Or *gospel*

Matthew. ¹⁴Then one of the twelve, who was called Judas Iscariot, went to the chief priests **(M)**(¹⁵and said,

Judas Iscariot. "What will you give me if I betray him to you?")

Matthew. They paid him thirty pieces of silver. ¹⁶And from that moment he began to look for an opportunity to betray him.

The Last Supper, 26.17-29
(Mk 14.12-16; Lk 22.7-13)

Matthew. ¹⁷On the first day of Unleavened Bread the disciples came to Jesus, saying,

Disciples. "Where do you want us to make the preparations for you to eat the Passover?"

Matthew. ¹⁸He said,

Jesus. "Go into the city to a certain man, and say to him,

Disciples. 'The Teacher says,

Jesus. My time is near; I will keep the Passover at your house with my disciples.'"

Matthew. ¹⁹So the disciples did as Jesus had directed them, and they prepared the Passover meal.
    ²⁰When it was evening, he took his place with the twelve;ᶜ ²¹and while they were eating, he said,

Jesus. "Truly I tell you, one of you will betray me."

Matthew. ²²And they became greatly distressed and began to say to him one after another,

---

ᶜ Other ancient authorities add *disciples*

215

Disciples. "Surely not I, Lord?"

Matthew. [23]He answered,

Jesus. "The one who has dipped his hand into the bowl with me will betray me. [24]The Son of Man goes as it is written of him, but woe to that one by whom the Son of Man is betrayed! It would have been better for that one not to have been born."

Matthew. (M)([25]Judas, who betrayed him, said,

Judas Iscariot. "Surely not I, Rabbi?"

Matthew. He replied,

Jesus. "You have said so.")

Matthew. [26]While they were eating, Jesus took a loaf of bread, and after blessing it he broke it, gave it to the disciples, and said,

Jesus. "Take, eat; this is my body."

Matthew. [27]Then he took a cup, and after giving thanks he gave it to them, saying,

Jesus. "Drink from it, all of you; [28]for this is my blood of the[d] covenant, which is poured out for many for the forgiveness of sins. [29]I tell you, I will never again drink of this fruit of the vine until that day when I drink it new with you in my Father's kingdom."

Gethsemane, 26.30-56

Matthew. [30]When they had sung the hymn, they went out to the Mount of Olives.
  [31]Then Jesus said to them,

---

[d] Other ancient authorities add *new*

Jesus. "You will all become deserters because of me this night; for it is written,

LORD. 'I will strike the shepherd, and the sheep of the flock will be scattered.' ᵉ

Jesus. ³²But after I am raised up, I will go ahead of you to Galilee."

Matthew. ³³Peter said to him,

Peter. "Though all become deserters because of you, I will never desert you."

Matthew. ³⁴Jesus said to him,

Jesus. "Truly I tell you, this very night, before the cock crows, you will deny me three times."

Matthew. ³⁵Peter said to him,

Peter. "Even though I must die with you, I will not deny you."

Matthew. And so said all the disciples.
³⁶Then Jesus went with them to a place called Gethsemane; and he said to his disciples,

Jesus. "Sit here while I go over there and pray."

Matthew. ³⁷He took with him Peter and the two sons of Zebedee, and began to be grieved and agitated. ³⁸Then he said to them,

Jesus. "I am deeply grieved, even to death; remain here, and stay awake with me."

ᵉ Zech 13.7

Matthew. [39]And going a little farther, he threw himself on the ground and prayed,

Jesus. "My Father, if it is possible, let this cup pass from me; yet not what I want but what you want."

Matthew. [40]Then he came to the disciples and found them sleeping; and he said to Peter,

Jesus. "So, could you not stay awake with me one hour? [41]Stay awake and pray that you may not come into the time of trial;[f] the spirit indeed is willing, but the flesh is weak."

Matthew. [42]Again he went away for the second time and prayed,

Jesus. "My Father, if this cannot pass unless I drink it, your will be done."

Matthew. [43]Again he came and found them sleeping, for their eyes were heavy. [44]So leaving them again, he went away and prayed for the third time, saying the same words. [45]Then he came to the disciples and said to them,

Jesus. "Are you still sleeping and taking your rest? See, the hour is at hand, and the Son of Man is betrayed into the hands of sinners. [46]Get up, let us be going. See, my betrayer is at hand."

Matthew. [47]While he was still speaking, Judas, one of the twelve, arrived; with him was a large crowd with swords and clubs, from the chief priests and the elders of the people. [48]Now the betrayer had given them a sign, saying,

Judas Iscariot. "The one I will kiss is the man; arrest him."

Matthew. [49]At once he came up to Jesus and said,

---

[f] Or *into temptation*

Judas Iscariot. "Greetings, Rabbi!"

Matthew. and kissed him. ⁵⁰Jesus said to him,

Jesus. "Friend, do what you are here to do."

Matthew. Then they came and laid hands on Jesus and arrested him. ⁵¹Suddenly, one of those with Jesus put his hand on his sword, drew it, and struck the slave of the high priest, cutting off his ear. **(M)**(⁵²Then Jesus said to him,

Jesus. "Put your sword back into its place; for all who take the sword will perish by the sword. ⁵³Do you think that I cannot appeal to my Father, and he will at once send me more than twelve legions of angels? ⁵⁴But how then would the scriptures be fulfilled, which say it must happen in this way?")

Matthew. ⁵⁵At that hour Jesus said to the crowds,

Jesus. "Have you come out with swords and clubs to arrest me as though I were a bandit? Day after day I sat in the temple teaching, and you did not arrest me. ⁵⁶But all this has taken place, so that the scriptures of the prophets may be fulfilled."

Matthew. Then all the disciples deserted him and fled.

Jesus before Caiaphas, 26.57-75

Matthew. ⁵⁷Those who had arrested Jesus took him to Caiaphas the high priest, in whose house the scribes and the elders had gathered. ⁵⁸But Peter was following him at a distance, as far as the courtyard of the high priest; and going inside, he sat with the guards in order to see how this would end. ⁵⁹Now the chief priests and the whole council were looking for false testimony against Jesus so that they might put him to death, ⁶⁰but they found none, though many false witnesses came forward. At last two came forward ⁶¹and said,

Witnesses. (two false) "This fellow said,

Jesus. 'I am able to destroy the temple of God and to build it in three days.'"

Matthew. [62]The high priest stood up and said,

Caiaphas. "Have you no answer? What is it that they testify against you?"

Matthew. [63]But Jesus was silent. Then the high priest said to him,

Caiaphas. (M)("I put you under oath before the living God,) tell us if you are the Messiah,[g] the Son of God."

Matthew. [64]Jesus said to him,

Jesus. "You have said so. But I tell you, From now on you will see

Daniel. (A)(the Son of Man seated at the right hand of Power and coming on the clouds of heaven." [h])

Matthew. [65]Then the high priest tore his clothes and said,

Caiaphas. "He has blasphemed! Why do we still need witnesses? You have now heard his blasphemy. [66]What is your verdict?"

Matthew. They answered,

Chief priests, Scribes and Elders. "He deserves death."

Matthew. [67]Then they spat in his face and struck him; **(M)**(and some slapped him,) [68]saying,

---

[g] Or *Christ*
[h] Dan 7.13

Chief priests, Scribes and Elders. "Prophesy to us, you Messiah!ⁱ Who is it that struck you?"

Matthew. ⁶⁹Now Peter was sitting outside in the courtyard. A servant-girl came to him and said,

Servant girl. "You also were with Jesus the Galilean."

Matthew. ⁷⁰But he denied it before all of them, saying,

Peter. "I do not know what you are talking about."

Matthew. ⁷¹When he went out to the porch, another servant-girl saw him, and she said to the bystanders,

Servant girl. (second) "This man was with Jesus of Nazareth."ʲ

Matthew. ⁷²Again he denied it **(M)(with an oath,)**

Peter. "I do not know the man."

Matthew. ⁷³After a little while the bystanders came up and said to Peter,

Bystanders. "Certainly you are also one of them, for your accent betrays you."

Matthew. ⁷⁴Then he began to curse, and he swore an oath,

Peter. "I do not know the man!"

Matthew. At that moment the cock crowed. ⁷⁵Then Peter remembered what Jesus had said:

Jesus. "Before the cock crows, you will deny me three times."

ⁱ Or *Christ*
ʲ Gk *the Nazorean*

Matthew. And he went out and wept bitterly.

Chapter 26 Notes
Jesus' death, 26.1-27.66

While many of the stories about Jesus and his teachings may have been independent accounts later compiled into a chronological account, the same was not true of Jesus' arrest and death. Even if the events did not follow the same order, there existed a clear relationship between John's gospel and the Synoptics. The passion narrative probably was the first to be placed in a fixed form and became the foundation for the gospel accounts. While Mark was the oldest account of the passion, Matthew and Luke were probably influenced by early customs and traditions. However, there was little reason to doubt the validity of these events.

1: *When Jesus had finished saying these things,* this (or a similar) formula marked the conclusion of each of the five main discourses in the gospel (see Introduction and 7.28; 11.1; 13.53; 19.1; 24.1-26.2). **2:** *The Passover* commemorated the escape from Egypt under Moses (Ex 12.1-20). It was celebrated on the 15th day of Nisan, and the eight-day Feast of the Unleavened Bread began on the same day (Ex 12.14-20). The Jewish day was from sundown to sundown and the paschal meal took place on the evening of the 14th, with the lambs having been killed in the temple earlier in the afternoon. *After two days the Passover is coming* so Mark and Matthew placed the conspiracy against Jesus on Wednesday the 13th (Mk 14.1-2; Lk 22.1-2; Jn 11.47-53). *Crucified* implied at the hands of the Romans, because the Jewish killed condemned persons by stoning. **3:** Joseph *Caiaphas* (*see* Caiaphas), son-in-law of Annas, was appointed high priest in 26 CE by the Roman procurator Valerius Gratus. **5:** During the festival Jerusalem would have been crowded with pilgrims, many from Galilee, and the nationalistic expectations were high as they remembered Israel's deliverance from Egypt. Therefore, the chief priests and elders planned to arrest and kill Jesus on the very night of their revered festival.

6-13: In John's gospel the anointing of Jesus' feet was done by Mary in the house of Lazarus at Bethany six days before the Passover (Jn 12.1-8). Matthew and Mark (Mk 14.3-9) made no connection between this incident and the previous one. There was no reason provided for the anointing, but the head, meaning to make him Messiah, not the feet as in Luke (Lk 7.36-50), was anointed. Was this an anointing similar to the private anointing of Saul (1 Sam 10.1), or Solomon (1 Kings 1.38-39), or Jehu (2 Kings 9.4-10) that might suggest a revolt with Jesus as the leader? If so, Jesus did not accept it as such, but as an anointing for burial.

6: *Bethany,* about two miles from Jerusalem, was where Jesus spent his last nights before his arrest. The identity of this Simon remains unknown other than he must have been a cured *leper.* If he still had the disease, people would have avoided contact with him. It could have been that he had the disease and was not at home, but others in the family acted as hosts. **7:** Nothing is known about the *woman* or if she was related to Simon (Jn 12.3; Lk 7.37). To sit or to recline was the customary position around the table except during the celebration of the Passover when all the participants would recline, "as a sign of freedom, we lean to the left when we partake of the wine and the symbolic food. In antiquity, slaves ate hurriedly, standing or squatting on the ground, while royalty, nobility and the wealthy dined on couches. Now we are free and we can recline." John reported the "house was filled with the fragrance of the perfume" and that the objection to the anointing was by Judas (Jn 12.3-5). Mark reported, "There were some who said to one another in anger" (Mk 14.4), while Matthew had the *disciples* joining in the protest, *"Why this waste?"* **9:** Matthews's use of *a large sum* of *money* to describe the *ointment* was defined by Mark as "more than three hundred denarii" or nearly a year's wages for a laborer. **10:** The *good service* represented what was good and fitting under these circumstances of impending death. The same Greek words were translated "good works" in 5.16. **11:** *You always have the poor with you, but you will not always have me* was

223

not being indifferent to the needs of the poor, but to rebuke those who criticized the woman's act of devotion and loyalty. **12-13:** The woman's act won higher praise from Jesus than any other mentioned in the NT (Jn 19.40).

14-16: The obvious question is why did Judas betray Jesus? It is not known for certain, but most popular ideas are centered on Judas' disappointment that Jesus would not openly accept the role of a military Messiah against the Romans, and he wanted to force him to defend himself and assume that kingly position. Luke added "then Satan entered into Judas" (Mk 14.10-11; Lk 22.3-6). **14:** *One of the twelve;* these words do not so much identify *Judas Iscariot* but intensify the horror of the betrayal. Judas made possible a change in the priest's plans. **15:** Ex 21.32; Zech 11.12. The value of the *thirty pieces of silver* was uncertain. Matthew's quotation referred to silver shekels; at four denarii to the shekel, this was one hundred and twenty days' wages (20.2). All of the Synoptics gospels imply that Judas merely identified Jesus for those the chief priests had sent to make the arrest. There was no evidence to support he gave the Sanhedrin any information about Jesus or that he was a witness against Jesus or even appeared at the trial. *An opportunity to betray him,* but it was not to be on the Feast day (verse 2) unless their plans had changed.

The Last Supper, 26.17-29

17: *The first day of Unleavened Bread* began after 6 p.m. on Nisan 14. In the later afternoon the Passover lambs were sacrificed at the temple and *the Passover* meal was eaten after sunset when the Passover day began (Ex 12.18-27; Deut 16.5-8). All of the gospels agree that Jesus was crucified on Friday. This date became one of dispute as questions were raised if the Judeans would have allowed the trial and crucifixion to take place on such a holy day as the Passover. It was permissible by Jewish law to try and execute someone convicted to be a false prophet on the Feast day. **18:** Matthew left out some of the details about the *certain man,* who must have been a friend, and the room. He added, *"My time is near; I will keep the*

Passover at your house with my disciples (Mk 14.12-16; Lk 22.10-11; Jn 7.6; 12.23; 13.1; 17.1). **19:** *They prepared* meant they purchased, slaughtered and roasted the paschal lamb, cleaned the room of leaven, made the unleavened bread, bitter herbs and had wine available (21.6; Deut 16.5-8).

20-25 The tractate *Pesakhim,* in the *Mishnah,* conveys the main features of the Passover celebration as it has been observed from Jesus' time until today. In addition to the roast lamb, the meal included unleavened bread, bitter herbs, a sauce known as haroseth, a hard-boiled egg and at least four cups of wine. *He took his place with the twelve* as it was the custom for the father of the family to preside over the meal. The ritual involved blessing the various elements of the meal, the wine and bread, while giving explanations concerning the ritual, singing songs of praises for God delivering his people out of Egypt. The only other Jewish meal that can be compared with the Last Supper is the cult meal of the Essenes (1QSa 2.17-22) reserved for only those men who belonged in the inner circle (Mk 14.17-21; Lk 22.14, 21-23; Jn 13.21-30). There was no evidence that Jesus had been influenced by the Essenes, but both the Essenes' cult meal and the Last Supper reflected Jewish religious practices. **21:** *One of you will betray me* did not require that Jesus used any supernatural knowledge, because he could have just observed the behavior and attitude of Judas. **22:** *Surely not I, Lord?* The response to the question by the disciples, *one after another,* may have suggested that each of the disciples thought he was capable of the act of betrayal. **23:** *The one who has dipped his hand into the bowl with me* did not identify Judas, but merely that the betrayer was present within this close group. **24:** *As it is written,* but Jesus did not indicate where it was written, and this verse may have expressed later thoughts by the church (Ps 41.9; Lk 24.25; 1 Cor 15.3; Acts 17.2-3; Mt 18.7). **25:** The disciples addressed Jesus as Lord while Judas calls him *Rabbi.* Did Matthew hint that Judas' loyalty was receding? *You have said so* was a common form of assent in Palestine, and it expressed accurately the situation.

26-29: These verses followed the order established by Mark where the bread was broken first and then the cup was passed. This order was reversed by Luke, but Mark seemed to reflect the earliest tradition (Mk 14.22-25; Lk 22.15-20; 22.17; 1 Cor 10.16; 11.23-26; Mt 14.19; 15.36). **26:** *The bread* and after it was blessed he *broke it* and *gave it to the disciples,* asking them to receive from him and *eat* this symbol of his broken *body.* **27:** The cup may have been the last of the four cups, the *cup* of Elijah, and after giving *thanks* and passing it to them, and they all *drink from it.* The *Didache,* known as the *"Teaching of the Twelve Apostles,"* appeared about 100 CE provided some brief rules for Christians. *Didache,* 9.1-5, [1]"Concerning the Eucharist, celebrate it in this way: [2]First, concerning the cup: 'We give thanks to you, our Father, for the Holy Vine of David your child, which you made known to us through Jesus your child; to you be glory forever.' [3]And concerning the broken bread; 'We give thanks to you, our Father, for the life and knowledge which you have made known to us through Jesus your child; to you be glory forever. [4]As this broken bread was scattered upon the mountains, but was brought together and became one, so let your church be gathered together from the ends of the earth into your kingdom, for yours is the glory and the power, through Jesus Christ, forever.' [5]But let none eat or drink of your Eucharist except those who have been baptized in the Lord's name. For concerning this also the Lord said, 'Give not what is holy to the dogs.'" **28:** The word *"new"* was added by some ancient authorities to make it the *blood of the new covenant* (Heb 9.20; Mt 20.28; Mk 1.4; Ex 24.6-8; Jer 31.31-34; Mk 14.24). It may not have been in the original text but the idea was presented that God was making a new covenant with his people by the death of Christ. *Poured out for many* was "a ransom for many" (20.28). The words *"for the forgiveness of sins"* were added by Matthew and not present in any of the other accounts. Whether Jesus said at the Last Supper that his death provided *forgiveness of sins,* he implied it and the disciples understood him to mean that and it was therefore taught from the early days of the church. **29:** The Last Supper was not only his farewell meal with the disciples, it was a promise that the *Father's kingdom* would be established and all of God's people would be united in that messianic banquet (14.13-21).

Gethsemane, 26.30-56

30: *The hymn* would be Pss 115-118, the second part of the Hallel Psalms. *They went out to the Mount of Olives* on the east side of Jerusalem. According to the Passover regulation, after the Passover had been eaten within the walls of Jerusalem, the rest of the night was to be spent inside a larger area of Jerusalem, and while Bethany was outside this prescribed area, Gethsemane on *the Mount of Olives* was included in it.

31: On the way to Gethsemane, Jesus told the disciples *you will all become deserters* and prepared for Peter's denial by quoting the word of the LORD (*see* Lord) in Zechariah (Zech 13.7; Jn 16.32). **32:** *But after I am raised up, I will go ahead of you to Galilee* was omitted from the third century *Fayum Fragment,* "while leading them out Jesus said, 'This night you will all fall away, as it is written, 'I will strike the shepherd, and the sheep will be scattered.'" When Peter said, "Even though all, not I," Jesus answered, "before the cock crows twice, you will this day deny me three times." **34:** *Before the cock crows* was during the third watch before dawn.

36-46: *Gethsemane* meant "olive press" or "olive grove" near the Kidron Valley where there were some very old olive trees. Jesus left all but three disciples at the edge of the grove, and he *began to be grieved and agitated.* **38:** The gospel writers rarely tried to describe Jesus' emotions, but here they revealed some strong feelings at the prospect of torture, rejection and *death* (Mk 14.32; Lk 22.40-46; Jn 12.27; Heb 5.7-8; Ps 42.6). Matthew and Mark say, *"I am"* which in the Greek meant literally "My soul is deeply grieved." **39:** Some question what Jesus prayed since he was alone. Matthew and Luke put little distance between Jesus and the three disciples and they could have heard, if they were awake. Mark (Mk 14.36) gave the Aramaic word Jesus used, "Abba, Father" asking if God's plan could be realized and his own work finished without suffering death (Ezek

23.31-34; Jn 18.11; Mt 22.20). Jesus did not desire death but accepted God's will even including death. *Cup* was a reference to the cup of suffering (20.22). It was possible that Jesus at Gethsemane faced the same temptations he encountered in the wilderness, where again he faced self-interest in contrast to God's will. Luke reported that "an angel from heaven appeared to him and gave him strength" as in the wilderness (Mt 4.11; Mk 1.13). **41:** The disciples were warned to stay awake and pray twice in Luke, but three times in Matthew and Mark. These warnings may have been to watch for those that might approach Jesus, but more likely it was to give support to Jesus in a *time of trial,* when one's best intentions may give way. **42-44:** Matthew provided the words that Jesus prayed again, *"My Father, if this cannot pass unless I drink it, your will be done* (26.39) then *for the third time* he agreed with Mark's words, "and prayed, *saying the same words"* (Mk 14.39) **45:** *The hour* of Jesus' arrest, trial and crucifixion *is at hand* (26.18n; Jn 12.23; 13.1; 17.1). **46:** Jesus must have seen Judas and the entire party with him, but in sorrow and disappointment he only spoke of Judas, *my betrayer is at hand.*

    47-56: Mk 14.43-52; Lk 22.47-53; Jn 18.2-11. **47:** *One of the twelve* only underscored the tragedy of being betrayed by a chosen follower of Jesus. *A large crowd with swords and clubs* as this crowd from the *chief priests and elders* evidently expected to encounter considerable resistance by Jesus and his followers. John identified those making the arrest as both Roman soldiers and the Jewish temple police (Jn 18.3). **48:** *The one I will kiss is the man* to make sure that they arrested the right individual. **50:** *Friend* was a term to mean "comrade" (11.16; 20.13; 22.12). The Synoptic Gospels did not report Judas' movements on this night (cf Jn 13.30; 18.3). In the Greek, *"Do what you are here to do"* could mean, "What are you here for?" or "Is this why you have come?" **51:** *One* of Jesus' disciples, identified in John as Peter and the slave as Malchus (Jn 18.10-11) *struck the slave of the high priest, cutting off his ear.* Luke said it was the "right ear" and that Jesus touched the ear and healed him, saying "No more of this," as fighting to defend Jesus would be self-defeating (Lk 22.50). **52:** Verses 52-54 were only found in Matthew (Gen 9.6; Rev 13.10). **53:**

Twelve legions would be seventy-two thousand angels. **54:** Jesus acted not in weakness but in strength placing his faith in God and his promise (4.6). The scripture referred to was probably Isaiah, "He was despised and rejected by others; a man of suffering and acquainted with infirmity" (Isa 53.5), where the Servants' vicarious suffering restored all people of God (Mt 8.17; 1 Pet 2.24-25). **55:** *Day after day* seemed to support the idea that Jesus taught in Jerusalem for a longer period than was presented in the Synoptic Gospels (see notes on Mt 21; Lk 19.47; Jn 18.19-21). **56:** Matthew continued with his emphasis, *that the scriptures of the prophets may be fulfilled,* while Luke presented this was the time of evil like the "power of darkness" (Lk 22.53). Mark added the account of a youth that ran off naked after they caught his linen cloth. Many identify this youth as Mark who added his own signature to the event. Others suggested it made a connection with the OT (Am 2.16), and that naked did not mean without any clothing, but only wearing an undergarment or tunic (Jn 21.7). **28:** Matthew closed this section with, *"then all the disciples deserted him and fled,"* but at least Peter did not go very far, because he followed at a distance to the courtyard of the high priest.

Jesus before Caiaphas, 26.57-75

57: The Sanhedrin (Jn 11.47) was the Jewish Supreme Court comprising seventy priests, scribes and elders, presided over by *the high priest.* While the Sanhedrin could condemn no one to death at night, this was not a formal trial but an attempt to find a serious charge that would enable them to put him to death. **58:** Peter was often considered weak but he had the courage to follow *at a distance to the courtyard of the high priest,* even to the point of going in and sitting *with the guards* to see what would happen. **59-60:** At least two witnesses who agreed were required by Numbers (Num 35.30) and Deuteronomy (Deut 19.15) (cf Mt 18.16; Mk 14.55) *to put* Jesus *to death. But they found none.* **61:** Jesus may have said that the temple would be destroyed, but not that he would destroy it and rebuild it in three days (24.2; 27.40; Acts 6.14; Jn 2.19). **62:** Jesus was invited by *the high priest* to defend himself, concerning the charge of destroying the temple. **63:** When Jesus remained silent, concerning the false charge, *the high priest* put him *under oath* and asked him, are you *the Messiah, the Son of God* (27.11; Jn 18.33)? **64:** *You have said so* were similar to the words Jesus told Judas (26.25). Mark had Jesus respond to this question with "I am" (Mk 14.62). Then without either using the title Messiah or the Son of God, Jesus referred to *the Son of Man seated at the right hand of Power* next to God, as *coming* to establish God's kingdom (16.28; Dan 7.13; Ps 110.1). **65:** *The high priest tore his clothes* but he was pleased because Jesus' response was considered *blasphemy.* **66:** In the rabbinic tradition, the only blasphemy punishable by death was that of cursing God by name, pronouncing the name of "YHVH" (Num 14.6; Acts 14.14; Lev 24.16). Here the only thing that Jesus said that could be considered blasphemy was in Mark he said, "I am." The rest of the Sanhedrin agreed with the high priest, *"he deserves death,"* but they did not have the legal right to carry out the sentence. **68:** Expressing their hate and contempt the Sanhedrin mocked Jesus, *they spat in his face, and struck him* and asked him to *prophesy.* In Mark and Luke Jesus was blindfolded, in Matthew the blindfold was omitted (Mk 14.65; Lk 22.64).

69-73: Peter spoke with a Galilean accent setting him apart from the Judeans (Acts 2.7). The oddities of the Galilean speech patterns and dress were ridiculed in the Talmud. *You are also one of them* was this regarding Judas or another disciple (Jn 18.15)? Or was it challenging Peter's courage to be present at the courtyard? With repeated curses and oaths, Peter denied that he even knew Jesus. **75:** *The cock crows* and it reminded Peter of what Jesus told him and his inability to remain faithful in the face of adversity (cf v 34), *and he went out and wept bitterly,* in bitter agony.

Chapter 26 Study Guide

1. Why do you think the woman anointed Jesus at the house of Simon the leper?
2. Why did Judas betray Jesus to the chief priests?
3. What is your understanding of Jesus' prayer in Gethsemane, "My Father, if it is possible, let this cup pass from me; yet not what I want but what you want"?
4. What were the Sanhedrin and the high priest expecting to receive from Jesus?
5. What charge was made against Jesus that deserved his death?

Chapter 27
Jesus before Pilate, 27.1-26

Matthew. When morning came, all the chief priests and the elders of the people conferred together against Jesus in order to bring about his death. [2]They bound him, led him away, and handed him over to Pilate the governor.

(**M**)([3]When Judas, his betrayer, saw that Jesus[a] was condemned, he repented and brought back the thirty pieces of silver to the chief priests and the elders. [4]He said,

Judas Iscariot. "I have sinned by betraying innocent[b] blood."

Matthew. But they said,

Chief priests and Elders. "What is that to us? See to it yourself."

Matthew. [5]Throwing down the pieces of silver in the temple, he departed; and he went and hanged himself. [6]But the chief priests, taking the pieces of silver, said,

---

[a] Gk *he*
[b] Other ancient authorities read *righteous*

Chief priests and Elders. "It is not lawful to put them into the treasury, since they are blood money."

Matthew. [7]After conferring together, they used them to buy the potter's field as a place to bury foreigners. [8]For this reason that field has been called the Field of Blood to this day. [9]Then was fulfilled what had been spoken through the prophet Jeremiah,[c]

Zechariah. "And they took[d]the thirty pieces of silver, the price of the one on whom a price had been set,[e] on whom some of the people of Israel had set a price, [10]and they gave[f] them for the potter's field, as the Lord commanded me." [g])

Matthew. [11]Now Jesus stood before the governor; and the governor asked him,

Pilate. "Are you the King of the Jews?"

Matthew. Jesus said,

Jesus. "You say so."

Matthew. [12]But when he was accused by the chief priests and elders, he did not answer. [13]Then Pilate said to him,

Pilate. "Do you not hear how many accusations they make against you?"

Matthew. [14]But he gave him no answer, not even to a single charge, so that the governor was greatly amazed.
[15]Now at the festival the governor was accustomed to release a prisoner for the crowd, anyone whom they wanted. [16]At that time they

---

[c] Other ancient authorities read *Zechariah* or *Isaiah*

[d] Or *I took*

[e] Or *the price of the precious One*

[f] Other ancient authorities read *I gave*

[g] Zech 11.12-13; Jer 32.6-9

had a notorious prisoner, called Jesus[h] Barabbas. **(M)**(¹⁷So after they had gathered,) Pilate said to them,

Pilate. "Whom do you want me to release for you, Jesus[i] Barabbas or Jesus who is called the Messiah?"[j]

Matthew. ¹⁸For he realized that it was out of jealousy that they had handed him over. **(M)**(¹⁹While he was sitting on the judgment seat, his wife sent word to him,

Pilate's wife. "Have nothing to do with that innocent man, for today I have suffered a great deal because of a dream about him.")

Matthew. ²⁰Now the chief priests and the elders persuaded the crowds to ask for Barabbas and to have Jesus killed. ²¹The governor again said to them,

Pilate. "Which of the two do you want me to release for you?"

Matthew. (M)(And they said,

Crowd. "Barabbas."

Matthew. ²²Pilate said to them,)

Pilate. "Then what should I do with Jesus who is called the Messiah?"[k]

Matthew. All of them said,

Crowd. "Let him be crucified!"

Matthew. ²³Then he asked,

---

^h Other ancient authorities lack *Jesus*
ⁱ Other ancient authorities lack *Jesus*
^j Or *the Christ*
^k Or *the Christ*

Pilate. "Why, what evil has he done?"

Matthew. But they shouted all the more,

Crowd. "Let him be crucified!"

Matthew. (M)([24]So when Pilate saw that he could do nothing, but rather that a riot was beginning, he took some water and washed his hands before the crowd, saying,

Pilate. "I am innocent of this man's blood;[l] see to it yourselves."

Matthew. Then the people as a whole answered,

Crowd. [25]"His blood be on us and on our children!"**)**

Matthew. [26]So he released Barabbas for them; and after flogging Jesus, he handed him over to be crucified.

The crucifixion, 27.27-44

Matthew. [27]Then the soldiers **(M)(**of the governor**)** took Jesus into the governor's headquarters,[m] and they gathered the whole cohort around him. **(M)(**[28]They stripped him**)** and put a scarlet robe on him, [29]and after twisting some thorns into a crown, they put it on his head. **(M)** **(**They put a reed in his right hand**)** and knelt before him and mocked him, saying,

Soldiers. "Hail, King of the Jews!"

Matthew. [30]They spat on him, and took the reed and struck him on the head. [31]After mocking him, they stripped him of the robe and put his own clothes on him. Then they led him away to crucify him.

---

[l] Other ancient authorities read *this righteous blood*, or *this righteous man's blood*
[m] Gk *the praetorium*

[32]As they went out, they came upon a man from Cyrene named Simon; they compelled this man to carry his cross. [33]And when they came to a place called Golgotha (which means Place of a Skull), [34]they offered him wine to drink, mixed with gall; but when he tasted it, he would not drink it. [35]And when they had crucified him, they divided his clothes among themselves by casting lots;[n] [36]then they sat down there and kept watch over him. [37]Over his head they put the charge against him, which read,

Charge against Jesus. "This is Jesus, the King of the Jews."

Matthew. [38]Then two bandits were crucified with him, one on his right and one on his left. [39]Those who passed by derided[o] him, shaking their heads [40]and saying,

Bystanders. "You who would destroy the temple and build it in three days, save yourself! If you are the Son of God, come down from the cross."

Matthew. [41]In the same way the chief priests also, along with the scribes and elders, were mocking him, saying,

Chief priests, Scribes and Elders. [42]"He saved others; he cannot save himself.[p] He is the King of Israel; let him come down from the cross now, and we will believe in him. [43]He trusts in God; let God deliver him now, if he wants to; for he said,

Jesus. 'I am God's Son.'"

Matthew. [44]The bandits who were crucified with him also taunted him in the same way.

---

[n] Other ancient authorities add *in order that what had been spoken through the prophet might be fulfilled, "They divided my clothes among themselves, and for my clothing they cast lots."*

[o] Or *blasphemed*

[p] Or *is he unable to save himself?*

The death of Jesus, 27.45-66

Matthew. ⁴⁵From noon on, darkness came over the whole land^q until three in the afternoon. ⁴⁶And about three o'clock Jesus cried with a loud voice,

Jesus. "Eli, Eli, lema sabachthani?"

Matthew. that is,

Jesus. "My God, my God, why have you forsaken me?" ^r

Matthew. ⁴⁷When some of the bystanders heard it, they said,

Bystanders. "This man is calling for Elijah."

Matthew. ⁴⁸At once one of them ran and got a sponge, filled it with sour wine, put it on a stick, and gave it to him to drink. ⁴⁹But the others said,

Bystanders. "Wait, let us see whether Elijah will come to save him."^s

Matthew. ⁵⁰Then Jesus cried again with a loud voice and breathed his last.^t ⁵¹At that moment the curtain of the temple was torn in two, from top to bottom. The earth shook, and the rocks were split. ⁵²The tombs also were opened, and many bodies of the saints who had fallen asleep were raised. ⁵³After his resurrection they came out of the tombs and entered the holy city and appeared to many. ⁵⁴Now when the centurion and those with him, who were keeping watch over Jesus, saw the earthquake and what took place, they were terrified and said,

---

q   Or *earth*
r   Ps 22.1
s   Other ancient authorities add *And another took a spear and pierced his side, and out came water and blood*
t   Or *gave up his spirit*

Centurion and Soldiers. "Truly this man was God's Son!"[u]

Matthew. [55]Many women were also there, looking on from a distance; they had followed Jesus from Galilee and had provided for him. [56]Among them were Mary Magdalene, and Mary the mother of James and Joseph, and the mother of the sons of Zebedee.

[57]When it was evening, there came a rich man from Arimathea, named Joseph, who was also a disciple of Jesus. [58]He went to Pilate and asked for the body of Jesus; then Pilate ordered it to be given to him. [59]So Joseph took the body and wrapped it in a clean linen cloth [60]and laid it in his own new tomb, which he had hewn in the rock. He then rolled a great stone to the door of the tomb and went away. [61]Mary Magdalene and the other Mary were there, sitting opposite the tomb.

[62]The next day, that is, after the day of Preparation, the chief priests and the Pharisees gathered before Pilate [63]and said,

Chief priests and Pharisees. "Sir, we remember what that impostor said while he was still alive,

Jesus. 'After three days I will rise again.'

Chief priests and Pharisees. [64]Therefore command the tomb to be made secure until the third day; otherwise his disciples may go and steal him away, and tell the people,

Disciples. 'He has been raised from the dead,'

Chief priests and Pharisees. and the last deception would be worse than the first."

Matthew. [65]Pilate said to them,

---

[u] Or *a son of God*

Pilate. "You have a guard[v] of soldiers; go, make it as secure as you can."[w]

Matthew. [66]So they went with the guard and made the tomb secure by sealing the stone.

Chapter 27 Notes
Jesus before Pilate, 27.1-26

1-2: Matthew and Mark reported a hearing at night by the Sanhedrin and the high priest to establish a charge and to obtain the proper witnesses (Mk 15.1; Lk 23.1; Jn 18.28-32). Jewish law required that the Sanhedrin take formal action by daylight and apparently, Matthew (Mt 26.57-68) described a pre-dawn hearing. Pilate was appointed Procurator of the Providence of Judea by Tiberius in 26 CE and was replaced in 36 CE. Pilate was not always on the best terms with the Jewish people. On one occasion, he brought troops into Jerusalem without removing their insignia that bore the emperor's picture. And another time, he used temple funds to construct an aqueduct.

3-10: The details of Judas' death were obscure. Each account connected him in death with a cemetery, the potter's field, for foreigners, not paupers, who died in Jerusalem. The plot of land came to be known as Akeldama, which in Aramaic meant "field of blood" (Acts 1.16-20). Judas repented (changed his mind) about what he had done, no matter what the purpose might have been, he had betrayed *innocent blood.* He received no help from the chief priests who were not interested in justice, *"what is that to us?"* Judas threw down the money, went out and hung himself (Acts 1.16-20). To the Jewish people suicide was the same as murder. **6:** See Deuteronomy (Deut 23.18) for scruples about ill-gotten gains for sacred purposes. **9-10:** Again, the formula so often used by Matthew was expressed, *"Then was fulfilled..."* However, the passage quoted was not from Jeremiah,

---

v Or *Take a guard*
w Gk *you know how*

but was freely interpreted from Zechariah, "I then said to them, 'If it seems right to you, give me my wages; but if not, keep them.' So they weighed out as my wages thirty shekels of silver" (Zech 11.12-13). The account in Jeremiah was about the potter who was working clay at his wheel (Jer 18.1-3) and later in Jeremiah where he purchased a field at Anathoth, for the right of redemption (Jer 32.6-15). *As the Lord commanded* (*see* LORD) was used by the church to stress that even in the dark events God's purpose was at work.

11-14: Mk 15.2-5; Lk 23.2-5; Jn 18.29-19.16. **14:** The governor was *greatly amazed* at Jesus' reaction, because most individuals, guilty or not, protested their innocence (Lk 23.9; Mt 26.62; Mk 14.60; 1 Tim 6.13).

15-26: To appease the crowd during a time of national enthusiasm, such as during a festival, the Romans followed a custom of the ancient world and permitted them to choose a prisoner to be released (Mk 15.6-15; Lk 23.18-25; Jn 18.38-40; 19.4-16). **19:** This verse was found only in Matthew and while Pilate's wife sent him a message, relating that she had a disturbing dream about the innocence of Jesus, the chief priests and elders were convincing the crowd to ask for *Barabbas and to have Jesus killed.* **21:** *Which of the two* and they choose Barabbas and called for the crucifixion of Jesus (Acts 3.13-14).

24: The ceremonial hand washing by Pilate was a Jewish custom rather than a Roman one and only found in Matthew (Deut 21.6-9; Ps 26.6). **25:** A lot of harm has been done by quoting this verse as if the entire Jewish nation was responsible for Jesus' death (Acts 5.28; Josh 2.19). **26:** *Flogging* with a multi-thronged whip ordinarily preceded execution.

The crucifixion, 27.27-44

27-31: Mk 15.16-20; Jn 19.1-3. **27:** *Soldiers of the governor* were those that accompanied the governor from Caesarea to Jerusalem and assisted in keeping order during the Feast. The governor's headquarters was the official residence of the governor. *The whole cohort* at full strength numbered about five thousand men. **28:** *A* *scarlet robe* was probably a soldier's scarlet mantle, an imitation of an imperial robe. **29:** *Twisting some thorns into a crown* was similar to the garland awarded to the victor in battle or at the games. It was used here in mockery of a royal crown, and a *reed in his right hand* might correspond to a king's scepter. **31:** Probably the soldier wanted his scarlet robe back, since the Roman soldiers had to purchase their own uniforms. Therefore, they *stripped him of his robe and put his own clothes on him* before they *led him away to crucify him.*

32-34: John said that Jesus carried his own cross, and this may have been so for a short distance (Jn 19.17). When they were outside the city and met Simon of Cyrene, *they compelled* him *to carry* Jesus' cross, perhaps because Jesus was weak from the flogging. Mark identified Simon of Cyrene as the father of Alexander and Rufus (Mk 15.21). The condemned individual did not carry the entire cross, but only the cross beam because the upright beam was usually standing ready to receive it (Mk 15.21; Lk 23.26, 33-43; Jn 19.17-24). The procession included Jesus, two other prisoners, a centurion, and a few soldiers. *Golgotha* in Aramaic meant *skull* or head that was located outside of the second wall of Jerusalem. **34:** *Gall,* any bitter liquid, possibly myrrh of Mark (Mk 15.23) was *mixed with wine* to ease the pain of crucifixion (Ps 49.4-21). It remains unclear if this mixture was the custom, requested by someone, or was an act of kindness. He *tasted it,* and when he realized what it was, *would not drink it,* but choose to endure the pain. Only Luke has the words of forgiveness by Jesus, "Father, forgive them, for they do not know what they are doing" (Lk 23.34). **35:** When they *crucified him* meant Jesus was probably laid down upon the cross beam, his hands nailed to each end and then the cross beam with Jesus on it was lifted and fixed to the upright beam. Perhaps the feet were then nailed to the upright beam. *They divided his clothes* as was the Roman custom. *His clothes* were mainly: head dress, cloak or outer garment; belt; shoes; tunic or inner garment. Since the soldier had already taken his robe back (v 31), contrary to public belief today it was not to be won by *casting lots.* The tunic was seamless like that of the high priest, which was symbolic of the controversy over Jesus as the high priest (Jn

19.23n; Ps 22.18) and was of some value. **36:** Only Matthew included the soldiers *sat down there and kept watch over him* probably to prevent anyone from rescuing him. **37:** It was a Roman custom to put a titulus around the neck of the criminal indicating the offense. Since the Romans recognized the ruling Herods, it implied that Jesus was alleged to be a pretender and revolutionary, and this was for the benefit of the pilgrims from many parts of the world. Jesus was crucified on the charge of having claimed to be the Messiah, a king (Jn 19.12-16).

38: *Two bandits* were identified in a later tradition as Zoatham and Camma. **39:** *Shaking their heads* was an Oriental gesture of scorn as in the Psalms, "All who see me mock at me; they make mouths at me, they shake their heads" (Pss 22.7; 109.25). **40:** *If you are the Son of God* was added by Matthew here and in verse 46 (26.61; Acts 6.14; Jn 2.19). **42-43:** The taunts stressed religious aspects of Jesus' works and words. *Israel* (rather than *the Jews,* v 37) referred to the religious community rather than the political state. **43:** The chief priests and elders mocked Jesus, *"He trusts in God"* from Psalms (Ps 22.8) where it states, "Commit your cause to the Lord; let him deliver – let him rescue the one in whom he delights", and "for if the righteous man is God's child, he will help him, and will deliver him from the hand of his adversaries" (Wis of Sol 2.18). If Jesus was the King of Israel, let him come down from the cross, and we will believe in him?

The death of Jesus, 27.45-66

45-51: (*Gospel of Peter,* 5.15-20), "Now it was noon, and darkness covered over all Judea, and they were afraid and distressed for fear the sun had set while Jesus was still alive. For it is written for them that the sun should not set upon one put to death. And one of them said, 'Give him gall with vinegar to drink.' And they mixed them and gave it to him. And they fulfilled all things and brought their sins to an end upon their own heads. And many went about with lamps, supposing it was night, and they went to bed. And the Lord cried out,

'My power, my power, you have forsaken me!' and saying this Jesus was taken up. In the same hour the curtain of the temple of Jerusalem was torn in two." **46:** *Eli, Eli, lema sabachthani,* was quoted from Psalms (Ps 22.1). **47:** *Some bystanders* (*see* Bystanders) may have been Judeans who knew about Elijah. Elijah (similar in sound to *Eli*) was expected to usher in the final period (Mal 4.5-6; Mk 15.35). **48:** The motive in offering the *sour wine* may have been to revive him and hence prolong the ordeal (Ps 69.21). **51:** *The curtain of the temple* before the Holy of Holies *was torn in two, from top to bottom.* By his death Jesus opened direct access to God for the people (Heb 9.8; 10.19; Ex 26.31-35; Mt 28.2; Mk 15.38). *Gospel of the Nazaraeans,* (in Jerome, *Letter,* 120 *to Hedibia* and *Commentary on Matthew,* 27.51), "Salome, and the women who followed Jesus from Galilee seeing Jesus who had been crucified. It was the day of Preparation, that is, the day before the sabbath, a man named Joseph of Erinmathaias, a city of Judea. Being a disciple of Jesus, he was good and righteous, but had been condemned secretly because of the fear of the Jews, and he looked for the kingdom of God. He had not consented to the purpose". **52-53:** These verses were only found in Matthew. *Bodies of the saints* those honored dead within the Jewish tradition *were raised. After his resurrection* implied a later addition to preserve the truth that Christ was the first to be raised (1 Cor 15.20). **54:** The words, *"Truly this man was God's Son"* for the Roman centurion might have implied the son of a pagan god, but for Matthew it was an expression of faith that Christians can hear with deep understanding. **56:** *James* was possibly the James of Mt 10.3; Lk 24.10; Acts 1.13.

57-61: Jesus died shortly after 3 p.m. on Friday and the sabbath would begin at sundown, and leaving the body of an executed criminal hang overnight was forbidden (Deut 21.23; Mk 15.42-47; Lk 23.50-56; Jn 19.38-42; Acts 13.29). *Joseph of Arimathea* who lived a little over twenty miles north-west of Jerusalem had moved to Jerusalem and being a *rich man* purchased his own *tomb, which he had hewn in the rock.* (*Gospel of Peter,* 2.3-5a), "Joseph, the friend of Pilate and of the Lord, was standing there; and knowing that they were about to crucify Jesus, he went to Pilate and asked for the body of the Lord for burial. And Pilate sent word to Herod and asked for the body. And Herod responded, 'Brother Pilate, even if no one asked for the body, we would bury it, since it is almost the sabbath. For it is written in the law, 'Let not the sun set on one who has been put to death.'" (*Gospel of Peter,* 6.21-24), "And then they drew out the nails from the hands of the Lord, and laid the body upon the earth. And the whole earth was shaken, and a great fear arose. Then the sun shone and it was found to be the ninth hour. The Jews rejoiced and gave Jesus' body to Joseph, to bury it, because he had seen all the good things that Jesus had done. And Joseph took the body of the Lord, and washed it, and wrapped it in a linen shroud and brought it to his own tomb, called the garden of Joseph." **58:** Ancient rulers sometimes gave the body of an executed criminal to friends for burial. **60:** Joseph rolled *a great stone* in place, perhaps with the help of his servants as there was no hint of any disciples being there (Jn 19.39; Mk 16.3-5; Acts 13.29). **61:** The two Marys were watching and later they could tell of the burial (27.56).

62-66: These verses were only found in Matthew and dealt with Pilate's relationship with Jesus. It centered on the Jewish people responding to the Christians claim that the empty tomb was proof of the resurrection because the disciples had stolen the body. Matthew provided the rebuttal because the tomb was watched, but the guards were bribed to say the body was stolen. **62:** *Next day* meant the sabbath (Mk 15.42). **65:** *You have a guard,* permission to use the temple police, under the authority of the Sanhedrin; or "Take a guard," i.e. granting them a squad of Roman soldiers.

Chapter 27 Study Guide

1. What do you make that Judas repented, returned the money and said, "I have sinned by betraying innocent blood"?
2. What role did Pilate play in the trial of Jesus? Could he have done more to stop the crucifixion?
3. Who choose Barabbas over Jesus? Why?

4. What does Jesus being crucified mean to you?
5. Explain the curtain in the temple being torn in two, from the top to the bottom.

Chapter 28
The first Easter, 28.1-10
(Mk 16.1-8; Lk 24.1-11; Jn 20.1-10)

Matthew. After the sabbath, as the first day of the week was dawning, Mary Magdalene and the other Mary went to see the tomb. [2]And suddenly there was a great earthquake; for an angel of the Lord, descending from heaven, came and rolled back the stone and sat on it. [3]His appearance was like lightning, and his clothing white as snow. [4]For fear of him the guards shook and became like dead men. [5]But the angel said to the women,

Angel. "Do not be afraid; I know that you are looking for Jesus who was crucified. [6]He is not here; for he has been raised, as he said. Come, see the place where he[a] lay. [7]Then go quickly and tell his disciples,

Mary Magdalene and Mary. 'He has been raised from the dead,[b] and indeed he is going ahead of you to Galilee; there you will see him.'

Angel. This is my message for you."

Matthew. [8]So they left the tomb quickly with fear and great joy, and ran to tell his disciples. [9]Suddenly Jesus met them and said,

Jesus. "Greetings!"

Matthew. And they came to him, took hold of his feet, and worshiped him. [10]Then Jesus said to them,

---

[a] Other ancient authorities read *the Lord*
[b] Other ancient authorities lack *from the dead*

Jesus. "Do not be afraid; go and tell my brothers to go to Galilee; there they will see me."

Bribing the guard, 28.11-15

Matthew. [11]While they were going, some of the guard went into the city and told the chief priests everything that had happened. [12]After the priests[c] had assembled with the elders, they devised a plan to give a large sum of money to the soldiers, [13]telling them,

Chief priests. "You must say,

Soldiers. 'His disciples came by night and stole him away while we were asleep.'

Chief priests. [14]If this comes to the governor's ears, we will satisfy him and keep you out of trouble."

Matthew. [15]So they took the money and did as they were directed. And this story is still told among the Jews to this day.

Jesus' commission to his disciples, 28.16-20

Matthew. [16]Now the eleven disciples went to Galilee, to the mountain to which Jesus had directed them. [17]When they saw him, they worshiped him; but some doubted. [18]And Jesus came and said to them,

Jesus. "All authority in heaven and on earth has been given to me. [19]Go therefore and make disciples of all nations, baptizing them in the name of the Father and of the Son and of the Holy Spirit, [20]and teaching them to obey everything that I have commanded you. And remember, I am with you always, to the end of the age."[d]

---

[c] Gk *they*
[d] Other ancient authorities add *Amen*

Chapter 28 Notes
The first Easter, 28.1-10

1: *After the sabbath, as the first day of the week,* Sunday *was dawning.* Matthew omitted Mark's statement of the women's intention to anoint the body (Mk 16.1) probably because the guards would have prevented this from happening. **2-3:** Matthew was the only gospel writer to introduce another *earthquake,* but the *stone* was *rolled back* by the *angel of the Lord,* (*see* Angel of the LORD) who *sat on it,* not the earthquake. The stone was rolled away not so Jesus might come out as Lazarus (Jn 11.43-44), but for the women to enter. **3:** The angel's appearance was as *lightning* (Dan 10.6). **4-5:** A blind, paralyzing fear seized the Roman guards, while the angel and Jesus told the women to not be afraid (vs 5, 10). **6:** *He is not here, for he has been raised, as he said* or as he predicted (16.21; 17.23; 20.19; Lk 24.6-7). The women in response to their love and devotion were invited to *"come, see the place where he"* was buried and be fully convinced that what he promised had really happened. **7:** Then they were to *go quickly* and tell the eleven what they have seen, that *he has been raised from the dead, and indeed he is going ahead of you to Galilee; there you will see him.* After saying this, the angel said, *"This is my message for you"* as if he had completed his mission (26.32; 28.16; Jn 21.1-23; 1 Cor 15.3-4, 12, 20). **8:** With mixed feelings of fear and joy, the women *ran to tell his disciples* (Cf Lk 24.9, 22-23). The sequence of events cannot be worked out as each account was a separate summary of early Christian testimony to the fact of Jesus' resurrection. **9-10:** Only in Matthew, did Jesus appear to the women and echo the angel's words. He must have appeared in human form as they recognized him immediately and bowing down wanted to *hold* on to *his feet and worship him* (Jn 20.14-18). *My brothers* were words that conveyed that the disciples were still tied up in the bonds of brotherhood with Jesus.

Bribing the guard, 28.11-15

11-15: Found only in Matthew, *some of the guard,* after recovering from their paralyzing terror, *went into the city and told the chief priest everything that happened* (27.62-66). They called for a full meeting of the Sanhedrin to prepare a report including plans of a sum *large* enough to persuade *the soldiers* to invent a story contrary to the truth, at their own peril. **14:** *We will satisfy him,* in the same way they had persuaded other soldiers by bribes. **15:** *This day* was the time when the gospel of Matthew was written. (*Gospel of Peter,* 11.45-49), "When those who were with the centurion saw what had happened, they hurried to Pilate at night, leaving the tomb that they were guarding. And being greatly disturbed, they reported everything they had seen, saying, 'Truly this one was a (the) son of God.' Pilate answered, 'I am free from the blood of the son of God, but this seemed good to you.' And they all went and asked him and begged him to order the centurion and the soldiers to tell no one what they had seen. 'For it is better,' they said, 'to commit the greatest sin before God than to fall into the hands of the Jews and be stoned.' Then Pilate commanded the centurion and the soldiers to say nothing."

Jesus' commission to his disciples, 28.16-20

16: Only Matthew reported the *disciples went to Galilee* where Jesus first appeared to the Eleven. *To the mountain* may have meant the mountain where the Sermon on the Mount was delivered (Lk24.11; Jn 21.1-23; 1 Cor 15.5-6). **17:** *When they saw him,* they recognized him, fell down and *worshipped him* that in the Greek literally means "prostrated themselves in worship"; they had not done this before the crucifixion. *But some doubted* may be regarding the fact that not all of the disciples had perfect faith (Lk 16.31). **18:** (11.27; Lk 10.22; Phil 2.9; Eph 1.20-22). *All authority,* cf Dan 7.14. **19:** *Go therefore and make disciples of all nations,* the mission to the Israelites (10.5; 15.24) was now to become a universal mission (Mk 16.15; Lk 24.27; Acts 1.8). Questions arise about the command to *baptize in the name of the*

Father and the Son and the Holy Spirit, language that reflected the Trinity, a later development by Tertullian (c 160-220 CE) who was the first Latin writer to use the term "Trinity." He wrote his Trinitarian formula after becoming a Montanist; his ideas were at first rejected as heresy by the church at large, but were later accepted as Christian orthodoxy. In the Hebrew, *in the name of,* meant in the possession and protection of someone (Ps 124.8). **20:** *Teaching them to obey everything that I have commanded you,* or educate them on what it means to be a follower of Christ. The gospel ended with a promise, *I am with you always, to the end of this age* (18.20; Acts 18.10). We come to Christ, we grow in Christ and we seek to serve others in the name of Christ.

Chapter 28 Study Guide

1. Explain the difference between Matthew and Luke's accounts of the resurrection.
2. What is the significance of the resurrection for you?
3. Why did Matthew include the bribing of the guard?
4. Why should the disciples "go to Galilee"?
5. What does the "Great Commission" mean to you?

Sources in Matthew

In both the cast and the notes following the Bible in Dialogue text, reference was made to several church fathers, books and manuscripts. Many of the sources, while taken for granted by many biblical scholars remain unknown to those sitting in the pews on Sunday morning, primarily because of a lack of exposure to them. Therefore, it seemed important to provide some historical information about these sources.

Acts of Philip. Fragments of this fourth century gnostic work were discovered with what appears to be later revisions.

Didache. The *Didache,* otherwise known as the *"Teaching of the Twelve Apostles"* first appeared *ca* 100-110 CE as a brief formulation of the rules of conduct Christians should observe.

Egerton Papyrus 2. The Egerton Papyrus, a group of fragments of an unknown gospel found in Egypt, were sold to the British Museum in 1934. The fragments were dated about the end of the second century CE, but the date of composition was perhaps 50-100 CE. It was one of the oldest known fragments of any gospel, or any codex. It was also called the *Unknown gospel,* since no ancient source referred to it.

Epiphanius of Salamis. Epiphanius was born in Palestine between 310 and 320 CE. He became an ascetic and later bishop of Salamis, the capital of Cyprus, in 367. He spent his life hunting heretics and died at sea on his way from Constantinople to Cyprus in 403. He wrote the *Ancoratus,* which was a defense of Christian doctrine, in 373; and, most importantly, the *Against Heresies,* his work against heresies - between 374 and 377. In this, he tracked down eighty heresies, twenty of which preceded the time of Christ, and the first of which was barbarism from Adam to the flood.

Fayum Fragment. This fragment identified as *Fayum Fragment,* from the third century contained words similar to Mark 14.27-30, except for verse 28. It was discovered by G. Brickell in Vienna in 1885, among the collection of Archduke Rainer. Scholars debated if the fragment came from a text of the gospel or if it was a homiletical paraphrase of Mark 14.27-30.

Gospel according to the Ebionites. This *Gospel according to the Ebionites*, written in Greek during the first half of the second century, may have been an abridged and altered form of the gospel of Matthew. The Ebionites, a Jewish Christian sect, who denied the virgin birth and believed that Jesus' sonship to God rested entirely on the union of the Holy Spirit with Jesus made at his baptism, used this gospel. The seven extant fragments of the work were found in Epiphanius, *Against Heresies* XXX. 13-22.

Gospel according to the Hebrews. The *Gospel according to the Hebrews,* written in the first half of the second century, was for Greek speaking Jewish Christians. It probably originated in Egypt, one reason for believing that was its main witnesses are the Alexandrians, Clement and Origen. The gospel was apparently not a development from any of the four canonical gospels. It contained traditions of Jesus' pre-existence and his coming into the world.

Gospel of the Naassenes. Hippolytus in Book V of his *Refutation of All Heresies* quoted the *Gospel of the Naassenes.* The origin of the Naassenes, or Ophites, i.e., Serpent-Worshipers, remains unknown. However, since they practiced heathen rites, they were heretics by Hippolytus.

Gospel of the Nazaraeans. The *Gospel of the Nazaraeans* appeared in the first half of the second century in Syrian and Jewish Christian circles. It was apparently an Aramaic translation of a Greek form of the Gospel of Matthew. It was first quoted by Hegesippus *ca* 180, and probably originated in Syria.

Gospel of Peter. Coming from the middle of the second century, the *Gospel of Peter* was a development in a Gnostic direction of the four canonical gospels. It was not, however, a full-blown Gnostic work. It was known by reference only (since there were no extant quotations from it) until the winter of 1886-87 when a fragment, coming from the eighth or ninth century, was found at Akhmim in Upper Egypt. The gospel began with Pilate's washing of his hands and ended with a unique description of Jesus' resurrection.

Gospel of Thomas. The *Gospel of Thomas* was a late fourth or early fifth century "gospel," consisting of sayings of Jesus, but with no narrative. It was discovered *ca* 1945 near the village of Nag Hammadi, up the Nile River in Egypt. The sayings, written in Sahidic Coptic, almost certainly originated in Greek, *ca* 140. An early Greek version of some of the sayings appeared in the *Oxyrhynchus Papyrus* fragments.

Hippolytus. Born *ca* 170 CE, Hippolytus spent much of his life in Rome as a presbyter and bishop for about seven years (222 - 23 to 230). He separated from Calixtus who had been elected bishop. He was sent into exile to the mines of Sardinia in 235 and died there or in Rome, probably the following year; he was buried on the road to Tivoli. He wrote many books but was known chiefly for his *Refutation of All Heresies,* which tried to prove that the heresies originated in Greek philosophy and in paganism.

Jerome. Jerome, born in Stridon, Dalmatia, between 331 and 342 CE, was educated in Rome where he was baptized *ca* 370 and later became an ascetic. In 385, he left Rome for Jerusalem where he presided over a monastery until his death in 420. His supreme gift to Christendom was the *Vulgate* - his translation of the whole Bible into Latin. Also of great importance are his many commentaries on biblical books, his dialogue, *Against the Pelagians* in three books (415 CE), and *On Illustrious Men,* written in 392 and 393, which was a list of ecclesiastical writers from the apostles to his own times with their main works. Many of his letters were also preserved.

Josephus. Joseph ben Matthias was born a Jerusalem Jew in 37 or 38 CE and died about 100 CE. At the age of sixteen, he explored the teachings of the Pharisees, the Sadducees, and the Essenes. Still not satisfied he studied under a desert ascetic named Bannus and upon returning to Jerusalem at nineteen, he became a Pharisee and served as a priest until the age of twenty-six. In the next year, he traveled to Rome to free several Jewish priests imprisoned by Felix the procurator of Judah. Through the acquaintance of a Jewish actor, Aliturus, he gained access to the imperial palace and was introduced to Poppaea, Nero's wife, and he was able to secure the release of the priests.

In 64 CE, the Jewish rebellion against Rome was rising, but his own involvement remains uncertain since his accounts of this revolt conflicted with each other. At twenty-nine (66/67) he was in Galilee in command of a Jewish army revolting against Rome and at Jotapata, he surrendered to Vespasian. He was placed under guard for a period in Caesarea, only to later accompany the Roman army to Jerusalem, where he served as an adviser and interpreter for Titus during the siege of the city and the destruction of the temple. He was an eyewitness and participant to many of the events of the Jewish War.

After the war, Josephus took the Roman name Flavius Josephus and accompanied Titus back to Rome where Vespasian gave him an apartment, honored him with Roman citizenship, granted him a pension, and a large tract of land in Judea. At the death of Vespasian, Josephus remained in favor with the two sons, Titus and Domitian, and was provided the freedom to write *The History of the Jewish War* and the *Jewish Antiquities*.

Josephus' writings are important because he was an eyewitness and he presented a different approach from Philo and the authors of 4 Ezra, 2 Baruch and the Apocalypse of Abraham. Yet, as a client of the Roman emperor, he wrote a history that later would be adopted as the empire's authorized version of the events. He did not hesitate to express Titus's goodwill toward the Jewish people and that he wanted to avoid the destruction of the temple. On the other hand, as a Judean he criticized the Judeans who he believed caused the revolt while he praised the virtue of the Jewish religion and God. He justified his desertion of the Jewish cause, and therefore the reader should practice some discrimination. However, Josephus presented an interesting account on the character of Herod the Great, what the temple and Jerusalem looked like in Jesus' days and why the Roman army was so invincible.

Mishnah. The Mishnah was essentially a collection of Jewish legal rulings and opinions. The Mishnah was divided into six orders, a structure that both the Babylonian and the Palestinian Talmuds followed. Each order had between seven and twelve subdivisions called tractates (each identified as Mishnah plus name of tractate), which are divided into chapters. It was said that to understand the Mishnah was to understand everything that was done, no matter how mundane, had a spark of the holy within it.

- Zeraim/Seeds dealt with the laws of agriculture.
  - Berakhot – 9 chs on prayers and benedictions.
  - Pe'ah – 8 chs on laws governing charity and gleanings.
  - Demai – 7 chs on doubtfully tithed produce.
  - Kilayim – 9 chs on seeds, trees and animals.
  - Shevi'it – 10 chs on laws of the sabbatical year.
  - Terumot – 11 chs on contributions to the priests.
  - Ma'aserot – 5 chs on tithes for the Levites and the poor.
  - Ma'aser Sheni – 5 chs on second tithe.

- ○ Khalah – 4 chs on dough offering to the priests.
- ○ Bikurin – 3 chs on offering of the first fruits.
- Mo'ed/Appointed Seasons covered the laws governing the festivals, fast days and Sabbath.
  - ○ Sabbath – 24 chs of laws governing the Sabbath.
  - ○ Eruvin – 10 chs of laws establishing permissive limits for carrying on Sabbath.
  - ○ Pesakhim – 10 chs to govern the khametz, matzah and the paschal sacrifice.
  - ○ Shekalim – 8 chs of laws governing the shekel donation to the Temple.
  - ○ Yoma – 8 chs of laws governing Yom Kippur sacrifice and fasting.
  - ○ Sukkah – 8 chs of laws governing the building of the sukkah, the Four Species and festival of Sukkot.
  - ○ Beitsah – 5 chs of general festival laws.
  - ○ Rosh Hashanah – 4 chs on fixing date of the New Year, blowing of the Shofar, Rosh Hashanah prayers.
  - ○ To'anit – 4 chs of laws on governing fast days.
  - ○ Megillah – 4 chs of laws governing Purim.
  - ○ Mo'ed Katan – 3 chs of laws governing intermediate festival days.
  - ○ Hagigah – 3 chs of laws concerning the pilgrimage festivals.
- Nashim/Women were primarily concerned with laws governing marriage, divorce, betrothal and adultery. It also contained the Nazirite vows of asceticism.
  - ○ Yebamot – 16 chs of laws on Levirate marriage, prohibited marriages.
  - ○ Ketubot – 13 chs on marriage contracts and agreements.
  - ○ Nazir – 9 chs of laws dealing with the Nazirite laws.
  - ○ Sotah – 9 chs of laws regarding adultery, war and murder in which the perpetrator is unknown.
  - ○ Gittin – 9 chs of laws on divorce and the *get*.
  - ○ Kiddushin – 4 chs of laws on the marriage act, genealogy.

- Nezikin/Damages were concerned with civil and criminal law, including the treatment of idolators and the Pike Avot/ Sayings of the Fathers, a collection of ethical maxims.
  - Baba Kama – 10 chs of laws on direct and indirect damages in civil law.
  - Baba Metzia – 10 chs of laws on losses, loans, work and wage contracts.
  - Baba Batra – 10 chs of laws on partnership, sales, promissory notes, inheritance.
  - Sahnedrin – 11 chs of laws regarding the courts, criminal laws, principles of faith.
  - Makot – 3 chs of laws regarding punishment by flagellation.
  - Shevuot – 8 chs of laws on oaths.
  - Eduyot – 8 chs in a collection of testimonies from the sages.
  - Avodah Zarah – 5 chs on laws regarding idolators.
  - Avot – 5 chs that contain the Sayings "of the Fathers".
  - Horayot – 3 chs containing cases involving errors by the court and their correction.
- Kedoshim/Holy Things covered sacrifices, ritual slaughter and the priesthood.
  - Zevahim – 14 chs of laws regarding sacrifice.
  - Menakhot – 13 chs of laws regarding meal offerings.
  - Khulin – 12 chs of laws on ritual slaughter and dietary laws.
  - Bekhorot – 9 chs of laws regarding firstborn child, firstborn animals, defective animals.
  - Arakhin – 9 chs of laws on valuation of Temple offerings and soil.
  - Temurah – 7 chs of laws on substituting an animal offering.
  - Keritot – 6 chs of laws regarding sins requiring expiation.
  - Me'ilah – 6 chs of laws regarding sins of sacrilege against Temple property.

- Tamid – 7 chs of laws on daily sacrifices in the Temple.
- Midot – 5 chs of laws regarding measurements of the Temple.
- Kinim – 3 chs of laws on procedure in the event of mixing sacrifices.

- Tohorot/Purities with a majority of the tractates dealing with the issues of ritual purity and impurity.
  - Kelim – 30 chs of laws regarding utensils and pollution.
  - Oholot -18 chs of laws governing the dead and ritual purity.
  - Nega'im – 14 chs of laws regarding leprosy.
  - Parah – 12 chs of laws regarding the sacrifice of the red heifer, purification after contact with the dead.
  - Tohorot – 10 chs of laws of purification.
  - Mikva'ot – 10 chs of laws governing the *mikveh* (water and purification before the Sabbath).
  - Niddah – 10 chs of laws regarding menstruation and ritual impurity in women.
  - Makhshirin – 6 chs of laws concerning ways in which food becomes ritually unclean.
  - Zavim – 5 chs of laws regarding gonorrhea and purification.
  - Tevul Yom – 4 chs of laws on other types of ritual impurity.
  - Yadayim – 4 chs of laws on ritual uncleanliness of the hands.
  - Uktsin – 3 chs of laws on things that are susceptible to ritual uncleanliness.

Oxyrhynchus Papyrus. This fragment of papyrus, discovered in Oxyrhynchus, Egypt in 1897, probably dated back to the middle of the second century and contained some sayings of Jesus in Greek. The sayings of Jesus found in this document were the same or similar to those found in the Coptic gospel of Thomas found about 1945 at Nag Hammadi. The sayings of Jesus in both these documents were similar, in varying degrees, to those found in the gospels of Matthew, Mark and Luke, but usually represent a later form of the sayings with their own particular characteristics.

Pesikta Rabbati. or P'sqita Rabbita was a collection of Aggadic Midrash (homilies) on the Pentateuchal and prophetic lessons, the special sabbaths, etc. It was composed around 845 CE and probably called *"rabbati"* (the larger) to distinguish it from the earlier Pesikta. The Rabbati contained about fifty-one homilies with seven or eight belonging to Hanukkah, and about seven each to the Feast of Weeks and New Year, while the older Pesikta contained one each for Hanukkah and the Feast of Weeks and two for New Year.

Peter of Laodicea. Peter was a bishop (although he was not always acknowledged as such) of Laodicea, in the seventh century, who wrote commentaries on the four gospels.

Tertullian. Quintus Septimius Florens Tertullianus, better known as Tertullian, was born in Carthage, in the Roman providence of Africa *ca* 150-55. He studied law and converted to Christianity *ca* 190-95. He has been called "the father of Latin Christianity." He broke with the "Catholic" Church *ca* 207 in favor of the asceticism of the Montanists. He was perhaps most famous for being the first to use the term "Trinity" (Latin trinitas), giving rise to a formal exposition of a Trinitarian theology. In his work there appeared "three Persons, one Substance" as the Latin "tres Personae, una Substantia." His Trinitarian formula was presented after he became a Montanist and therefore, his ideas were at first rejected as heresy by the church at large, only to be later embraced as Christian doctrine. When he died *ca* 223, he had left the Montanists and founded a sect of his own. His chief polemical work was *Against Marcion* in five books written over a period of about twelve years, 200-12.

Testament of the Twelve Patriarchs. This is a pseudepigraphic work from 200 BCE to 200 CE to have contained the deathbed speeches of the twelve sons of Jacob. The Testaments of Asher, Benjamin, Daniel, Issachar, Judah, Levi, and Naphtali are referenced in the notes on Mt 8.29 and Mark 5.7.

Tobit. The book of Tobit was named after a generous and God-fearing Jewish man whose blindness and poverty in Nineveh resulted directly from his performing one of his most characteristic good deeds burying an executed fellow-Judean. Thanks to the courageous efforts of his devoted son, Tobias, who was assisted by the angel Raphael, disguised as Azariah, Tobit not only recovered his sight and fortune but also gained a pious daughter-in-law, Sarah. From her, Tobias exorcised Amadeus, the demon who had claimed the lives of her seven previous husbands on their wedding nights. On his deathbed, Tobit had Tobias promise to move the family from Nineveh to Ecbatana, where Tobias lived to a rich old age.

The author used three well-known secular folktales: (1) the tale of the Grateful Dead (the story about a man impoverished but ultimately rewarded for burying an abused corpse); (2) the tale of the Monster in the Bridal Chamber (the story of a demon who killed the bride's husbands on their wedding nights); and (3) the tale of Ahiqar (the account of a wise courtier who, though falsely incriminated by his adopted son, was vindicated).

The author of Tobit was a Judean, writing originally in Hebrew or Aramaic (copies in those languages have been found at Qumran), probably somewhere between 225-175 BCE, and, possibly, in Palestine. Tobit was represented by three major Greek recensions and two Latin translations. Unlike the RSV, the NRSV of Tobit was based upon the Sinaiticus family as supplemented by the Old Latin. There were also some late Hebrew translations, which were based upon a Greek text, as were the older Syriac, Ethiopic and Sahidic versions.

Additional Reading

Barrett, C. K., *The New Testament Background*, New York, Harper and Row Publishers, 1961.

Burrows, Millar, *The Dead Sea Scrolls*, New York, Gramercy Publishing Company,1986.

Burton, Ernest DeWitt, and Goodspeed, Edgar Johnson, *A Harmony of the Synoptic Gospels,* New York, Charles Scribner's Sons, 1945.

Buttrick, George A., Editor, *The Interpreter's Dictionary of the Bible*, Four Volumes, Nashville, Abingdon Press, 1986.

Buttrick, George A., Editor, *The Interpreter's Bible, A Commentary in Twelve Volumes*, Nashville, Abingdon Press, 1957.

Dupont-Sommer, A., *The Essene Writings from Qumran*, New York, The World Publishing Co., 1967.

Eisenman, Robert, *The Dead Sea Scrolls and the First Christians,* New York, Barnes & Noble Books, 2004.

Filson, Floyd V., *The Gospel according to St. Matthew,* Harper & Row, New York, 1960.

Fuller, Reginald, *Interpreting the Miracles*, Philadelphia, The Westminster Press, 1963.

Gaster, Theodor H., *The Dead Sea Scriptures*, Garden City, New York, Doubleday & Co., 1976.

Hunter, Archibald M., *The Work and Words of Jesus*, Philadelphia, The Westminster Press, 1950.

Jeffers, James S., *The Greco-Roman World of the New Testament Era*, Downers Grove, Illinois, InterVarsity Press, 1999.

Josephus, *Thrones of Blood, A History of the Times of Jesus 37 BC to A.D. 70*, A Barbour Book, 1988.

Major, H. D. A., Manson, T.W., Wright, C. J., *The Mission and Message of Jesus*, New York, E. P. Dutton and Co., Inc., 1961.

Mack, Burton L., *The Lost Gospel the Book of Q & Christian Origins*, San Francisco, Harper, 1993.

Metzger, Bruce M., and Murphy, Roland E., Editors, "Matthew," *The New Oxford Annotated Bible with the Aprocryphal/Deuterocanonical Books*, New Revised Standard Version, New York, New York, Oxford University Press, 1994.

Moule, C. F. D., *The Birth of the New Testament, third ed.*, San Francisco, Harper & Row Publishers, 1982.

Robinson, James M., Editor, *The Sayings Gospel Q in Greek and English*, Minneapolis, Fortress Press, 2002.

Wise, Michael; Abegg, Martin, and Cook, Edward, *The Dead Sea Scrolls, A New Translation*, San Francisco, Harper, 1996.

Cast Index

A

Aaronic priesthood. 1, 193
Angel. 24, 30, 244
Angels. 1
Asaph singer. 2, 108

B

Blind. 2, 77, 164
Bridegroom. 2, 207
Bridesmaids. 2, 207
Bystanders. 2, 221, 235, 236

C

Caiaphas. 2, 220
Centurion. 3, 68, 237
Chief priests. 3, 29, 171, 172, 214, 220,
    231, 232, 235, 237, 245
Children. 3, 92, 170
Christ. 3
Citizens. 3, 170
Congregation. 3
Crowd. 4, 48, 60, 170, 233
Crowds. 78, 97, 170

D

Daniel. 4, 200, 220
David. 4, 186
Demon. 99
Demoniac. 4
Demoniacs. 71
Disciples. 5, 70, 76, 105, 108, 118, 133,
    140, 141, 146, 155, 169, 171, 183,
198, 214, 237
Disciples. (John the Baptist's) 90

E

Editor. 5, 154
Elders. 5, 172, 214, 220, 231, 232, 235

F

Father. 5, 140, 173

G

God. 5, 37, 139, 154, 184

H

Herod. 6, 29, 117
Herodians. 6, 183
Homeowner. 6, 107

I

Isaiah. 7, 25, 31, 35, 42, 69

J

Jairus. 7, 77
James. 7, 164
James and John. 7
Jesus. 8, 36, 41, 46, 58, 64, 68, 75, 83,
    91, 96, 105, 124, 131, 139, 146,
    154, 161, 169, 182, 191, 197, 206,
    214, 232, 235, 244
John. 164
John the Baptist. 8, 35, 36, 117
Judas Iscariot. 9, 215, 216, 231

K

King. 9, 182, 210

L

Lawyer. 9
Leper. 9, 68
Lord. 9, 29, 30, 47, 49, 76, 91, 96, 105,
124, 156, 169, 170, 217
Lord God. 9
Lord GOD. 10

M

Magi. 10, 28
Mary. 10, 11, 244
Mary Magdalene. 10, 244
Matthew. 12, 23, 28, 35, 41, 46, 68, 75,
96, 104, 117, 123, 131, 139, 146,
154, 163, 169, 182, 191, 197, 214,
231, 244
Meander. 12
Messenger. 12, 35, 91, 100, 207
Messiah. 12, 198
Moses. 13, 41, 42, 49, 156, 184, 185

N

Nobleman. 13, 208

P

People. 13, 92
Peter. 13, 119, 125, 133, 134, 139, 148,
157, 217, 221
Pharisees. 14, 36, 76, 78, 96, 99, 123,
131, 154, 186, 192, 237
Pilate. 14, 232
Pilate's wife. 233
Pilates wife. 14

R

Rich young ruler. 14, 156
Righteous followers. 14, 209

S

Sadducees. 15, 36, 131, 184
Salome. 15, 117, 163
Scoffer. 65
Scoffers. 15, 199
Scribes. 15, 29, 75, 99, 123, 171, 192,
220, 235
Servant girl. 15, 221
Slave. 15, 148, 201, 208
Slaves. 106, 182
Soldiers. 16, 234, 237, 245
Son. 16, 173
Synagogue members. 16, 109

T

Temple singer. 16, 41, 171
Temple tax collectors. 16, 142
Tempter/Devil. 17, 41
Tenants. 17, 174
Those at the left hand. 17, 210

U

Unemployed. 17, 162

V

Vineyard owner. 17, 161

W

Witnesses. 17, 220
Woman. 18, 77, 125
Workers. 162

Z

Zechariah. 18, 169, 232

Printed in the United States
By Bookmasters